A Drastic Turn of Destiny

A MEMOIR

A Drastic Turn of Destiny

Fred Mann

FIRST EDITION

Copyright © 2009 The Azrieli Foundation and others

The Azrieli Foundation
164 Eglinton Avenue East, Suite 503
Toronto, Ontario
Canada, M4P 1G4
www.azrielifoundation.org

Cover and book design by Mark Goldstein
Cartography by Karen van Kerkoele

Library and Archives Canada Cataloguing in Publication

Mann, Fred, 1926–2008
    A drastic turn of destiny/ Fred Mann.

(Azrieli series of Holocaust survivor memoirs. Series II)
Includes bibliographical references and index.
ISBN 978-1-897470-08-4

1. Mann, Fred, 1926–2008. 2. Holocaust, Jewish (1939–1945) – Germany. 3. Jewish children in the Holocaust – Germany – Biography. 4. Refugees, Jewish – Biography. 5. Holocaust survivors – Canada – Biography. I. Azrieli Foundation II. Title. III. Series: Azrieli series of Holocaust survivor memoirs. Series II

D804.196.M35 2009   940.53'18092   C2009-901399-1

© **Mixed Sources**
Product group from well-managed forests, controlled sources and recycled wood or fiber
FSC   www.fsc.org Cert no. SW-COC-002080
© 1996 Forest Stewardship Council

Printed in Canada

The Azrieli Series of Holocaust Survivor Memoirs

Contents

Series Preface:
In their own words. . .

In telling these stories, the writers have liberated themselves. For so many years we did not speak about it, even when we became free people living in a free society. Now, when at last we are writing about what happened to us in this dark period of history, knowing that our stories will be read and live on, it is possible for us to feel truly free. These unique historical documents put a face on what was lost, and allow readers to grasp the enormity of what happened to six million Jews – one story at a time.

David J. Azrieli, C.M., C.Q., MArch
Holocaust survivor and founder, The Azrieli Foundation

Since the end of World War II, over 30,000 Jewish Holocaust survivors have immigrated to Canada. Who they are, where they came from, what they experienced and how they built new lives for themselves and their families are important parts of our Canadian heritage. The Azrieli Foundation-York University Holocaust Survivor Memoirs Program was established to preserve and share the memoirs written by those who survived the twentieth-century Nazi genocide of the Jews of Europe and later made their way to Canada. The program is guided by the conviction that each survivor of the Holocaust has a remarkable story to tell, and that such stories play an important role in education about tolerance and diversity.

Millions of individual stories are lost to us forever. By preserving the stories written by survivors and making them widely available to a broad audience, the Azrieli Series of Holocaust Survivor Memoirs seeks to sustain the memory of all those who perished at the hands of hatred, abetted by indifference and apathy. The personal accounts of those who survived against all odds are as different as the people who wrote them, but all demonstrate the courage, strength, wit and luck that it took to prevail and survive in such terrible adversity. The memoirs are also moving tributes to people – strangers and friends – who risked their lives to help others, and who, through acts of kindness and decency in the darkest of moments, frequently helped the persecuted maintain faith in humanity and courage to endure. These accounts offer inspiration to all, as does the survivors' desire to share their experiences so that new generations can learn from them.

The Holocaust Survivor Memoirs Program collects, archives and publishes these distinctive records and the print editions are available free of charge to libraries, schools and Holocaust-education programs across Canada, and to the general public at Azrieli Foundation educational events. Online editions of the books are available on our web site, www.azrielifoundation.org.

The Israel and Golda Koschitzky Centre for Jewish Studies has provided scholarly assistance and guidance in the preparation of these memoirs for publication. The manuscripts as originally submitted are preserved in the Clara Thomas Archives and Special Collections at York University, and are available for review by interested scholars.

The Azrieli Foundation would like to express deep appreciation to Tamarah Feder, Managing Editor and Program Manager 2005–2008 for her contribution to the establishment of this program and for her work on Series i and ii. We also gratefully acknowledge the following people for their invaluable efforts in producing this series: Mary Arvanitakis, Elin Beaumont, François Blanc, Aurélien Bonin, Florence Buathier, Mark Celinscack, Nicolas Côté, Jordana de Bloeme, Darrel Dickson (Maracle Press), Andrea Geddes Poole, Sir Martin Gilbert, Esther Goldberg, Mark Goldstein, Elizabeth Lasserre, Lisa Newman, Carson Phillips, Susan Roitman, Judith Samuels, Randall Schnoor, Erica Simmons, Jody Spiegel, Mia Spiro, Erika Tucker and Karen Van Kerkoerle.

Introduction

Fred Mann's account of his own and his family's journey from Germany to Belgium, France, Portugal and then to Jamaica before coming to Canada is an extraordinarily well-remembered memoir of a young boy who was forced to grow up – and grow more Jewish – under the mortal pressure applied by the Nazis and their helpers. Fred Mann recounts, sometimes humorously, frequently unabashedly, what he saw and experienced as a teenager. Told from the perspective of the adolescent boy of the day, Mann's story includes (as truth demands) his conflicts with his father (to whom he is nevertheless bound in deep affection and respect); his biting disdain for those who seek to take advantage of the precarious situation of Jewish refugees; his gratitude to the Christians and Jews who help when helping is not easy; his dedication to school and work; and his remarkably varied, prolific, and literally "pre-mature" erotic life.

Singular as Fred Mann's chronicle is, it also contains many familiar elements. At times it is reminiscent of *The Odyssey* and also has aspects of *Casablanca*. But the memoir's chapter titles indicate that, to its author, his journey was actually a twentieth-century version of the biblical exodus. It is indeed a story of "going forth" from the hand of tyranny and destruction to a new land of freedom. At the same time, it is an account of a boy's coming of age – religiously (with the celebration of Fred's bar mitzvah, a year late, in Belgium), sexually, and in terms of the responsibility Fred assumes for the well-being of his family. Ultimately, it is a relatively positive story, despite tragic losses within Fred's family and in the larger context.

The personal account is enriched by the political contextualization that Mann provides. The Mann family's journey takes place amidst the unfolding repression, exclusion and, finally, murder of a large part of European Jewry. The centrifugal stations of the journey give Fred Mann important information on specific situations at specific times, but he never loses sight of the larger context. In fact, the Manns' ability to realistically assess the state of their relative vulnerability or safety was an important factor in keeping them alive by allowing them to decide whether to stay where they were or move on (and if to move, then where they should go).

Fred Mann's story is unique in the perspective it brings to the events, processes and experiences of the Holocaust – in the closely observed and detailed description it provides of life under tyranny, occupation, and mortal danger; and in the range of people, places and events it portrays. The author is blessed with the intelligence, determination and ingenuity (and luck) to exploit opportunities and avoid potentially disastrous traps. He is also possessed of the natural storyteller's sense of how to weave a complex but fascinating narrative from many intertwined strands, all the while keeping the reader's empathy and interest.

∼

Fred Mann, whose German name was Manfred Lothar Mann, was born at his parents' home in Leipzig on February 28, 1926. Fred (or Fredi, as he was known to his German family) was the second son of Emanuel Mann, who was born in Vienna in 1889, and Zelda Mann, née Waldmann, who was born in Zgierz, Poland, north of Lodz, in

1896.[1] Emanuel and Zelda Mann met in Leipzig and married there in 1922. Thus, although Fred was a "German Jew," his family history made him and his relatives both sensitive and susceptible to the fates of Jews in Poland and Austro-Hungary.

Leipzig, located in eastern Germany, was both a thriving city and a favoured commercial and immigration destination for Jews from Poland, the Habsburg Empire, and points east. When Fred Mann was born, more than two-thirds of Leipzig's Jews had been born outside Germany.[2] In this regard, the Manns were typical. They were also typical in that Mann's grandfather was a furrier. After the commercial laws and restrictions on Jewish settlement had been liberalized in the nineteenth century, more and more Eastern European Jews, particularly those in the fur business, having been drawn initially to the city's trade fair, made Leipzig their home.[3] Here the Manns flourished, although they moved away from the fur trade and the core of the Jewish district to other enterprises and a neighbourhood that was not identified or identifiable as Jewish.

Before the rise of National Socialism, Fred's extended and nuclear family was already well-integrated into the majority Christian society, with relatives having served in the Austro-Hungarian army and in the Polish Sejm. The language of the Mann household in Leipzig was German, although Fred's paternal grandparents knew Yiddish.

---

1 On the history of Jewish Zgierz, see the Memorial Book of the city, available in English translation on the Web at: http://www.jewishgen.org/Yizkor/Zgierz/Zgierz.html.

2 Solvejg Höppner and Manfred Jahn, *Jüdische Vereine und Organisationen in Chemnitz, Dresden und Leipzig 1918 bis 1933*. Ein Überblick (Dresden: Sächsisches Druck- und Verlagshaus, 1997), 9; cited in Robert Allen Willingham II, "Jews in Leipzig: Nationality and Community in the 20th Century," Diss. University of Texas at Austin 2005, 19, note 25.

3 Steffen Held, "Juden in Leipzig. Ein geschichtlicher Überblick" (www.juedischesleipzig.de).

The sons received quintessentially German names – Heinz Arno and Manfred Lothar. They attended public school until they were forced by the Nazis to go to a Jewish school. Fred's father had non-Jewish as well as Jewish friends and wanted his family to live a life more-or-less "indistinguishable from the non-Jewish population."[4]

Gradually, the family grew less strict in their Jewish observance. There was no doubt in their own or anyone else's mind that they were Jewish, but when they attended services, it was at the liberal synagogue headed by Dr. Felix Goldmann, who espoused religious Judaism in the diaspora, as opposed to either Zionism or assimilated, ethnic or culinary Judaism.[5] The Manns celebrated the Jewish holidays and major life-cycle events. Yet on Shabbat they also drove, frequented the Café Heiner and listened to the radio; the boys were sent out for a snack during the Yom Kippur fast. Fred's mother maintained a kosher kitchen out of respect for her husband's parents, but she and her family also ate non-kosher food (occasionally, at her insistence, even ham).

In all these respects, the Manns illustrate a lifestyle that attempted to be simultaneously German and Jewish. Then the balance tilted, and the Manns were sent in a different direction by National Socialist Germany. In effect, it was the Nazis who forced the family to become more Jewish. They received the compulsory middle names "Israel" and "Sara" and had to dismiss their Christian maid. Heinz and Fred were expelled from the public school system and compelled to associate only with Jews – for example, in the Jewish Scouts or the Bar Kochba sports club. At the same time, it was the family's non-Jewish connections, including Emanuel's old school friend (a convinced and active Nazi) and the Polish consuls in Leipzig, Eduard Tulasziewicz

---

4 1926: PowerPoint presentation for Fred Mann's eightieth birthday (cited hereafter as Mann, "Eightieth Birthday PowerPoint").

5 Michael A. Meyer, "Liberal Judaism and Zionism in Germany," *Judaism within Modernity: Essays on Jewish History and Religion* (Detroit: Wayne State University Press, 2001), 240–241; 250, note 8.

and Feliks Chiczewski, who provided them with information and a safe haven and, ultimately, allowed them to escape.[6] Moreover, the family's (and particularly Fred's) ability to "pass" – physically, culturally and linguistically – in various gentile settings was crucial to their ultimate survival.

Fred Mann's intimate portrait of Jewish communal and family life in Leipzig and Berlin (including the café scene in the German capital) provides important insights into the extremely diverse communal structures, institutions, and practices that resisted all attempts to reduce and homogenize them. What we can say is that young Fred's personality, education, embeddedness in his family and skills prepared him to play a key and crucial role in leading his family out of Germany and to ultimate safety in the New World.

~

The first quarter of Fred Mann's account brings to life his early youth and the circumstances which he, his family and his fellow Jews had to endure as German society became more and more openly hostile to Jews. Jewish life appeared to thrive as members of the community who had once considered themselves fully "German" were forced back to Jewish institutions that in turn benefited from their participation. But this was merely one side of coin, one that could be considered positive only by ignoring the larger context of growing discrimination, exclusion and repression.

As the pace of anti-Jewish policy and practice accelerated and the trend became impossible to overlook, the Jewish community of

---

6 Chiczewski also saved many Jews during the expulsion of Polish Jews from Leipzig in the fall of 1938. See Bernd Karwen, "Porträt: Ein polnischer Diplomat half verfolgten Juden in Leipzig," *Dialog. Magazyn Polsko-Niemiecki*, 60 (2002), 52–53; English summary at http://www.znak.org.

Leipzig became increasingly attenuated. Some members were deported; others fled. The situation in Leipzig was more complicated than in many other cities because two-thirds of the community were not German citizens. By 1938 the "non-German" Jews were excluded from holding positions within the Jewish community, depriving them of income and the community of their services. Then came the deportation order for Jews with Polish passports in October 1938 (the so-called *Polenaktion*), in the course of which Fred's paternal grandmother Fannie (Feige) Mann died.[7] And finally there was the November pogrom that has come to be known as Kristallnacht (Night of Broken Glass) and the resulting violence to places and persons. By 1939 the Jewish population of Leipzig had fallen from over 11,000 in 1933 to just under 4,500.[8]

The Manns were fortunate in having the foresight and the means to leave Germany, although Fred's paternal grandfather, Ferdinand (Feiwel) Mann, had to stay behind.[9] Fred Mann's older brother, Heinz, opted to go to England with the Kindertransport but the British government subsequently removed him to Canada as an "enemy alien." Fred himself, then thirteen years old, remained in Germany with his parents while the family prepared to flee to what they hoped was a safer place.

That place was Belgium. For Fred Mann, it was the beginning of an odyssey that was to last until the war was over – and beyond, since

---

7 See page 41 of the memoir. A notation of Fannie's death on October 28, 1938, exists in the records of the Leipzig Jewish Community; we are indebted to Ms. Klaudia Krenn of the Leipzig Jewish Community for the information on Fred's grandparents.

8 Willingham, 118; for a more complete description of the November pogrom in Leipzig, see Willingham, 102–111.

9 According to the records of the Leipzig Jewish community, he died in Leipzig in 1941, having applied to emigrate in June 1940. At that time he believed his son's family was still in Belgium, although they had already gone to France.

the family was not reunited in Canada until 1948.[10] From Brussels, the family moved away from the epicentre of Nazi tyranny in a south-westerly direction, with side-trips and the retracing of steps covering more than three thousand kilometres from Brussels to Lisbon between July 1939 and January 1942.

The Manns' journey took place in a critical period during which Nazi Germany and its allies and collaborators extended their control over Europe and set in motion the organized mass murder that was at the heart of the Holocaust. In July 1939 Germany was still enacting measures aimed at getting Jews to emigrate from its territory, but by the end of September, Germany had invaded, conquered and occupied Poland. As a result, Germany brought millions of Jews within its grasp, established the first ghettos, instituted discriminatory practices and carried out executions of Polish intellectuals through special killing squads (*Einsatzkommandos*). Even more ominously, the Germans began experimenting with mobile gas vans that used carbon monoxide to carry out their mass slaughter.[11]

There was an interval of almost ten months between the Manns' arrival in Belgium on July 20, 1939, and the German invasion of that country. But this respite was full of warning signs. Having begun to settle in, the Manns registered with grave concern and fear the treatment of Jews in German-occupied Poland. In this, they were no different from other Belgian Jews, many of whom had arrived from Eastern Europe after World War I. The threat that the Germans would attack their western neighbours was tangible. Mr. Mann decided to

---

10 As noted earlier, Heinz (Heini, later Howard) Mann was sent to Canada from England in 1940. He graduated from the University of Toronto in 1947, the year Fred came to Canada. Their parents arrived in May 1948: Mann, "Eightieth Birthday PowerPoint," slides 81–82.

11 A timeline is available at http://www.deathcamps.org, which focuses on to the Aktion Reinhard camps but also includes the genesis and broader workings of Nazi genocide.

stay in Brussels rather than move to Antwerp, which had an apprecia-
bly larger but more religiously conservative Jewish population.[12] Mr.
Mann also decided that Fred should learn French, not Flemish, and
his son's linguistic and cultural competence in French were to prove
vital to the family in the months to come.

In 1940, as a new concentration camp was set up on German territory in the city of Auschwitz (in Polish, Oświęcim), killing centres for
people who were handicapped and otherwise deemed "useless" were
established in Germany and Poland. As spring progressed, so did the
German armies into the Low Countries. Belgium surrendered in late
May, some two weeks after the Netherlands. Unlike Paul-Henri Rips,
whose account of life as a Belgian Jew under Nazi occupation appears
in the Azrieli Foundation's series of Holocaust Survivor Memoirs, the
Manns succeeded in getting out of Belgium and so did not really experience the occupation there.[13]

The Mann family left Brussels on May 15, 1940. They moved southwest through France in stages – from Reims to Limoges to Toulouse
– before finding a temporary abode in Rodez on June 18. Again,
because they were in Vichy-controlled France, they escaped direct
German occupation, although the Vichy regime not only complied
with German orders and wishes, but shared with the Germans important assumptions and policies regarding the Jews.[14] Indeed, Vichy
France moved quickly to enact antisemitic and anti-foreigner legislation not quite a month after the Manns arrived in Rodez. Before the

---

12 See the introduction to Paul-Henri Rips, *E/96: Fate Undecided* (Toronto and
Montreal: Azrieli Foundation, 2009).

13 For literature on Belgium and the Holocaust, consult the list of sources in the
volume by Paul-Henri Rips.

14 Michael R. Marrus and Robert O. Paxton, *Vichy France and the Jews* (Stanford,
CA: University Press, 1995); Richard H. Weisberg, "Vichy Law and the Holocaust
in France," *Studies in Antisemitism*, ed. Yehuda Bauer, vol. 3 (Amsterdam: Har-
wood, 1996).

Manns left France on November 3, 1940, just under six months later, the government had extended the definition of who was "Jewish" and granted itself authority to intern, confine or press into labour foreign Jews.[15] Scholars have shown that the Vichy authorities were in some cases going beyond what the Germans demanded in an attempt to ingratiate themselves with their masters and allies.[16] This might not have been evident to the Manns, but they did know that they were in danger, and that the risks of fleeing were less than the risks entailed in staying.

That they succeeded in fleeing can be credited to their own fore-sight, Fred's crucial and inspired interventions, and certain coura-geous and benevolently disposed officials in Marseille, including Bishop Jean Delay and unknown members of the Portuguese consul-ate.[17] With the aid of these individuals and others, the Manns made it to Portugal, officially in transit on their way to Siam (as Thailand was then known). Portugal was to provide the longest sojourn during their exodus; they were in Lisbon a little over fifteen months, from November 6, 1940 to January 24, 1942. Like Vichy France, Portugal was not occupied. It was nominally a neutral, non-combatant coun-try, although its leader, António de Oliveira Salazar, was a totalitar-ian dictator who both admired and feared Hitler even as he tried to maintain a relationship with England, to which Portugal was bound by tradition, trade and treaty.[18] As a neutral country, Portugal could

---

15 Susan Zuccotti, *The Holocaust, the French, and the Jews.* (New York: Basic Books, 1993), 53–57.

16 Marrus and Paxton, 16–21; Ryan, 28–29. For a concise summary of the anti-Jewish measures, see Richard Vinen, *The Unfree French: Life under the Occupation* (New Haven: Yale University Press, 2006), 135–137; on 29–38 Vinen explores the French concept of the "exode" (exodus) of refugees.

17 Donna F. Ryan, *The Holocaust & the Jews of Marseille* (Urbana and Chicago: University of Illinois Press, 1996).

18 Avraham Milgram, "Portugal, the Consuls, and the Jewish Refugees, 1938–1941," trans. by Anna Shidlo, *Yad Vashem Studies* 27 (1999), 123–155.

jockey for position between the opposing camps, doing business with both while hoping to preserve its autonomy. That way, when the tide did shift, Portugal could end up backing the winner.[19] During the Manns' sojourn in Portugal, personal circumstances, Portuguese policy interests and the larger developments in the war combined to determine their relative – and constantly shifting – position of vulnerability or security.

In June 1941 Germany invaded the Soviet Union, further extending the Nazis' control over a huge Jewish population. But before then, the Nazis had solidified their hold over Jews in the occupied parts of Western Europe as well as over the ghettos in the East. By the summer and fall of 1941, Nazi policy toward the Jews moved into its final phase – the systematic murder of European Jewry. Ironically, the attack on Pearl Harbor and the United States' declaration of war in December 1941 caused the cancellation of a meeting scheduled at a lakeside villa on the outskirts of Berlin. The so-called Wannsee Conference, convened by Reinhard Heydrich to consolidate his control over the "final solution of the Jewish question," as Nazi parlance had it, was postponed until January 20, 1942. Two days after it took place, the Mann family left Europe for Jamaica. Over the next two years, at the height of the gassings of Jews in the Aktion Reinhard camps and the gas chambers of Auschwitz II-Birkenau and Majdanek, the Manns were in the relative safety of the New World.

∼

In addition to a wealth of details about his travels from Nazi Germany to the ultimate safety of Jamaica, Fred Mann has woven a retrospective and reflective strand into his text. His manuscript was completed

---

19 See David Birmingham, *A Concise History of Portugal, Cambridge Concise Histories* (Cambridge: Cambridge University Press, 1993), esp. 156–167.

in 2006 and as such it is the work of an eighty-year-old who has seen, experienced and accomplished much in his life. As a person who never stopped learning – even during the Holocaust – Fred Mann was an avid reader who brought the fruits of his later reading and thinking into his memoir. What makes his account so valuable, though, is that it was personally experienced and witnessed. Accordingly, the editors of this volume have opted to cut or pare down many of the manuscript's historical excurses, some of which contained extensive quotations from speeches or documents by historical figures of the day.

As readers we need to bear in mind that, just as there are limits to memory, there are limits to what the author could have known at the time – much of what we know today only came to light after the end of the war. At the same time it is also true that the Manns were often in a position to know more about what was happening during the war than many other survivors – they were well connected to a fluid community of refugees from all over Europe and Fred Mann himself regularly dealt with and even worked for various levels of officials in France and Portugal – officials in both the civil and military authorities and Jewish organizations such as American Jewish Joint Distribution Committee (JDC). In 1940–1941, when the Manns were living there, Lisbon was the largest refugee centre in Europe, the city to which the JDC had relocated its European headquarters. Nonetheless, their interpretations of what they heard were necessarily subjective – what the Manns thought and felt and did at any given time was circumscribed by the situation in which they were living.

At the time of the Manns' sojourn in Belgium, France, Portugal, and in individual cities and regions, the political situation varied considerably, affected as it necessarily was by such factors as whether the particular area was free, under direct occupation by the Germans, governed by a collaborationist regime or neutral. Whether there was any formal or informal resistance or opposition to National Socialism and its policies toward the Jews and how effective it was also had a significant impact on the people living there. The experience of Jews living in Vichy France in 1940, for example, was dramatically different from the experience of those living in Occupied France; in Belgium, living in Antwerp, where the Jewish community was subject to much more overt antisemitism, was not at all the same as living in Brussels, where the Association of Jews in Belgium continued to function until very close to the end of the war.

The Manns' circumstances and sources of information were also influenced by the varying extent to which they were able to connect with people outside the refugee community – which Fred Mann himself was able to do in Vichy France, in particular – and with various groups within the Jewish community. The make-up of the Jewish community was very different in each place they passed through, depending on the size of the established Jewish community, the number of Jews who had come as refugees and the relationship between the two. The Manns' situation (and that of their fellow refugees) was also inevitably affected by the state of Jewish-Christian relations in a particular country, region or city, which included the attitudes and actions of the organized churches and their leaders.

Throughout his memoir Fred Mann shows remarkable resourcefulness under terrible conditions of oppression, hatred and violence. As the same time, he was certainly no angel – particularly when it came to his budding sexuality and his youthful practice of the art of seduction. He was also bound by the cultural limitations of the time and places in which he was living. While his references to "coloured" people in Jamaica would be grossly offensive today, for example, they reflect the culture and vocabulary of the times. To excise them would no doubt diminish the offensiveness of these episodes, but it would also mean pretending that the prejudices of half a century ago did not exist.

Reading critically, which interestingly enough goes hand-in-hand with reading empathetically, is one of the most important things a free society can teach and support. There can be no doubt that Fred Mann's account provides remarkably vivid first-hand testimony about how events were experienced and perceived, and thus also about how things *really were*.

~

Fred Mann concludes his memoir with details of his family's life as refugees in Jamaica and his much-anticipated reunion with his brother in the US. After the war, he travelled to the United States and Europe, during which he retraced his European itinerary and took steps to establish a business. While in Europe he met Veronica (Ronnie) Klein, a fellow Holocaust survivor from Hungary. Their son, Larry, was born in Salzburg, Austria, in 1949. Fred, Ronnie and Larry emigrated to Canada in 1952, meeting up with Fred's parents, who had come in 1948, and Fred's brother, Heini (now Howard), who had been in the country since 1940. Fred began his professional career in the import/export business, but then became a financial-market consultant and international financier, with projects and partners in the Caribbean, West Africa, the Pacific Rim and Europe. Ronnie Mann died on April 28, 2006, having valiantly endured Parkinson's disease for thirty-six years.[21] Fred lovingly tended to her during her illness. He also doted on his grandchildren Jeffrey and Jennifer, the children of his son, Larry, and Larry's wife, Lyn.

To the end, Fred Mann retained his sense of realism that was paired with a rare and dry sense of humour. The last slide of the PowerPoint presentation for his eightieth birthday is headlined "Our future permanent residence in a brand new building." The slide shows a (still unmarked) tombstone and gives the new address. Fred Mann died on March 24, 2008.

---

21 See Veronica Mann's obituary, *Globe and Mail*, March 27, 2008.

~

Fred Mann and his immediate family experienced relative good fortune – they never had to endure a concentration camp or worse. They were able to escape to life and freedom, although some members of the extended family were murdered (directly or indirectly) by the Nazis. These include Fred's paternal grandmother; his uncles Dadek Waldmann, Willy Mann and (by marriage) Kurt Berliner; and his maternal aunt Anja and her family. One of the lessons of this book is that the Holocaust was not confined to the gas chambers of Nazi camps or the operations of the mobile killing squads (*Einsatzgruppen* and the like). Those who identified themselves as Jews or were considered to be Jews by the Nazis and their helpers, and who were displaced, persecuted and/or discriminated against by the racial, religious, ethnic and political policies of the Nazis and their allies – including the Mann family – are also Holocaust survivors.[22]

Fred Mann's memoir provides the details of how refugee life operated – its psychology, sociology and political economy – in a variety of settings. In addition to its own immediate value, the manuscript represents a rich primary source for future research on life during the Holocaust.

Beyond this, precisely because the account is set in places as far away from each other as Germany and Jamaica, it offers unique insights into the construction of identity as defined by race, nationality and ethnicity. To the Nazis and their sympathizers, the Manns were not "Aryan," nor could they ever be. To Fred's new schoolmates in Belgium, he was at first the "filthy German," and Fred's brother, Howard, was interned in Canada as an enemy alien after having escaped to England. In Jamaica Fred is suddenly so "white" that he can redefine as "equally white" a fellow Jewish refugee from the

---

22 See the definition offered at: http://www.kindertransport.org/history09_FAQ.htm.

Netherlands who is banned from an all-white hotel swimming pool because of her dark complexion. Indeed, though he was a victim of racism at its worst, and aware of the hierarchies of race in Jamaica, the young Fred Mann does not question the hierarchical construction of race (or gender).[23] The irony of the entire affair, however, is the extent to which Nazi racialist policy enforced and reinforced the Jewish self-identification of those whose family trajectory was probably heading toward greater assimilation into Christian society. This is, of course, out of all proportion to the destruction that European and world Jewry experienced at the hands of those who had set out to murder them.

Finally, Fred Mann also documents the ways in which World War II resulted in peregrinations and international relations that had globalizing effects. Even more important to the Manns, they sensed not just dangers but the potential opportunities that presented themselves in the course of their wanderings. Their awareness of the positive within the negative was among the factors that contributed to their survival. And that is the spirit that permeates and characterizes Fred Mann's account of the "drastic turn" of his destiny and his exodus to freedom.

Mark Webber
Toronto, 2009

---

23 On the constructedness of Jewish "colour," see Karen Brodkin, *How Jews Became White Folks & What That Says About Race in America* (New Brunswick, NJ: Rutgers University Press, 1998).

Growing Up under Hitler

I was only six years old when my destiny took a drastic turn on January 30, 1933. It was a wintry day in Leipzig, and my father was in bed with the flu. He asked me to go downstairs to the newsstand and fetch the daily newspaper – there was no home delivery in those days. When he read the headline pronouncing the news of the day, he just shrugged. Little did he know that this shrug was probably the most significant gesture of his entire life – that was the infamous day that Field Marshal Paul von Hindenburg, president of Germany, appointed Adolf Hitler chancellor.[1]

A few days later my father received news that the Sturmabteilung, the SA Brown Shirts, were looking for him.[2] One of his old school friends who had been very active in the Nazi party since the late 1920s

---

1 Following two years of deepening political crisis and social instability that threatened the survival of the Weimar Republic, Hindenburg appointed Adolf Hitler, leader of the National Socialist German Workers' (Nazi) Party, chancellor of Germany. Within weeks, Hitler had consolidated power and established himself as absolute dictator of Germany's totalitarian Third Reich, setting in motion a chain of events that both launched the Nazis' brutal campaign against the Jews of Europe and resulted in World War II.

2 The Sturmabteilung (SA), or storm troopers, were known as Brown Shirts because of the colour of their uniforms. For more information, see the glossary.

and who later became a major player in the Gestapo, telephoned my father to tell him that his name was prominently featured on the pickup list for a manual labour assignment.[3] He was to be escorted to the so-called Brown House, the Brown Shirts' headquarters on Eisenbahnstrasse, to carry coal from the basement to the top floor of the building. They were going to teach this chauffeur-driven, fur-coated Jew a lesson.[4] As soon as he received this information, my father immediately drove his car to Berlin, where he stayed until his old schoolmate could get the order rescinded. This took about a week. My mother, assisted by a neighbour in our apartment house who was an old-time Nazi, very courageously made a personal representation to some of these SA leaders.

Those who were not as fortunate as my father were forced to scrub toilets with toothbrushes, clean floors with their own shirts, wipe urinals with their hands, all under the supervision of the Brown Shirts standing there with their whips, ever ready to apply a few strokes to a laggard. They were the lucky ones – they at least were doing their work indoors, unlike people who were forced to scrub walls outside in the winter cold, whitewashing remnants of political graffiti like the hammer and sickle or slogans besmirching the German National Socialist German Workers Party (Nationalsozialistische Deutsche Arbeiterpartei), the Nazis. Most were not allowed to wear their overcoats or gloves, and some were even deprived of their jackets. If they were not lucky enough to get something to scrape with, they had to use their fingernails, although some of them were handed toothbrushes.

---

3 The Gestapo were the secret police. For more information, see the glossary.
4 Even before the establishment of concentration camps within Germany and the outbreak of World War II, the Nazis used forced manual labour – often pointless and humiliating work to be performed without proper equipment, clothing, nourishment or rest – as a means of punishing and degrading Jews and "re-educating" those they identified as opponents of the Third Reich.

For some German Jewish citizens, these events were their first introduction to the new regime, but still most Jews didn't believe that what they were witnessing was the beginning of a well-defined campaign against them. The evidence was there, though – a considerable part of Hitler's *Mein Kampf* explains the "necessity" of making Germany *judenrein*, purified of Jews.[5]

Assimilated German Jews argued that they had fought in World War I for their "Fatherland" and many proudly displayed their military medals, including Germany's famous Iron Cross, even after Hitler came to power. Although my father had served in the Austro-Hungarian army and could not match the German medals, he long maintained his belief, as did many of his friends, that Hitler's era world be short-lived.

A month after Hitler was made chancellor, on February 27, 1933, the German parliament building in Berlin, the Reichstag, was set on fire, damaging the first floor and part of the roof of the building. I vividly remember the date since the following day was my seventh birthday. Hermann Goering, who was then a cabinet minister without portfolio, announced the arrest of all one hundred Communist members of parliament. The Nazis blamed the fire on a mentally impaired, twenty-four year-old Dutchman, Marinus van der Lubbe, who allegedly confessed to being a member of the Dutch Communist Party. Within a few days, almost five thousand people were detained, creating an overflow in the jails.[6] To accommodate this expanded prison

---

5 For more information on Hitler's *Mein Kampf* and the meaning of *judenrein*, see the glossary.

6 To consolidate their power, on February 4, 1933, the Nazis issued a Decree for the Protection of the German People that placed constraints on the press and banned all political meetings and marches. This arson attack on the Reichstag by an alleged Communist gave Hitler's government the rationale for shutting down all remaining political opposition and civil rights. For more information, see the glossary.

population, the Nazis opened their first official concentration camp in Dachau, near Munich, where they hastily erected wooden barracks on the grounds of an abandoned munitions factory.[7] On February 28, Hitler convinced Hindenburg to sign an emergency decree that effectively gave him complete power.[8]

After a few months, the impact of this first encounter with Nazi barbarism seemed to fade and, in Leipzig at least, the Jews wrote off these first incidents as the work of a few hotheads, unlikely to be repeated. Even the September 1933 trial of the alleged arsonist van der Lubbe, held before the Federal Court of Leipzig, did not arouse much attention. He was convicted, condemned to death and executed in January 1934.

It is interesting to note that the persecution of Jews manifested itself differently in various parts of Germany. After this first skirmish with the Nazi party in February 1933 until the end of 1935, when the Nuremberg Laws were published, Leipzig experienced almost a laissez-faire attitude and the Jewish population was left in relative peace.[9] Our city didn't experience the book burning that took place in Berlin that May, when university students fuelled huge bonfires with the books of writers who were declared to be enemies of the people. This broad category encompassed such writers as Lion Feuchtwanger, Jakob Wassermann, Arnold and Stefan Zweig, Albert Einstein and Thomas Mann, all towering figures of twentieth-century literature and science. A century earlier Heinrich Heine wrote in his play *Almansor:*

---

7 Established in March 1933 to house primarily political prisoners, Dachau, located about sixteen kilometres northwest of Munich in southern Germany, was the Nazis' first concentration camp. For more information, see the glossary.

8 The Order of the Reich President for the Protection of People and State – more commonly known as the Reichstag Fire Decree – suspended essential civil rights in Germany and helped establish the Third Reich as a one-party totalitarian state. For more information, see the glossary.

9 The Nuremberg Laws, announced in September 1935 at the party rally in that city, legalized discrimination against Jews. For more information, see the glossary.

A Tragedy, "Dort wo man Bücher verbrennt, verbrennt man auch am Ende Menschen." (Where they burn books, in the end they will end up burning human beings.)[10]

When Rabbi Dr. Felix Goldmann, chief Reform rabbi in Leipzig, died in 1934, Leipzig's lord mayor, Carl Friedrich Goerdeler, and the chief of police of attended his funeral.[11] The Jewish Boy Scouts stood honour guard for the last kilometre on the road to the Jewish cemetery, starting from the Bar Kochba Platz, a Jewish outdoor sports facility. Even after 1935, the Bar Kochba Platz was allowed to operate and sports festivals and competitions took place regularly. We had our soccer and handball competitions there, as well as the annual races with Jewish athletes coming from all over Germany. In 1937 I was a member of the main soccer team and we played many of the other Jewish teams visiting Leipzig.

Ours was not the experience elsewhere in the country. To create an acceptable scapegoat for the German populace and divert attention from their existing misery, Hitler cleverly promoted the idea of a Jewish "cult" that was harming the public. Not only did he promulgate propaganda that Jews were responsible for all of Germany's economic problems, but he promoted a newspaper that was entirely devoted to this subject, the infamous antisemitic newspaper *Der*

---

10 In April 1933 the Nazi German Student Association's Main Office for Press and Propaganda launched a nationwide "Action against the Un-German Spirit" that culminated in a massive book-burning. On May 10 university students burned about 25,000 volumes of "un-German" books and right-wing students marched in torchlight parades in opposition to the "un-German spirit." All in all, between May 10 and June 21, students in thirty-four university towns across Germany took part in similar actions. Among the authors whose works were burned that night were Bertolt Brecht, Karl Marx, Ernest Hemingway, Thomas Mann, Jack London and Theodore Dreiser.

11 From 1917 to 1933 Dr. Felix Goldmann served as rabbi of the Reform synagogue in the Gottschedstrasse; the synagogue was founded in 1854 to serve Leipzig's growing Reform community.

Stürmer, founded by Julius Streicher in 1923. By 1938 the weekly paid
subscriptions numbered 500,000; by 1939 it had a national distribution and became one of the most widely read papers in Germany. The
newspaper specialized in Jew-baiting and printed photographs that
depicted "Jewish atrocities" against the German public. It spoke of
a "Jewish conspiracy" to control German economic life and society.
Nobody was spared, including statesmen like Rathenau and scientists such as Einstein. Even Thomas Mann, though not Jewish, was
attacked for his written condemnation of the Hitler crowd.

In addition to individuals, *Der Stürmer's* smear campaign extended to all the aspects of Jewish life, art, science and culture. Jews had
earned their place in the arts and sciences of Germany, which made
them easy targets. According to the newspaper there were no "average" income Jews, only wealthy ones who profited from the ignorance
and gullibility of the German public. The stereotypical Jew was cari-
catured as having a hooked nose – anybody who looked like that was
declared Jewish and was an open target. In Berlin, an Italian man
who looked "Jewish" was almost killed by a crowd in a department
store because he dared, as a "Jew," to question the Aryan saleslady
about the change he received after a purchase. A logical mistake considering that about 170,000 Jews lived in Berlin.[12]

My existence, however, continued on a more or less even keel in
the first years of Hitler's regime, although there were a few exceptions. In school some of the teachers singled us out as undesirables
and made sure that the class understood the difference between blue-
eyed blond Germans and the propaganda picture of the greasy, hook-
nosed Jew. Only a few months earlier I had been a happy youngster
marching into school with my *Zuckertüte*, a cone-shaped container

---

12 Originally a nineteenth-century anthropological term used to describe an Indo-
European ethnic and linguistic grouping, the word "Aryan" was changed by the
Nazis to denote a Germanic "master race." Here, Mann echoes the Nazi usage in
the sense of "non-Jew," member of the German "racial community."

filled with chocolates and sweets. This was a German custom to help a youngster experience the first day in school with sweetness and thereby lessen the shock of the transition into an organized existence. Kindergarten didn't exist in my day and being suddenly removed from one's parents' home and put into strange surroundings and a regimented school day required some inducement.

My first teacher was a middle-aged lady whose hair was drawn back into a severe-looking bun; her eyeglasses were almost smaller than her eyes. She walked along the rows wielding her cane and liberally hitting the desks with it, making us dread an encounter with her. Nevertheless, the first few months of school life in 1932 passed uneventfully. I learned the first letters of the alphabet and the rudiments of the number system. My teacher was horrified to learn that I had acquired this knowledge before coming to school and my parents were called in and reprimanded for teaching me these basics ahead of time.

We continued to attend services at the Gottschedstrasse Synagogue and Rabbi Felix Goldmann's sermons almost mirrored the words spoken by Rabbi Leo Baeck of Berlin, who preached calm and reason and who stayed in Berlin even after the great wave of immigration that followed the events of Kristallnacht.[13]

The German Pfadfinderbund (Boy Scouts) were dissolved and replaced by the creation of the Hitlerjugend (Hitler Youth) and Bund Deutscher Mädel (Organization of German Girls) or B D M – better known to some as "Bubi Drück Mich" (Laddie, Squeeze Me).[14] This

---

13 Leo Baeck (1873–1956) was a rabbi, scholar and leader of Progressive Judaism in Berlin. Although many American institutions offered him refuge, he refused to abandon his community. On the night of November 9–10, 1938, the Nazis instigated widespread pogroms – state-sanctioned, anti-Jewish riots – against German Jewish communities. In the wake of these events, Jewish emigration from Germany rose dramatically. For more information, see Kristallnacht in the glossary.

14 For more information on the Hitlerjugend and Bund Deutscher Mädel, see the respective glossary entries.

left a void for Jewish youth and brought about the formation of the Jüdischer Pfadfinder Bund (Jewish Boy Scouts). This organization was very Zionist oriented and promoted the idea of aliyah, emigration to Palestine. We wore the traditional Boy Scout uniform – minus the hat since that attracted too much attention – but had to hide it under our jackets or overcoats so the Hitler Youth wouldn't attack us. There were some glorious fights in the forest since the Jewish Boy Scouts owned a club house there that the Hitler Youth coveted. After many broken noses and limbs, the Hitler Youth came accompanied by the dreaded SA, making withdrawal the wiser choice. While the older boys had boxing and kicking fights, we were very much aware that the SA wouldn't be averse to setting an example by killing a few Jewish boys.

I remember that one of the last movies I saw before we were prohibited from entering the theatres was the 1934 film *Gold* starring the famous German actor Hans Albers. It was the story of a scientist seeking a method to change lead into gold and depicted the harnessing of atomic energy for the purposes of scientific progress. In the film, the scientist constructs a gigantic atomic reactor for that purpose but destroys it when commercialism attempts to take over his invention.

$\sim$

The City of Leipzig has a long and rich history, its growth and prosperity arising from its trade fairs. By the eighteenth century Leipzig was a city of Baroque splendour, in the words of Goethe, "a little Paris," with more than thirty park-type gardens with orangeries, dance pavilions and restaurants. Musicians and stallholders called out their wares and the streets were congested with heavy covered wagons, riders, chaise-bearers and pedestrians, with ladies and gentlemen, dandies and students dressed in the latest fashions promenading around the town or in its gardens.

Jews had been living in Leipzig from the beginning of the thirteenth century and the community grew through the intervening centuries to the point that by 1932 the Jewish population numbered about 30,000 Jews and of those, only seven thousand could immigrate to other countries. At the time of Hitler's appointment one year later, there were about 600,000 Jews living in Germany, with the majority residing in Berlin.

~

We lived at 22 Lutherstrasse in Reudnitz, a suburb in the eastern part of Leipzig, on the third floor of a six-storey apartment building. The staircase wound around the one elevator located in the centre of the building and the apartments were located off one side of the hallway. Our building was on a corner with the main entrance on Lutherstrasse and the driveway on the side street. When you came in from the side street you entered through a covered archway onto a cobblestone drive. Another smaller apartment building sat at the end of the driveway. Once you cleared the archway there was a large fenced-in backyard play area that was part of the apartment building where we children spent our spare time. There was also a bicycle shed where we chained our bicycles to a cemented steel frame, since bicycles were not allowed inside the building. Past the playground along the drive were garages and my father's car was parked in one of those.

The janitor's lodgings, a grocery store and a restaurant/bar were on the ground floor of the building. We bought most of our food in that grocery store where my parents maintained a charge account. We could enter the backdoor of the store from within the building. The restaurant was also accessible this way and my father occasionally would send us down to fetch a bottle of malt beer, or my mother would send us for some prepared food. There were five apartments on each floor and our apartment was a corner unit. Directly to the left of the entrance was the bedroom I shared with my brother. The beds in that room were placed in an L-shaped formation with my brother's bed at the window and mine close to the door. The room also contained a big wooden wardrobe where we kept all our clothes and a small desk. To the right of the entrance, off the hallway, was the living room and adjoining that, accessible by passing through a multicoloured glass-bead curtain, was the family room. To the left of the living room was the dining room, which we could enter from either the hallway or the living room. My parents' bedroom was at the end of the hall and the kitchen was across from the living room. Next to that was a small bedroom occupied by our maid. The windows of the family room, living room and dining room faced the Lutherstrasse, while the windows of the other rooms faced the backyard playground. In between the kitchen and my parents' bedroom was the only bathroom in the apartment. When that was occupied and somebody else required its services, the person had to use the small room with a toilet and washbasin at the end of the hallway. The shared bathroom was reserved for the tenants of that particular floor; each floor had the same arrangement.

Our storage lockers were in the basement. Most of them were large since many people stored utilitarian items such as coal and potatoes there. My mother preserved a great number of fruits in the summer and the big glass containers had to be taken down to the basement and fetched up again during the winter. It was a scary place for a little boy – there were no lights and we had to take candles or a kerosene lamp with us. Our locker was about halfway down a long hallway. The walls were concrete and a simple lock secured the entrance door. Nobody worried about theft since only the tenants had access to this basement. The walls of the locker were lined with shelves that held my mother's large selection of preserved fruit. In the centre there were usually two piles: one of coal and the other the German food staple – potatoes.

~

Once the Nazis were ensconced in power, school teachers began encouraging their students to denounce parents who didn't adhere to the new Nazi politics. Teachers told students that if they overheard any conversation at home or anywhere else criticizing the Führer or the Nazi party, they should be patriotic and report such deviationism. The report would bring the Gestapo to the door and the offending parent or parents would be hauled off for investigation. Many of them were forced to confess to offences they hadn't committed and to apologize to their children in front of the Gestapo officer. This, of course, encouraged more denunciations as the children bragged to their friends about what had happened to their parents. In one case I remember that the father of one of my schoolmates was kept in jail for more than a month and his "loving" son made sure that everybody in school knew about it. He was very proud of his contribution to the building of a proper German Reich.

When the new race laws of 1935 started to be enforced, everything quickly escalated. Jewish children were no longer allowed to mingle with the "Aryans" in schools and had to enrol in a Jewish school. In Leipzig the only Jewish day school was the Carlebach Schule, which was ill equipped both in staff and facilities to accommodate this influx of new pupils. For my brother and me, it meant a thirty-minute bicycle ride twice a day because we didn't live close to the school, which was located toward the centre of the Jewish residences and community life. One benefit of the long bicycle ride was that it gave us time to review our lessons and mentally prepare for examinations. Rain, snow or shine, we pedalled to school five days a week through traffic, at times quite heavy, because our route led us past the central railroad station. My parents, but mainly my father, didn't believe in us ever being driven to school at any time, even though our car and chauffeur were standing idle. I do, however, have very fond memories of sitting on the chauffeur's lap when I was eight years old and proudly manoeuvring the steering wheel while the chauffeur let the car move slowly forward. On the weekends, when my father drove, my mother always insisted on sitting in the back between my brother and me holding us firmly by the shoulder.

The principal, Dr. Weigersheimer, did a superb job incorporating all these newcomers into the academic life of the school but was greatly hindered by the rapid emigration of teachers. He was helped by the fact that all Jewish university professors were dismissed from the "Aryan" universities and persuaded them to teach at his school. I clearly remember my mathematics teacher, Professor Dr. Levy, who instilled in me a love for numbers. Professor Dr. Kassewitz was my homeroom teacher and taught us German and history. Mr. Lampel, a cantor, was our music teacher. These teachers adapted quickly to teaching children instead of university students and we profited from their educational skills.

School life became easier when we no longer had to confront the bullies whose parents taught them that all Jews were evil and who punctuated this teaching with their fists and feet. It gave us some peace of mind to know that we no longer had to worry about defending ourselves against an unexpected attack when we arrived at school. There were not many of these rowdies, but even one made our existence uncomfortable.

There was one very welcome side effect that came from switching to the Carlebach Schule. At the time that my brother and I started public school we had also been attending Hebrew school to learn Hebrew, Jewish culture and prepare for our respective bar mitzvahs. This meant that twice a week we were deprived of afternoon playing. Once we were enrolled at the Carlebach Schule, Hebrew lessons became part of our regular school curriculum and our afternoons were returned to us.

Weekend afternoons were the time when we visited family at the coffee house. Almost every Saturday and/or Sunday afternoon we would proceed to Café Felsche where my parents would meet their friends and, of course, their children. This was also the time when our table manners were put to the test. My mother would again sit between us watching carefully how we used our cutlery. She would never reprimand us in public – instead, when we did something wrong, she would pinch us under the table. We paid close attention to our manners to be spared the pinching.

Uncle Josziu, who was my mother's brother, and his wife, Aunt Karolin, owned a well-known coffee house in Berlin, Café Garai on BelleAllianceplatz, that was frequented by the "arty" set of Berlin, such as famous film producers, writers and painters. The coffee house had two sections: the left section was for the "peons," while the one on the right was reserved for those who had already made a name for themselves. Both sections were furnished in round, marble-topped tables that seated two or four people and red, plush-covered comfortable chairs. Guests at the café were welcome to stay as long as they liked, even if they were having just one cup of coffee. There were also the usual wooden hangers on the wall holding the main German newspapers for people to read.

The maitre d' at the Café Garai had a thorough knowledge of who was who and rarely made a mistake. At the end of the right section was the *Stammtisch*, the table reserved for the owners and their friends and favourite guests. It was strictly "by invitation only" and quite a few guests aspired to sit at that table. It was like King Arthur's round table and there were two main requirements for being invited into this inner sanctum reigned over by my Aunt Karolin. One was impeccable manners as demanded and practiced by my aunt, and the other was recognition of one's achievements. I never did discover which of these two was more important to my aunt, but I do know from personal experience that she was an absolute stickler for good manners. Many a well-known Berlin celebrity could be found at the Café Garai was accommodated and even in my early youth I appreciated, while not fully comprehending, the conversations taking place there.

Aunt Karolin was a regal-looking woman who carried her 250 pounds with great dignity; her weight gave her distinction comparable to that of Queen Wilhelmina of Holland. She had earned high respect for her self-possession and kindliness from all who knew her. Her husband, my Uncle Josziu, by comparison, was a meek man who danced to her tunes and who, I believe, was very much afraid of her wit and intelligence. It was undoubtedly her intellect and regal composure that attracted the type of guest who frequented the coffee house. Everybody clamoured to be invited to the round table and pay homage to Aunt Karolin. Whenever my brother and I visited Berlin and frequented Café Garai, we always got a refresher course in proper manners and behaviour. She never looked upon us as children to be pampered but rather as individuals to be moulded. Her personality was so forceful that even a child could not help but try to please her. Her corrective measures and reprimands were never expressed in anger but always with kindness and compassion.

My brother and I sometimes visited our uncles in Berlin during school holidays. While we usually stayed at our Uncle Arno's residence – he was another of my mother's brothers – I loved to visit the coffee house. Not only were there all the goodies such as pastries and specialty foods at our full disposal but, even more enticing, there was also a movie house next door to which we had free and unrestricted access. Uncle Arno had an apartment that was also located on BelleAllianceplatz and the coffee house was within walking distance. Another attraction was the fact that Uncle Josziu owned a beautiful German shepherd dog that I was occasionally allowed to walk outside. He was a most gentle animal and in retrospect I believe that he took even better care of me than I took of him. He had a great dislike for Brown Shirts and street sweepers.

One day my brother was walking down the aisle in the café before regular opening hours with a broom slung over his shoulder. The dog came around the corner and lunged at my brother, biting him in the thigh. It wasn't a deep bite – I think that midway through the attack the dog recognized my brother. After my brother was treated at the hospital, he was taken up to Uncle Josziu's apartment, located in the same building as the coffee house, and except for his outings to relieve himself, the dog didn't leave my brother's side.

~

My father, Emanuel Mann, was born in Vienna on April 14, 1889, and, as I have said, during World War I he served in the Austro-Hungarian army. He attained the rank of corporal and was attached to the finance section. As such he was responsible for the pay of the Austrian soldiers stationed in Italy. He graduated from the Commercial High School and after the war moved to Leipzig with his family, where he went into business.

My mother, Zelda Waldmann Mann, was born in Zgierz, Poland on May 24, 1896, and came to Leipzig in 1920 to join her brother Dadek, who was running a dental clinic. She worked as a dental assistant until she married my father in 1922. My brother Heinz (Heini) was born in 1923, and I was born in 1926. My brother was always the studious type and was never satisfied unless he was at the top of his class. Most of the time he was either first or second and my parents were very proud of his scholastic achievements. I, on the other hand, was always in the first third of my class because the work came naturally to me without a lot of studying that could have upgraded my ranking.

My mother had three brothers and two sisters – Arno, Josziu, Dadek, Anja and Rena – all of them born in either Zgierz or Lodz, Poland. Her brother Josziu was born on the same day as my mother, only three years earlier, in 1893. The three brothers had emigrated to Germany, as did my mother and one of her sisters. My Aunt Rena worked as a bookkeeper in my Uncle Arno's factory in Berlin and was a frequent visitor to our home in Leipzig. My mother's youngest brother, Uncle Dadek, also lived in Leipzig. He was a bachelor but had many girlfriends. Interestingly, all his girlfriends were very obese, while he was an exceptionally thin and small person. It would have been easy for him to hide behind any one of them without being noticed. Dadek was always short of money and my father helped him out constantly. One of the reasons for Dadek's pecuniary problems was that he believed anybody who came to him with a good story and would invest in their ventures. He never refused help to anybody who approached him, whatever their cause or reason.

Like my father, his three brothers – Arno, Hermann and Willy – were all born in Vienna, Austria and were Austrian citizens. The oldest, Arno, was killed in World War I while serving in the Austro-Hungarian army. When the family moved from Vienna to Leipzig after World War I, my grandfather practiced his trade as a furrier. Leipzig was the fur centre of Germany and the Brühl was the street of wholesale furriers. The fur trade attracted a great number of Jewish owners and operators, as did the textile industry. German Jews were not welcome in certain fields and professions – including public service – but there were a number of Jewish-owned merchant banks such as Oppenheimer, Warburg and Mendelssohn.

It is interesting to note that Leipzig never regained its status as a fur centre after World War II – Jewish furriers who did return to Germany after the Holocaust settled mainly in Frankfurt rather than the Communist-controlled Leipzig. A relatively small fur centre developed in Frankfurt after the war with some Jewish participation. My grandfather had prospered in Leipzig's fur trade, but his three sons entered different fields. My father went into the textile industry, first as a shirt manufacturer and then as a men's underwear wholesaler. When the law deprived him of these activities, he became an independent wine merchant buying wine from German vineyards and selling it in large quantities to wealthy individuals.

I never met my maternal grandparents, Israel and Machla Waldmann, and really know very little about them. My only recollection is seeing photographs of both of them – my grandfather wrapped in a *tallis*, a traditional prayer shawl, and my grandmother wearing a *sheitel*, the conventional wig worn by Orthodox Jewish women. My grandfather was apparently ultra-Orthodox, but this religiosity was certainly not practiced by any of his children living in Germany. My maternal grandparents were living in Lodz, Poland when they died. My grandfather died on a trip to Warsaw, where he was visiting his cousin who, I was told, was one of the few Jewish members of the Sejm, the Polish parliament. My grandmother died in 1935 and I remember my mother making the trip to Poland for her funeral and remaining to sit shiva for the usual seven days.[15]

My paternal grandparents, on the other hand, remain vividly imprinted in my memory. My grandfather, Ferdinand Mann, was a patrician-looking gentleman who invariably wore shirts with wing collars. My grandmother, Fannie Mann, was all of five feet tall but carried her size so well that one could almost be fooled into believing she was much taller. She was always well dressed but never ostentatious in either her choice of jewellery or clothing. By the time I was really conscious of their existence, my grandfather had retired and they had moved into a smaller apartment not far from the Carlebach Schule. Before that they had maintained the apartment where my father and his brothers were brought up. Their move closer to our school meant my brother and I frequently went to their place for lunch and my grandmother would always have something special for us, be it sweets, small gifts or money; we never left their apartment without a little something in our pockets.

My paternal grandmother's brother was an Orthodox Jew who married in Poland before coming to Leipzig. It was only a religious marriage and was not recognized under German law. This created an interesting situation since the first two of their six children car-

---

15 In Judaism, shiva (meaning "seven" in Hebrew) is the seven-day mourning period that is observed after the funeral of a close relative.

their mother's maiden name, Reiter, and the next four had their father's name, Gang. After the birth of their first two children, Mr. Gang gave in and went through a civil marriage ceremony in Leipzig and while it "legitimized" their last four children, the first two kept their mother's name. Their oldest boy, Hermann, became a well-known boxer and won the Leipzig middleweight boxing championship. He left Germany shortly after Hitler came to power since he was on the blacklist of the German Athletic Society and would have been subject to severe beatings had they caught him.[16] He emigrated to South America, where he became a successful furrier in Buenos Aires. The youngest two spent a lot of time at our apartment and at times considered my mother to be theirs as well. They even called her Mami and both my parents gave them a lot of moral and financial support.

We never really got to know the Polish side of my mother's family. One of her sisters from Lodz frequently visited us, but I never met the other sisters. One of my mother's married sisters lived in Lodz and my mother made annual treks to Poland, for about a fortnight each, to visit her. My mother's three brothers were all in Germany, two in Berlin and one in Leipzig. One of her sisters immigrated to Berlin and was living with and working for her oldest brother, Uncle Arno.

Uncle Arno was an engineer who held about seventy technical patents registered in Germany. He owned a tool-and-die factory in Berlin and did most of the development and special part manufacturing for Deutsche Lufthansa and other factories. His factory was declared an essential industry by the Germans and was thus exempted from the German racial laws. It continued in operation, employing Aryans up to the time of his departure for London in 1939. He was deported in the infamous *Abschiebung* (deportation) of 15,000 to 17,000

16 The Nazification of all aspects of German life even extended to sports, as the Reich Sports Office systematically excluded "non-Aryans" from sports facilities and associations. Like other official sports bodies, the German Boxing Association expelled Jewish and Sinti champion fighters.

Polish-born Jews in October 1938, when most of the Jews of Polish birth living in Germany were forcibly repatriated to Poland.[17] The irony was that this was only a couple of months after he had returned from a visit to the United States.

During this roundup the Germans proceeded to take people from their homes and herd them into a central assembly place. There was clearly no definite plan to this mass deportation and the arrest procedure varied from city to city. In some places, the whole family was arrested, even though only one member of the household was of Polish origin. In others they concentrated only on the Polish-born member. In still other cities they arrested the husband and wife, but not the German-born children. My Aunt Rena, for example, one of mother's sisters who was Polish-born but living in Berlin, wasn't targeted for deportation and fled with us to Brussels in 1939. My mother's brother Arno was also one of the few permitted to return to Berlin from Poland since German industry required his services. My coffee-house uncle, Josziu, who was also deported at this time, was not allowed to return to Berlin. Aunt Karolin's sister was married to a very prominent Greek politician who arranged for my uncle to be admitted to Greece and Aunt Karolin had to liquidate their assets before following him to Athens. From there they travelled to Southern Rhodesia, now Zimbabwe, from where my uncle emigrated to Canada after Aunt Karolin's death.

Uncle Arno's wife, Herta, was a compulsive poker player and a chain smoker. She would come to my uncle's factory three times a week to look after the company accounts since she didn't trust anybody else to do it. Herta was in her late thirties when she gave birth in May 1930 to their only child, Alfred, who was born with Down's syndrome. No effort or money was spared to try to find a cure and they

---

17 On October 27–28, 1938, the Nazi government expelled Jews with Polish passports from Germany in what has come to be known as the *Polenaktion* or Zbaszyń deportation.

were told that if the child lived past eighteen years of age, he could have a normal life span. Uncle Arno doted on that boy and tried everything to allow him to live as normal a life as possible. They travelled all over Europe to visit anybody who offered even the remote possibility of a remedy. Uncle Arno never recovered from the pain of having an only child with this condition and this pain was heightened whenever my brother and I, his only nephews, visited Berlin or he came to Leipzig. He always believed that his wife's self-indulgent lifestyle during her pregnancy had contributed to their son's disorder.

We were well off and most of the wishes we had as children were fulfilled. I remember that we were the first among our friends to own a galena (lead sulfide) crystal radio in which the connection was established by moving a wire to a certain point on the crystal. It required really fine-tuning because the tiny wire, called a cat's whisker, had to be very precisely centred on a given spot on the crystal detector. This was the basis of the first radio receivers. The sound was, of course, scratchy, but in the early 1930s, even this was heaven. One wire hanging outside the window served as an antenna and another connected to the water faucet as the grounder. Our friends telephoned us regularly to hear the voices and music emanating from our crystal radio, and our telephone lines would often be tied up for hours. Every Saturday afternoon we listened to a symphony concert aired from the Leipzig Gewandhaus, turning up the volume to its highest level so that our friends could listen to it through the telephone. The melodious voice of tenor Joseph Schmidt made his rendition of "Ein Lied geht um die Welt" (A Song Heard 'Round the World') one of the most popular songs in Germany. It was quite exceptional in those days to own a radio and not too many young people possessed one. It added to our popularity with the other children but dismayed all the parents because everyone's telephones were tied up for long periods. My father also bought me a mini camera – a Minox – that produced photographs measuring about 4 centimetres by 4 centimetres. While it created a fairly sharp image, you needed good eyesight to recognize the people in the pictures. It was definitely made for children because the film was so tiny that it took small fingers to load the film.

My brother got his first bicycle when he was about ten years old. I was so envious and even though I was told that when I reached the same age I would be able to have one as well, I cried my heart out trying to persuade my parents I was responsible enough now. Nothing worked and both my parents were adamant about their decision. I started saving my pocket money until I had enough to buy a bicycle pump. As soon as I got one I showed it to my parents telling them that since I already had the pump for my bicycle, I shouldn't have to wait too long to be able to use it. Somehow this logic impressed my father enough to buy me a bicycle a few months later. The bicycle opened up new vistas for exploration. I no longer needed to take the streetcar to school but could ride along with my brother. At first I was only allowed to bicycle on my own on our street, but once I had passed this trial period, my restrictions were lifted and I was free to roam. The Bar Kochba Platz sports centre was about a forty-five minute ride from our apartment. This meant I could go there without having to be driven. Also, we could reach the Skeudnitz airport in about an hour and a half from our apartment and watch planes take off and land. The longest ride we would take was to visit the town of Halle, which was about a four-hour ride. A new world opened when I could ride anywhere and visit places that were otherwise difficult to reach. We visited the zoo more frequently and attended the weekly outdoor concert in the summer at the Rosenthal Park on Sunday afternoon. Twice a year we went to the Leipzig fairgrounds to see what was, in those days, the largest European industrial fair, where the world came to present its goods and seek new customers. The various languages we heard were amazing to a child and that's when I really began to realize that the world was larger than just Germany.

~

The charmed life I had led began to disappear forever when the Nazis passed the Nuremburg race laws in 1935. I've already mentioned some of the effects – at school and in the Boy Scouts – but in 1936 my parents had to dismiss our maid who had been with us for over thirteen years. Else was like a member of the family and couldn't understand why she had to leave, particularly when she had no other employment. After she had gone a tenant in our apartment building laid charges against my father, saying that he had observed my father making love to Else on the stairs of the building. *Der Stürmer* was delighted with this information and published my father's photograph, accusing him of *Rassenschande*, desecration of race. Fortunately it never came to trial since Else refused to corroborate the charges. It took a lot of courage for her to do so because the pressure put for her to testify to these false accusations was enormous.

This event reminds me of a story my father told me when I was already grown up. Every Thursday he had a regular poker game with the same participants, the location of the game changing every week to another player's residence. During the summer they played in residences where the maids were still working. The reason for this was that most of the families would go to the seashore almost for the whole summer and the maids would go with them. The fathers came to visit on the weekends and spent maybe a week or two with the family during the summer, so the poker game was transferred to the home of those players who still had a maid in attendance. One of these locations was the home of my father's friend Oscar R, and there was a new player for that particular evening. During the course of the evening he asked Oscar where the bathroom was and Oscar told him that it was "down the hallway, the second door to the right." After a short while the man came back laughing hilariously and Oscar asked him what was so funny. The man said that he had opened the door and a female voice in the dark room said, "Oscar, is that you?" using the intimate word *Du* for "you." Needless to say the ensuing outbreak of laughter by all the other players was universal – except for Oscar, who didn't appreciate this revelation at all.

After 1936 we could no longer go away for the summer because the owners of the summer seashore residences weren't allowed to lease to Jews. We could still visit most places in Berlin in 1936, particularly during that summer's Olympic games. On Hitler's personal orders all the signs that said "Juden sind hier unerwünscht," (Jews Not Wanted Here) were removed before the start of the games and the world should have recognized then that Hitler still cared about world opinion. Had the nations of the world showed unity at the time, they could have prevented the oncoming disaster of the Holocaust.

Part of our summer and some other school holidays were usually spent visiting my uncles in Berlin, and during the summer of 1937 my brother and I were bundled off to Berlin to stay with Uncle Arno. Aunt Rena was requisitioned from her job in my uncle's factory to look after us, but the opportunities to entertain Jewish children were rather restricted. We couldn't visit museums, go to movie theatres or visit a swimming pool. Even the boat ride down the river Spree was not allowed. Uncle Josziu, my coffee-house uncle, could arrange for us to sneak into the movie theatre in his building and my brother and I went in and out through a side door. We didn't have any companions, though, because the "Aryan" children were not allowed to play with us. Unfortunately my cousin Alfred not only suffered from Down's syndrome, but was four years younger and therefore not a playmate. Somehow my aunt found enough ways to keep us occupied and the few weeks we spent there passed quickly.

After we were enrolled in the Carlebach Schule in 1936, my parents decided that Heini and I should take music lessons. I picked the violin as the instrument I wanted to master and my brother elected to learn to play the piano. My music teacher – a man of about seventy-five years who taught both violin and piano – lived halfway between the school and our apartment. Once a week after school we proceeded to the teacher's apartment, where we would both take our lessons on the same afternoon. It was quite a feat for my parents to arrange this because the teacher was "Aryan" and was not legally allowed to teach us. He knew we were Jewish and I never discovered if whether my father paid him a princely sum to overlook our religion or the man did it out of his own conviction. The lessons proceeded satisfactorily, although at times our teacher used a conductor's baton on our hands to reinforce his instructions. We became proficient enough in our playing to be required to perform for our parents' friends, and especially for my paternal grandparents when they came for dinner every Friday night.

We had no school orchestra even though our music teacher at school was a conductor and former professor of music at the Leipzig academy of music. One of the main reasons for this was the steady departure of children as their families left Germany. While our music teacher would at times have us perform individually before the whole class and would correct some of our errors, it wouldn't have been feasible to organize an orchestra. He did expose us to classical music and taught us how to interpret the music and appreciate the composer's intent. Our music teacher, Mr. Lampel, was also a synagogue cantor and had a very melodious voice with an incredible range. He made sure we were well trained in the scales and could read music. In this regard Hitler did us a favour in banning Jewish professors from German universities because under normal circumstances we would not have been taught at the high school level by instructors of such high calibre. They understood how to bring the learning process to life and make it interesting. Many Jewish children from that era benefited from this unusual situation and continued willingly and gladly through the educational process. We learned our do-re-mi voluntarily, without being pressured to do so and that generation grew into lovers of classical music.

During this period we were all fascinated with the writing of the German "Indian" writer Karl May. In his seventy years he had never actually met a real "Red" Indian, but his writings seemed authentic to us. He wrote some seventy books, of which the most widely read is probably the novel *Winnitou*, the story of an Indian chief and his white friend "Old Shatterhand."[18] Reading it made us participants in the life in the West of the great land America. We heard our parents speak of moving to America and we could visualize encountering Karl May's Indians there. To cement their friendship, Winnitou and Old Shatterhand became blood brothers by cutting into a finger of one hand and pressing the bleeding digits together. The flow of blood from one to the other not only assured their eternal friendship but also made them inseparable.

My two best friends and I decided we too should be blood brothers. We had to find a way to go about this secretly since we didn't want to invite others into our blood brotherhood. So our first blood mingling took place in a closed toilet cubicle in the boys' washroom. The three of us crowded into this small cubicle, pierced our index fingers with a pin and then press them together. We didn't know how long to apply the pressure nor did we know if you could perform this ceremony with three people instead of two, so to be sure we decided to repeat the ritual three times. As it happened, because we couldn't use the cubicle for the third attempt for some reason, we did it in the bicycle shed after school. We thought that everybody else had left, but little did we know that one of the boys who was suspicious of our actions in the cubicle and wanted to join our group had spied on us. Midway through our ceremony he appeared and demanded to be let in on our ritual. We adamantly refused and told him to get lost.

It turned out not to be a wise decision on our part. The boy told his parents what we were doing and they reported us to the headmaster, Professor Dr. Weigersheimer. We were called to the headmaster's office and he asked us point blank if we were performing the act of blood brotherhood, assuring us he would go easy on us if we admit-

---

18 Karl May (1842–1912), one of the most popular German authors of the day, based his *Winnetou* series of books on the fictional Native American character, Winnetou, a wise Apache chief, and his white blood brother, Old Shatterhand.

ted it. He told us that, according to Jewish law, the blood brotherhood procedure that required the spilling of human blood was one of the great sins and could not be tolerated in a Jewish high school, lest it grow into a fad. We were afraid of the consequences if our parents found out what we had done and admitted the transgression to the headmaster with great regret and promised never to do it again. We believed that our admission would end this whole affair without our parents knowing about it.

When I returned home after school and told my mother that I was going out to play, however, I was told to stay home in my room and wait for my father to come home. I realized then that the telephone had been used for a purpose other than just listening to music with my friends. When my father arrived he called me into the family room and asked me about the matter. He wanted to know whose idea it was and why we had thought it necessary to perform the act. When I explained that it was my idea and that we had done it to cement our friendship under these trying times, that we didn't know what was going to happen to us or if we would always stay together. My father explained to me the Jewish religious reasons for considering the act to be a transgression, which the headmaster had not done. He also explained that friendship is earned and not created through blood brotherhood. He made me promise never to do it again and to tell the other boys to stop. When I told my friends that we must desist, they were quite happy to comply because their parents had disciplined them severely, including a beating administered by the father of one of them.

∼

Over the years, my parents had, like others, consulted with our teachers to plan for our future occupation. In those days career counsellors and career testing were unknown, so unless a child displayed some clear early signs of aptitude in a particular field, the parents simply selected a career based on their imagination. In my early youth I showed great interest in chemistry and tried to develop my skills in this field. My parents bought me a chemistry set with test tubes, Cadmus paper, microscope and a Bunsen burner. I'm sure that the thought of my turning out to be another Robert Wilhelm Bunsen, the famous German chemist, crossed their mind. The set had a great number of chemicals in vials and tubes, as well as instructions on how to conduct various experiments. It was something I really enjoyed and looked forward to using after school. For days I spent all my free time doing experiments and searching for new ways to change colours and smells by mingling the various chemicals.

One Saturday afternoon when my parents did not insist on my accompanying them to the coffee house, I came up with the brilliant idea of seeing what would happen if I boiled urine. I had read somewhere that urine is a composition of various salts and I wanted to separate the salts and examine them under the microscope. After I had filled a test tube with urine – mine of course – I held it over the Bunsen burner to vaporize the liquid. This took quite some time and when I had finished, there was some crystallization, but there was another side effect: the whole apartment was filled with a foul stench. At first I couldn't smell it; I had become accustomed to the odour. By the time I realized what had happened, it was hard to clear out the stench. Even opening all the windows in the apartment couldn't get rid of it. My parents weren't too enchanted with that phase of my experimentation and suggested that I stick to the instructions in my chemistry set and restrict my creativity to ideas that I had checked out with my physics teacher at school.

Another experiment I conducted was making facial creams for my mother. I learned from a book that the underlying ingredient of all facial creams is lanolin, the fat obtained from the sheep's wool, with the other substances governing the absorption, aroma and consistency of the cream. Lanolin itself has a terrible smell and the various perfumes used to kill this odour fools the public into thinking that there are different varieties of facial creams in the marketplace. My mother really liked the facial cream that I produced and even gave some to her girlfriends. It wasn't a commercial venture, but this production confirmed my parents' belief that I was suited to studying chemistry. These dreams were shattered by being forced to emigrate and to this day I still wonder if I would have become a chemist had Hitler not appeared on the scene.

∼

My father's sense of security was severely shaken when Hitler carried out the *Anschluss*, the annexation of Austria to Germany on March 12, 1938. As result of this action, my father lost his status as a foreigner. On March 26 Hermann Goering declared the Nazis' intention of ridding Vienna of all Jews within four years and on April 1 my father learned that the first transport of Austrian Jews to Dachau had taken place.[19] Any remaining sense of security that my father had evaporated on April 10 when a plebiscite was held in Austria and over 99 per cent of the ballot-casters voted in favour of the already completed annexation. Up to that time he had felt relatively protected, even as a Jew, because he firmly believed the Germans would respect his nationality. In February 1933, when the order had come for him to be picked up to perform menial tasks in the Brown House, the order had been revoked precisely because the German authorities had learned of his Austrian citizenship. His service in the Austro-Hungarian army during World War 1 had also entitled him to Austrian government protection up to the time of the annexation. Suddenly he found himself without this security blanket and he started to feel at risk.

---

19 Hermann Goering, Hitler's designated successor and commander-in-chief of the Luftwaffe (German air force), played an important role in the annexation of Austria. For more information on Goering and Dachau, see the glossary.

I believe that even more instrumental in my father's decision to leave as soon as possible was the famous meeting on September 29, 1938, between Adolf Hitler, Benito Mussolini, Edouard Daladier and Neville Chamberlain.[20] The breathing space created by the Chamberlain Declaration had proved to be as futile as the earlier meeting in Evian-les-Bains, in France that was held July 6–15, 1938, when delegates from thirty-two countries, including the United States, Great Britain and France, failed to arrive at a solution to the Jewish refugee problem and had essentially said "Jew, help yourself." The undisputable fact of the concentration camps in Germany did not induce these representatives to seek a solution that would safeguard German Jews.

It was not the supposed assurances of "peace for our time" uttered by Chamberlain but the fact the world chose to ignore the cruelties perpetrated on Jews and others by Hitler and his cronies that convinced the German and Austrian Jewish communities that there would be no help forthcoming from outside. It must also have convinced the Nazis that the world didn't care what happened to the Jews. This was demonstrated when the Nazis decreed that all Jews in Germany would have to carry specially marked identity cards beginning on January 1, 1939. Jewish passports would be marked with a red letter J and it would become compulsory for all Jews whose first names were not recognizably "Jewish" to add the names "Israel" for men or "Sara" for women. The decree had been issued on July 23, 1938, just days after the Evian meeting. By then the majority of the German

---

20 The Munich Agreement of September 30, 1938, was a pact signed between the governments of Germany, France, Britain and Italy to settle Germany's claims to the Sudetenland region of Czechoslovakia. Czechoslovakia was not permitted to participate in this conference, which took place in Munich. Large portions of Czechoslovakian territory were granted to Germany by France and Britain in order to avoid a war. Following the Munich Conference, Neville Chamberlain declared that he had secured "peace for our time."

citizenry was solidly behind Hitler. In my eyes, he had catered to their love of uniforms, parades and military formations, and they were only too willing to submit to this style of absolute authority.

The loss of my father's citizenship was somehow mitigated by the fact that his friend Kuba Ader had persuaded him to get a Polish passport in 1937. Kuba Ader had excellent relations with the Polish consul, Mr. Edward Tulasiewicz, in Leipzig and could get anything done there. The fact that my father obtained a Polish passport was quite a feat considering that he didn't speak a word of Polish and was born in Vienna; only my mother was fluent in the language. The Aders were close friends of my parents and together they contemplated the possibility that my brother would marry their daughter Ursula.

Even with these events unfolding around us, though, life retained some aspects of normalcy – particularly from a child's perspective. Every Saturday morning at around 11 A M, my father would drive to Café Heiner to meet with Ader and other friends at their usual round table. This was a solemn ritual not to be changed by Hitler's actions against Jews. Even after the 1935 Nuremberg race laws were published, these Saturday meetings were inviolate. He would sometimes take my brother and me along and we would walk around downtown. One place we visited frequently was the Kroch Building, Leipzig's tallest building at the time, where they had a paternoster lift that replaced the traditional elevator.[21] It consisted of cabins of about two metres in height and one metre in width stacked one on top of the other. It was in perpetual motion and passengers jumped in and out of the cabins on the desired floor. We were always afraid to ride it all the way around because we thought it would go upside down at the top and we would land on our heads. One day we got brave and decided to ride it all the way. We were ready for any eventuality, but to our sur-

---

21 A paternoster lift is so named because its connected compartments move in a continuous loop like a rosary, the string of beads used in the traditional Christian Pater noster prayer ("Our Father," or Lord's Prayer).

prise the cabin remained upright when it moved across to the down position. On one occasion I tripped when jumping into the cabin and my brother had to pull me in before my leg got caught by the floor above.

My grandparents continued to come to our apartment for Friday night dinners. My mother continued to adhere to the Erev Shabbat (Sabbath evening) ceremony even after Else, our maid, had to leave because of the race laws. The white tablecloth spread over the dining room table was laid with the Rosenthal china dishes and the silver cutlery all neatly placed in the required order of usage from the outside inward. The challah (egg bread) in its silver basket was placed in front of my grandfather so that he could recite the blessing over it before the beginning of the meal. On those Friday evenings, a heavy silver chalice was substituted for the usual crystal wineglass at my father's place at the table. The candelabras with their two white candles were placed in the centre of the table. My mother lit the candles and covered her face with her hands as she recited the blessing over the candles. Although my mother had a very liberal outlook on dietary laws she kept a kosher household so that my orthodox grandparents would eat in our home.[22] She did this out of respect for her husband's parents, but did not necessarily adhere strictly to Orthodox dietary laws in all circumstances. Let me illustrate this more clearly. Somebody mentioned to my mother that ham was healthy for children. Since she would not bring ham into our home, once a week she took my brother and me for a walk past a butcher shop. She would march us in, buy two Kaiser rolls and a quarter kilogram of ham and evenly divide the meat between the two rolls and give one to each of us. She swore us to secrecy and we were happy to comply so that we wouldn't lose this delicious weekly treat.

---

22 For more information on the Jewish dietary laws and on the Jewish Sabbath, see the entries *Kashruth* and Shabbat in the glossary.

During one of our Friday night dinners, while we were eating the first course of boiled carp, a fishbone lodged in my grandfather's throat. He started to choke and began to turn blue. My father hit him squarely between the shoulder blades a number of times and almost at the very last second managed to dislodge the bone. There is very little doubt the man would have suffocated shortly had his breathing not been restored just in time. This had a very strong psychological effect on my brother and me – to this day, neither of us eat any fish with bones. While I will eat sardines, I remove the spine before putting them in my mouth.

Chicken was always the main course at the Friday night dinners. It was the easiest kosher meat to purchase since there were more kosher poultry stores than kosher meat markets and it was a staple food item in kosher German households. People also generally thought that chicken was healthier to consume than red meat. My childhood experience with it, however, has resulted in my developing an utter dislike for chicken; I still avoid eating it as much as I can.

There were no refrigerators, only iceboxes, and the daily delivery of ice that we relied on was suspended to Jewish households after 1936. We were lucky because our next-door neighbour – who was not Jewish – would purchase extra quantities and we were able to get it from him. Other Jews had to go down to the street to purchase blocks of ice and cart them back to their apartments or houses. Iceboxes were relatively small and did not permit too much storage. As a result, people had to buy meats and vegetables on a daily basis. Even butter was usually bought one hundred grams at a time to reduce the possibility of it turning rancid. The fact that there was a grocery store in our apartment building made it easier for us to get provisions even when Jews had problems frequenting the non-Jewish stores. My parents had had a charge account at the store for years, but now the owner informed them that he could no longer let them put things on account because he was afraid of being audited and the authorities would discover that he dealt with Jews.

~

Once a year the family would gather in either Berlin or Leipzig and sometimes even one or two members from Poland joined us. These were always joyous occasions for everybody except for me and my brother – we were the centre of attention and thus had to be on our best behaviour. We also had to endure the inevitable kissing and face-stroking by our aunts. My cousin Alfred was spared these expressions of tenderness. On the bright side, though, was the presents we received – our uncles and aunts all had to outdo each other in the gifts they gave us. Nonetheless we found that the best way to annoy members of the family was for me and my brother to converse in Hebrew. We had acquired enough knowledge of the language at Hebrew school and the Jewish Boy Scouts to be able to carry on a fairly fluent conversation. While everybody in the family could read Hebrew, they certainly didn't speak the language. Everybody spoke German because assimilation had taken its toll in our family as well as others. Yiddish was not considered acceptable and proper German usage was a must in our circle.

My brother's bar mitzvah in August 1936 was the occasion for the last family gathering. My uncles Arno and Josziu drove in from Berlin with their wives, along with my Aunt Rena. Uncle Arno drove in his Opel Admiral and was full of praise for the new Autobahn between Berlin and Leipzig, a distance of about 160 kilometres.[23]

The celebration of my brother's bar mitzvah was held in the Gottschedstrasse synagogue during a regular Saturday morning service in August 1936. The religious teacher at the Carlebach Schule had prepared him for the ceremony. Heini was called up to read a certain section of the Torah and recite the various blessings and chants asso-

---

23 The Autobahn was Germany's four-lane divided highway system; construction on it started in 1933 and the first stretch was opened to traffic in 1936.

ciated with this event. He performed excellently, justifying the many days and hours of study it took to perfect this. My parents, grandparents, uncles and aunts were very proud of him on this day when a Jewish boy enters manhood.

After the service, it is customary for the boy's parents to pay for a kiddush, a celebratory gathering at which the whole congregation is invited to enjoy alcoholic beverages and food. At the kiddush following Heini's bar mitzvah there was an ample supply of all sorts of herring, chopped liver, cheeses and a sweet table. From there, we proceeded to our apartment where the family celebration took place. Aside from my Berlin relatives, there was also my father's parents and his two brothers, Uncle Hermann and Uncle Willy. At that time, Uncle Willy was divorced from his last wife, a practicing pharmacist, and I heard snatches of conversations that he was having an affair with a married woman.

Uncle Hermann's wife was an alcoholic and I don't remember ever meeting her when she was sober or didn't smell of alcohol. My Aunt Anja, my mother's sister, had travelled from Poland for the festivities and, to the best of my knowledge, this was the last time my mother and her brother Dadek saw her alive. Aunt Anja and her family disappeared during the Holocaust and despite many inquiries, we were never able to find any information about what became of them or their many offspring.

The bar mitzvah was a very joyous day and for a while we were able to block out the outside world with its inherent dangers. A sumptuous lunch was ready on our return from the synagogue and the twenty or so people enjoyed, for what was to be one of the last times, a euphoric feeling about the future. Since hotels were not allowed to accommodate Jews, my Berlin uncles and their wives had to drive back the same day.

This was the year that various members of our family began to emigrate, starting with my Uncle Willy leaving for Paris and my Uncle

Hermann and his wife for the Free City of Danzig, as it was known.[24] After World War I, the League of Nations had declared Danzig to be a free city in accordance with the Versailles Treaty. This had always rankled the Germans, who keenly resented the loss of this historic city along with the war. So it came as no surprise when Hitler annexed Danzig in 1939, reclaiming it as part of Germany.

Uncle Willy, my father's youngest brother, had always been considered to be a bon vivant in the family. He was the only one who had married and divorced twice and, much to my grandparents' chagrin, his second wife was both a gentile and a working woman. As I mentioned, she was a trained pharmacist whom my uncle met when he was having a prescription filled. My grandparents objected vigorously to this misalliance and threatened to cut my uncle out of their will. He had always stayed with my grandparents between his marriages since his mother catered to every whim. During these fights about his marrying "out of the faith," many words were spoken that later created resentment. One of these was my grandfather's statement that he would rather be dead than see one of his children marry a shikse, a gentile woman.

One morning during this harrowing period, my uncle didn't come out of his bedroom for breakfast. My grandmother went to his room and found him lying on his back with his mouth open and his arm hanging lifeless over the side of the bed. When she went to the bedside she could see that my uncle wasn't breathing and an empty medicine bottle was lying on the night table. Her loud cry brought my grandfather to her side and my grandmother immediately starting berating

---

24 After more than one hundred years of mostly German and Prussian rule, Danzig (in Polish, Gdańsk) was made a Free City by the Treaty of Versailles and placed under the jurisdiction of the League of Nations. The city was to have its own constitution, national anthem, parliament and government. When Nazi Germany invaded Poland on September 1, 1939, the Germans regained control of the city. For more information, see the glossary.

my grandfather for causing of their son to commit suicide. Filled with grief, my grandfather said he wished he had not been so hard on my uncle and let him marry the woman. At that point my uncle opened his eyes and thanked my grandfather for giving his blessing to the nuptials, which took place a week later at the city hall.

The marriage lasted only a short while, however, since my uncle could not contain his extra-marital activities. His bright yellow Opel convertible, along with his roving eye, made a good combination for all sort of trysts. When my father questioned him, my uncle replied that while he liked to eat at home he occasionally needed to eat out. The divorce, which took place at the end of 1935, was partly caused by (and easy to obtain through) the newly decreed race laws. Willy's wife was told that she would lose her pharmacist position if she stayed married to a Jew. This was a tragic development for my uncle since it now became dangerous to have affairs with gentile women. He couldn't legally enter most restaurants or hotels since they were off-limits for Jews.

Sometime in the middle of 1936, though, he started an affair with the wife of a prominent Jewish furrier. While he was discreet about it, the news leaked out and came to my grandfather's attention. My grandfather knew the furrier from his own professional days and was disconcerted by his son's latest escapade. I believe this contributed to my uncle's decision to leave Germany and at the end of 1936 he and Mrs. Jedlicki, the furrier's wife, left Leipzig for Paris together. My grandparents didn't appear in public for at least six months thereafter because they felt so ashamed that their son had committed such a heinous act. But my father took it in stride, declaring that he wasn't responsible for his brother's actions. I know that it took a long time for my grandparents to be able to speak about the whole affair and even my Uncle Willy's frequent telephone calls from Paris didn't alleviate their pain or assuage their feelings of shame.

My Uncle Hermann and his wife, Else, also decided to leave for Danzig in 1936. This marriage was one of more downs than ups. As

I said, my Aunt Else was an alcoholic and a chain smoker. My father frequently had to support them and at various times employed Uncle Hermann so that he could earn a living. In January 1938 my father rushed to Danzig as soon as he heard that Uncle Hermann was dying from blood poisoning. He had apparently been suffering from this for almost week and had become too weak to visit the hospital. Aunt Else was too drunk to fetch a doctor and by the time she was sober enough to do so, it was too late. They had no telephone and she called my father from the post office in Danzig to tell him his brother was dying in the hospital. My father arrived just in time and my uncle's last affectionate words to my father were, "You are a faithful dog." After my father arranged for the funeral and gave Aunt Else money, he returned to Leipzig, which was only possible because he had obtained a re-entry permit from the police prior to his departure. He was away for four days and when he returned it was his sad task to inform my grandparents of their son's death.

~

Our last visits to the synagogue took place on September 25–27, 1938, for the High Holidays of Rosh Hashanah, the Jewish New Year, and October 4–5 for Yom Kippur, the Day of Atonement. In prior years we attended every High Holiday as well as the more joyous occasions such as Simchat Torah, when lots of sweets were handed out to the children.[25] We went to at least one Shabbat service a month, and this was always followed by a visit to the Rosenthal Park where we met with our school friends. Unlike all the previous years, in 1938 not a single man appeared in the customary morning coat or top hat.

---

25 The Jewish holiday of Simchat Torah is a joyous autumn celebration that marks the conclusion of the annual cycle of public Torah readings and the beginning of a new cycle. For more information, see the glossary.

After the 1938 conference in Berlin between Hitler and Chamberlain, the prime minister of England, our fears of war and of being caught in Germany were assuaged and we believed – or rather we wanted to believe – in Chamberlain's "peace for our time." During Yom Kippur the conversations centred mainly on Chamberlain's declaration and the consequences of peace. People were surprised that Chamberlain didn't intervene for the safekeeping of Jews in Germany or discuss their emigration.

The longest day of the High Holidays was Yom Kippur, when my parents remained in synagogue for almost the whole day. The services lasted until late afternoon and my brother and I were sent off to a restaurant for lunch only to return after eating to slip in and out of the ongoing religious services.[26] In previous years the men's attire was probably as unusual as one would see anywhere. Many men wore top hats, morning coats and striped pants, and on the lapel of their morning coats they proudly displayed their German World War I medals. This, they thought, marked them as good Germans. They looked as if they were presenting their credentials to God and requesting another year of accreditation. The synagogue had an excellent choir and a very harmonious organ that played during the service. The reverberations and echo were so well tuned that the synagogue was sometimes used for choral performances. The cantor had a most resonant voice and could easily have qualified as an opera singer.

Until 1936 the pulpit had been occupied by Rabbi Dr. Felix Goldmann, an outstanding orator and a most respected scholar. It is indeed a pity that his sermons were never published and are now lost to the public. I clearly remember the effect that his reasoning and explanations had on me and I'm convinced that, while I can no longer remember all the details, they left their mark. He would stand on the pulpit, wrapped in a huge prayer shawl that was bordered with

26 Yom Kippur, the Day of Atonement, is a solemn day of fasting and repentance. For more information, see the glossary.

gold embroidery, and preach to a sea of top hats, ignoring the world outside the temple. Rabbi Goldmann was the author of a number of books on Jewish life in Germany, most of them praising the assimilation of Jews in Germany. It was almost as if we had entered a different world that was freed from the restraints placed on Jewish life by the German antisemitic ordinances. The meeting place for our Boy Scout gatherings was not far from the synagogue and I recall that whenever I passed the building it always filled me with pride and awe. My brother Heini's bar mitzvah in August 1936 was one of the last times that Rabbi Goldmann preached before his death from blood poisoning.

During the infamous Kristallnacht that took place on November 9–10, 1938, the synagogue was burnt to the ground along with 250 others in Germany. Only the caretaker's residence, which was to the side of the synagogue and occupied by a non-Jew, was left standing. The wealth of information and symbols of tradition that not only recorded Jewish life in Leipzig but across Germany went up in smoke that night.

~

Friday, October 28, 1938, started out like any other day. My brother had left for school before me and before I left that morning, my father received a telephone call from his Gestapo school-friend. My father's friend told him about the German government's plan to deport all Polish-born Jews back to Poland and said that my mother's name was on the list for deportation. He suggested that we proceed immediately to the Polish consulate and seek refuge there. At that time the German government still respected international law regarding diplomatic immunity and the fact that the Polish consulate building was also the consul's residence assured that the grounds were inviolate. My parents decided to follow this suggestion and told me to go to school to get my brother. They also wanted me to stop by my grandparents' apartment – both of them were Polish-born – and advise them to also go to the consulate. When I arrived at school I found my brother and told him the news. He went to find my grandparents but he returned shortly to tell me that they had already been arrested by the police and taken to the collection centre. The gymnasium in our school, a separate edifice across the yard from the main school building, was being used as the collection centre. My brother said that he was going to try to enter the gymnasium to speak to my grandparents, but when he approached the entrance, the policeman standing guard told him that he could go in but wouldn't be allowed to come out.

At that point we thought that it was wiser to proceed to the Polish consulate. We got on our bicycles, but when we arrived at the consulate, police were outside along with a Polish vice consul who was advising the police who to let in and who to keep out. Since we knew that our parents were already inside, we had no problem being admitted. The building wasn't large enough to accommodate all the people taking refuge there and the conditions inside were not suited for the influx of so many people. This created all kinds of sanitary and medical problems. The other difficulty was the inadequate food supply – the consulate kitchen didn't have anywhere near enough food to provide for these masses nor the facilities to prepare it. A collection was taken up to give funds to the consul to purchase food supplies – there were no fast-food take-out restaurants in those days. It was impossible to find a place to sleep; people slept on chairs, on the ground or in some cases even standing up. My father's friend Kuba Ader, who was a friend of the consul, made arrangements for my mother to share one of the bedrooms with some of the other "privileged" ladies.

The consulate had a huge garden, but it couldn't be used at night because the weather was already freezing cold. The first evening we were there, I went for a walk in the garden and sat down on one of the benches. Apparently, I was tired enough to fall asleep sitting there in the cold. My Uncle Dadek, who had free access to come and go, brought us food and while he and my father were walking in the garden my uncle said, "Look at the person sleeping there on the bench; we'd better wake him up before he freezes to death." As they approached, they realized with horror that I was the person sitting there. Had they not passed by, I might have become what we would soon learn was the second death in the family caused by this deportation.

On the second day of our stay at the consulate, Uncle Dadek returned to the consulate with news that my grandmother had suffocated in the train before it had even pulled out of the railway station. When the roundup of Polish-born Jews had been completed, they had all been taken from the school gymnasium to the railway station in open trucks and herded into the trains. The stress was apparently too much for my grandmother and she couldn't breathe. After she was declared dead, her body was taken off the train and my grandfather was allowed to return to their apartment while my grandmother's body was delivered to a funeral parlour. The funeral had to be delayed until we could leave the consulate, which took three days.

The Polish consul negotiated with the German authorities and finally received their assurances that those of us leaving the consulate could safely return to our dwellings without further danger of deportation. I learned about the gruesome scenes of the trains moving from various points in Germany to the Polish-German border from eyewitnesses, including my uncles from Berlin who had been caught up in that net. The railway cars had disgorged thousands of people onto the grasslands as the German soldiers stood with machine guns telling them to march forward toward the Polish border-control area. The Poles, not knowing what was happening, stood with machine guns refusing to allow the people to cross into Poland. One thing was certain, the Poles were not interested in accommodating all of these Jews, many of whom could hardly speak Polish or had had anything to do with Poland for most of their lives. They were forced to remain in a no-man's-land on the German-Polish border in Zbąszyń for several months before the Polish and German officials finally reached an agreement that allowed the Jewish deportees into Poland after they had returned to Germany to liquidate their assets.

This clear and unmistakable proclamation that Hitler intended to live up to his commitment to make Germany free of Jews definitely left its mark on my father. Since the end of 1936 he had begun to think that our days were numbered if we didn't leave Germany very soon. He made arrangements for my grandfather to move into an old folks' home in Leipzig since, at eighty-two years of age, he was too old and weak to travel. Leaving him there was very hard on my father, knowing he may never see him again, but it was the only solution. My grandfather died in that old folks' home in 1942 and was spared the gruesome hardship of concentration camps or freight-train transports.

German and Polish Jews were increasingly deprived of their civil rights. Nazi decrees required the declaration of all Jewish property worth more than five thousand Reichmarks and made it illegal for Jews to place a non-Jewish figurehead at the head of a company to camouflage the fact that it was a Jewish corporation. Next came the *Asozialen-Aktion* (actions against antisocials) – the arrest of all "previously convicted" Jews, even including those who were prosecuted for minor traffic violations, and their detention in concentration camps. Lists of wealthy Jews were drawn up at treasury offices and police districts. Board certification of all Jewish physicians was revoked and Jewish physicians were only allowed to function as nurses to Jewish patients. All Jewish lawyers were confined to acting as "Jewish consultants for Jews." German passports held by Jews were confiscated and, when available, reissued with the J stamped inside to designate Jewish ownership. Rumour had it that this was done at the behest of the Swiss government who had no legal restrictions on Germans entering the country. After this measure, however, people with a J in their passports were refused admission to Switzerland – the Swiss welcomed the Jews' monetary assets but not their physical presence. German Jews were now forbidden to attend any public cultural events, prohibited from attending movies and concerts. Driver's licenses were confiscated and restrictions were imposed on freedom of movement and travel. Jews with industrial enterprises and businesses were forced to relinquish their ownership.

Many German Jews didn't have the financial means to leave Germany and were consequently condemned to the fate that eventually befell them. Jewish individuals and institutions with the financial means to have helped their coreligionists to leave bear some of the responsibility for the deaths of those who could not get out. In the early days of the Third Reich, Hitler only wanted a Germany that was free of Jews; if help had been forthcoming then, a great number of Jews living in Germany could have been saved.

~

My father was beholden to his Gestapo friend for extending a helping hand to us on three occasions. The first was in 1933, the second was during the Polish deportation in October 1938, and the third was just before Kristallnacht. In the early afternoon of November 9, 1938, he telephoned my father to warn him of what would be happening that evening. He suggested again that we seek refuge in the Polish consulate because he was sure that they would arrest my father and send him off to a concentration camp. This time, however, not only were there not as many people in the consulate but we only had to spend one night there. This was even more fortunate because we no longer had the good services of Uncle Dadek – he had already fled to Brussels, Belgium.

The persecutions continued with Jews being rounded up. The elderly were most affected – in Leipzig the SS dragged them to a rivulet near the zoological garden and made them jump from one side to the other while the officers whipped the old people ferociously.[27] Many of them couldn't make it across and fell into the icy-cold water. Onlookers,

---

27 The SS began as Adolf Hitler's elite corps of personal bodyguards, but later expanded its ambit significantly. For more information, see the glossary.

mainly youngsters, stood on the bridge off Humboldtstrasse laughing, encouraging the SS as if this were a display of trained animals. Witnessing this was one of the most sickening memories that is indelibly engraved in my mind. Even today, I can still see this picture as vividly as if it happened yesterday. It was probably the first real exposure I had to seeing man's cruelty to man. As Boy Scouts we had had fist and kicking fights with the Hitler Youth and during the last years of my attendance at the public school, we had been singled out by teachers and ridiculed, but I had never seen this type of barbarism displayed by fellow human beings.

Walking through the city it was incredible to discover the burned synagogues and the Jewish-owned stores smashed and plundered. The Jewish district of Leipzig, in the vicinity of the Gustav-Adolf-Strasse, Humboldtstrasse and Gerberstrasse, suffered the worst fate. There was hardly a Jewish store owner or wholesaler who did not lose all his or her assets that night. The destruction was not only total but systematic – one could see the old German edict of thoroughness in its execution. It was hard for me – a twelve-year-old boy – to grasp the logic or reason behind such intentional and planned wanton behaviour.

Were these the very same people whose culture had produced Schiller, Haydn, Schumann, and Goethe, who Lord Byron said was the greatest genius his age had produced? Or was this a new breed producing Hitler, Streicher, Goebbels, Heydrich? Was Goethe prophetic when he said, "The Germans should be transplanted and scattered all over the world, like the Jews, in order to bring to full development the good qualities that lie in them, and for the health of all nations?" Kristallnacht was not only the burning of synagogues and the destruction of Jewish property but a test that demonstrated the effectiveness of many years of anti-Jewish propaganda used to brainwash the population. The general population showed no reluctance to participate in the destruction and the photographs of German people's faces taken during this unpunishable "freedom to destroy" speak volumes. We are frequently told that not everyone engaged in the horrendous events of that night, but when one looks at the spectators, one realizes that their facial expressions aren't very different from those of the perpetrators. Nor can one excuse the rest of the world for not taking measures to challenge the Germans and to express the total unacceptability of these acts. When could we expect decent human beings to take a stand on matters of wilful and planned destruction and death? Ninety-one Jews were killed that night and 25,000 carted off to concentration camps to a fate worse than death. In those days the concentration camps were still located within Germany – Dachau, Buchenwald and Sachsenhausen. But the world remained silent and the Germans realized that nobody from the outside world was concerned about the Jews.

On November 12, 1938, Field Marshal Goering announced a fine of one billion Reichmarks to be levied against the Jews, labelling it an "atonement payment for the killing of Ernst vom Rath in Paris."[28] Goering also ordered Jews to pay for cleaning up the debris from the burnt synagogues and for the repairs to the destroyed Jewish storefronts of shops. It's ironic that the Nazis perpetrated these crimes and then ordered the Jews pay for them. In order to meet this penalty, every Jewish community across Germany was organized to collect funds from all the Jews still living in Germany. I believe that the German Jews were aware that there would be dire consequences if they didn't comply. Gold, silver, ornaments, paintings and any other valuables that could be turned into cash were delivered to the Jewish community centres to settle this blackmail demand.

One of the final blows to German Jewry in 1938 was the creation of a ban against Jews living in Berlin. The capital of Nazi Germany was

---

28 Ernst vom Rath was the junior German diplomat in Paris whose assassination in November 1938 by Herschel Grynszpan provided the pretext for Kristallnacht. Grynspan's family, though German residents, were Polish citizens and had been deported to Poland.

to now become *judenrein*. The year 1939 turned out to be no better for Jews. The newspaper *Der Stürmer* continued its unrelenting smear attack against Jews, advocating that any action against Jews, in whatever fashion, was legal and commendable. Early in January a decree was issued forbidding all Jewish dentists, veterinarians and pharmacists to practice. The Germans established a National Central Office for Jewish Emigration, with offices in Vienna and Prague. There was strong pressure on Jews to emigrate. The gas chambers had not yet been conceived. The emphasis was on getting Jews out of Germany and its annexed territories.

In April we learned that we no longer had eviction protection and the incontestable cancellation of all rent agreements with Jews was permitted. The underlying reason for this was to create Jewish houses where all Jewish families would be lodged. Fortunately, the enforcement was delayed by a few months and this allowed us to stay in our apartment until we left Germany.

~

The Keren Kayemet L'Israel (Jewish National Fund JNF) had placed a great number of coin collection boxes in Jewish homes, but toward the end of 1938 many Jews were disappearing daily.[29] Some of them were being sent to concentration camps, while others were fleeing Germany. The Fund was losing the income from these boxes because the last thing on anybody's mind was returning them to the JNF office. At the request of the JNF in Berlin, I volunteered to collect the boxes from Jewish households. It was a most tedious job because of the incomplete lists of households where these boxes were placed. I was given addresses of households to visit every day but often the

---

29 Established in 1901 by the Fifth Zionist Congress, the prime purpose of the Jewish National Fund (JNF) was to purchase land (and to raise money for the purchase of land) in Ottoman Palestine for Jewish settlement.

people listed were no longer there. The dwelling was either occupied by another Jewish inhabitant or, worse, by a non-Jew. When I met with non-Jewish occupants, the door was frequently slammed in my face since anything Jewish was dirty and might contaminate them – at least according to *Der Stürmer*, the newspaper that they all read. However, a lot of money was recovered and the Fund benefited. My work was so effective that I was invited to Berlin a number of times to speak to other collectors and tell them how I went about it. Before my departure I received a letter of commendation and thanks from the Jewish National Fund in Berlin for my ingenuity and perseverance in making those collections. It resulted in a lot of money being used for the poorer Jews in Germany and to send some of them to Palestine. By then I was all of thirteen years old.

~

Our family doctor was Dr. Kapauner. He had assisted at the births of my brother and me since my mother gave birth at home. My brother was born in the midst of depression and hyperinflation in Germany in 1923 and Dr. Kapauner had held my father's cheque for three days before depositing it at his bank. My father told me that at the time of deposit it was worth just one-tenth of its value from three days earlier. Dr. Kapauner was caught up in the first wave of Jewish arrests in 1935 and sent to Dachau, the concentration camp near Munich. His wife wasn't Jewish and his two children were never educated in the Jewish faith. It was a tremendous blow to the family pride to suddenly discover not only that the father was Jewish but that the children were considered Jewish as well. When one no longer considered oneself of Jewish faith, when, without warning, Hitler reclassified you as a Jew, it was a great shock not only to your mental outlook but also to your social life. Dr. Kapauner was not only our family physician but also a friend of my parents, and we played with his children even though they were older than we were. Dr. Kapauner was eventually released and no longer allowed to treat non-Jewish patients under the German racial laws. Over the next year, his practice shrank since he had previously treated mostly non-Jewish patients and the Jews were not about to change medical care to help Dr. Kapauner to survive. At the beginning of 1936, Dr. Kapauner and his family emigrated to Costa Rica and we lost track of them.

Hitler managed to reclassify people as Jews even though they no longer had ties to Judaism and were almost completely assimilated into the non-Jewish majority society. All of a sudden, they were entirely identified with a faith they no longer practiced, a faith they may have had little familiarity with. Their association with Judaism was not only painful but completely unfamiliar. Some of them committed suicide rather than experience the "shame" of being Jewish. The fully assimilated even looked down on Jews and made sure that any trace connecting them with their past was completely eradicated. Many wives left their husbands when they discovered them to be of Jewish ancestry – the German courts encouraged this by granting quick divorces to these women while penalizing Jewish husbands with monetary fines. Children were uprooted and educated to hate their "Jewish" fathers. Many families living an idyllic social life were split apart shortly after Hitler's racial laws took effect. The consequences were devastating to many people who suddenly discovered they were Jews. Some had to reach back two and three generations for that discovery.

The desire for assimilation was so great among many German Jews that it led to excessive efforts in trying to achieve it. Many were of Polish or Russian Jewish descent whose forefathers had spoken Yiddish as their main language. The largest component of the Yiddish language is German, with a thousand-year history of being spoken and written by the Jews of Central and Eastern Europe. Yiddish was the language common to all inmates of the concentration camps, regardless of their national origin.

Yet for many of those assimilated households, not a word of

Yiddish was ever spoken. Mixed marriages were not encouraged and German Jews who were very assimilated considered marriage to religious Jews to be mixed marriages. Insofar as they addressed it at all, they thought of their Jewishness as social and cultural rather than religious. They made every attempt – and some very successfully – to integrate into the fields of science and art, but to a large extent remained the nation's traders. Jews were business leaders in many department stores and in the textile industry. Assimilated Jewish army veterans had shared the German defeat in World War I along with their countrymen and felt that the gulf of difference was bridged through their valour during that debacle.

In World War I, for the first time, European Jews had been pitted against other European Jews. French or British Jews had fought the German Jews. What better proof for assimilated Jews that being Jewish was not a brotherhood but strictly a religious belief. It put a crimp into the propaganda machine that espoused "domination" by a world Jewry. A Jew could be as good a German as his Protestant brethren. Given this premise, the shock that German Jews experienced when Hitler appeared on the scene can be readily understood. For fifteen years German Jews had laboured under the belief that they were equal German citizens. Suddenly, overnight, they were "reduced" to being Jews again, not Germans. The disbelief of assimilated Jews manifested itself best when the World War I veterans displayed their war medals and citations, waiting to be recognized as Germans. After all, they thought, it was the Jew who spoke Yiddish (or Yiddish-accented German) who was really Jewish; they were "truly" German and should be recognized as such. But the Nazis didn't differentiate between Jews who fought in the German armed forces during World War I and Jews who, according to *Der Stürmer*, disadvantaged "Aryans."

The *Winterhilfswerk* (Winter Aid Program) was a creation of the Nazi Party to assist the unemployed and poor. The so-called *Eintopfgericht* (stew pot) regulation ordered that once a month each household cook the main meal in one pot and the savings derived from this be contributed to the Winter Aid Program. My coffee-house uncle proudly displayed a citation from the Winter Aid program in the café for his considerable contribution to that institution. Jews either had no perception of what was happening around them or they deluded themselves with the belief that the Nazis weren't after them. Like my father, many believed that Hitler would not last and so did not see any point in dislodging themselves for what would be a temporary situation. It was really only after the proclamation of the 1935 Nuremberg laws that the realization that Hitler was not transient and that he meant it when he stated that he intended to rid Germany of Jews fully sank in. But by this time, many Jews were caught in this net with no escape.

Up to that time it was still relatively easy to liquidate businesses and leave Germany with most of one's funds and household goods. The forerunner of what we know as a shipping container today was the "lift" – a large wooden box, almost the dimensions of a container, used to transport household belongings. Once the Nuremberg laws were enforced Jews were only allowed to take household goods and cash totalling to no more than ten Reichmarks per person. Businesses had to be assigned to German "Aryan" citizens for free, together with all their assets but none of their liabilities. What liabilities there were had to be liquidated and all taxes paid before the former owner could obtain a permit to leave the country. To even take household goods Jews had to submit a written application that listed every item to be included in the lift. Once the permit was obtained, arrangements had to be made to have a customs officer in attendance when loading the lift. Needless to say, the German authorities were not very cooperative with Jews and packing dates had to be changed many times because the customs officers decided not to attend. One could only assure a smooth operation by giving the customs officer extra money – he had the power to demand that the lift be unloaded if he hadn't been adequately compensated.

While the Germans did issue exit permits, it was very difficult to obtain entrance visas to other countries. The United States or England only granted entry permits if the applicant had some special skill to offer, which is how my engineer uncle, Arno, was able to emigrate to London. Far off places like Costa Rica, the Dominican Republic and Cuba were more receptive to Jewish immigrants, and some chose those destinations out of desperation rather than intent. My father didn't want to make this long trek and I think he still secretly thought that Hitler wouldn't last. Consequently, his decision was to remain in Europe.

~

As I've mentioned, after 1933 all youth organizations other than the Hitler Youth were banned in Germany. Most of the members of the other organizations had to merge with the Hitler Youth and only those of a political nature – such as the communist youth groups – were excluded. The Jewish Boy Scouts, Kadima Hazair, were a direct outcome of the dissolution of the German Boy Scout organization. The Jewish Boy Scouts wore the traditional uniform originally designed by Lord Baden-Powell, but our orientation was different. Kadima Hazair placed more stress on Zionism and on convincing us to make aliyah to Palestine. We would sing primarily Zionist songs such as "Chai-Chai Trumpeldor," and "Hatikvah," now the State of Israel's national anthem, was sung at the beginning and end of every meeting.

My troop was called Seev (Wolf) and my Boy Scout name was Eli. My uncle in Berlin made a steel die for me that contained a wolf's head and had an opening for a pin. I would melt lead, pour it into the opening of the die and clamp it together to produce beautiful silver-looking wolf's-head pins. Everybody in my troop wore one of these pins, which greatly added to my popularity. We would go on Sunday marches to the countryside and, up to the time it was stolen from us, spend many afternoons in our clubhouse in the woods. Some of us spoke Hebrew fairly well and were encouraged to hold conversations in that language. Although there was no religious aspect to the organization, children of both Orthodox or conservative Jewish orientation also belonged. It gave us a feeling of moral wellbeing to be part of this group and many members did think about emigrating to Palestine. The children who did decide to go were usually transported to Italy and made their way from there to Palestine. Many parents agreed to this, particularly those who had no hope of leaving Germany due to financial limitations. Little did I anticipate that membership in the Boy Scouts would play a major part in my life later on.

People came to speak to us on various subjects, but the group was mainly geared toward making good Zionists out of us and convincing us to emigrate to Palestine. Somehow this was not an aspiration in my family and no real consideration was ever given to this exit possibility. One of the lectures that left an imprint on me was a talk Rabbi Goldmann gave in July 1935 about the death of Lieutenant-Colonel Alfred Dreyfus. The infamous Dreyfus affair had come to a head in 1894 when Dreyfus, a captain in the French army who had served on the general staff, was falsely convicted and sentenced to life imprisonment for selling military secrets to Germany. Although Dreyfus was eventually exonerated, as a Jew – and thus an "alien" – he had been an easy target for the French military machine. Rabbi Goldmann drew a parallel between the German and French newspapers *Der Stürmer* and *La libre parole*, both published for the sole purpose of Jewish hate-mongering, one published by Streicher and the other by Edouard Drumont, who had also published a bestselling book *La France juive* (Jewish France). *La libre parole* had maintained that there was a "Dreyfus syndicate," financed by Jewish money, that was out to purchase all the newspapers in Europe.

∼

One by one I began to lose my friends to emigration. The process was slow before 1936 but most decidedly accelerated after that. It got to the point where from one day to the next class attendance at school shrank until there were only about ten boys in my class. Not only the pupils disappeared but also the teachers. It became harder for the school to fill teaching positions and many teachers had to cover more than one subject. My good friends like Manpel, Lichtenstein and Sonnabend were all gone one day without my knowing where they went or if I would ever see them again. Sonnabend's father had a wholesale clothing business and on weekends the showroom became our indoor playground. Buried under the clothes during a hide-and-seek game I experienced my first kiss. Ruth Markise and I, at twelve years of age, were in love and swore eternal friendship. Our mothers, prior to her mother's early death, were close friends. It became difficult to form a lasting friendship when one never knew how long the friend would be around.

Those were hard times that left a lasting impression on me. After all, we form our most durable friendships during our school years and if those are interrupted, what happens? In due course, since my family was one of the last to leave, I found myself alone without friends to play, share thoughts, go on bicycle rides with or even to study with. Prior to their departure, some children were not allowed to say they were leaving because their parents intended to escape illegally. Those were the ones who hadn't been able to acquire entrance permits to countries but simply fled across the borders, seeking asylum. As it turned out, in 1939 my family became one of them.

~

Both my older brother, Heini, and I were given a choice to flee with my parents or make a legal exit to England. The British government allowed Jewish children who had no relatives outside Germany the opportunity to come to England.[30] While I elected to stay with my parents, my brother decided to go to England. At that time we already knew that Uncle Arno would emigrate there after so that my brother wouldn't be alone. The idea was that my brother would move to London and stay with my uncle and aunt. Nobody gave any thought to an imminent world war when those plans were laid – the best laid plans of mice and men. As it turned out, my brother was among the approximately two thousand German and Austrian, mostly Jewish, refugees who were interned in England in 1940 as "enemy aliens" and shipped to Canada. What a feeling it must have been for a seventeen-year-old to be uprooted and not know where he was going and what would happen when he got to wherever he was being sent. Fortunately, Heini ended up in an internment camp in Fredericton, New Brunswick rather than in Australia, where some were sent. A few teachers and scholars accompanied them to ensure the continuation of the children's education in the camp.

By the end of June 1939 my father had obtained all the necessary permits to ship our household belongings to Brussels, Belgium. He had also paid the required emigration tax that the Nazis exacted from all those leaving. Needless to say, we didn't posses an entrance permit to Belgium. The German customs officer attended the loading of the lift and was handsomely rewarded for his presence. Part of his duty was to check our papers to assure that we could go to Belgium, but the remuneration he received covered that oversight. When the back panel of the lift was nailed into place and the customs officer affixed his official seal, our apartment had been stripped of all our material assets, including all our clothes other than the ones we had packed in a few suitcases and the ones we were wearing.

---

30 A government-sanctioned but privately financed initiative to bring German Jewish children to the UK, the Kindertransport rescued nearly 10,000 children under the age of seventeen between December 1938 and September 3, 1939. For more information, see the glossary.

That evening we left for Berlin to visit Uncle Arno and pick up my mother's sister Rena, who was leaving with us. This was the last time, for a long spell, that our immediate family was together because of my brother's imminent departure for England. None of us could predict what the future would bring and whether we were going to survive as a family or even individually. We stayed in my uncle's apartment. Heini was to leave for London from Berlin a few days after our departure, and my uncle would follow a few weeks later.

A year earlier Uncle Arno had made a trip to New York to investigate whether it was advisable for us to attempt to emigrate there. He returned to say that he found the place terrible and could not recommend that we go there. It was at that time that he made the decision to move to England. He had been given permission to move most of his machinery to Britain, enabling him to set up a factory there. He had dismantled some of his machinery and drilled holes into the columns, where he secreted money and then welded the columns back into place. As it turned out he was never able to benefit from this deception. The machinery reached Hamburg toward the end of August 1939 and was booked on a freighter to be shipped to England on September 4, 1939. The invasion of Poland took place on September 1, 1939, and by September 3, England and France were at war with Germany. Whoever used that machinery was never aware of the fortune it was hiding. Luckily, both my brother and my uncle and his family were already in England at the outbreak of the war.

After a few days in Berlin we took the eight-hour train ride to Cologne during the first week of July. We almost retraced part of the journey we had already made since Berlin is northeast of Leipzig and Cologne southwest of Berlin. There was always the danger of being accosted on the train by Nazis seeking the usual Jew-baiting entertainment, and even a first-class compartment provided no security.

My father had engaged a border-crossing smuggler who was to meet us in Cologne. We had an address of what we would call today a "safe house," where we would stay until our departure across the German border into Belgium. We arrived at the house and were shown to two rooms. My father and I slept in one and my mother and aunt in the other. So far we were still on safe ground and had not broken any laws. My mother and aunt were leaning out of the window in the late afternoon and when men stopped on the street and looked up and whistled, they quickly became aware of where we were lodged – it was one of Cologne's brothels. We spent two nights there and left in the middle of the second night.

At about midnight on the second night, we were told to get ready and within half an hour we were in a car driving toward the German-Belgian border. We each carried a suitcase with only the most necessary paraphernalia such as toiletries and a change of clothes, but the driver objected even to that. Accepting this ride was a matter of blind trust; we really didn't know if the smuggler might take our money and deliver us to the Gestapo. The only insurance policy we had was that my father's payment was undoubtedly higher than the reward the smuggler would receive from the Gestapo for turning us in and that the smuggler also ran the risk of punishment for consorting with Jews.

So, after more than six years of exposure to Hitler's Third Reich, we were leaving Germany behind us. We were quitting the country that, prior to Hitler, had offered us security and a feeling of a natural state of existence. At the age of fifty my father was leaving the surroundings that he had grown up in, facing not only new ventures but the obligation of looking after his family in a country whose language, culture and business life were totally unfamiliar to him.

Our main purpose in making this journey was to escape the clutches of Hitler's forces and escape the almost-certain death that was hanging over every Jew who remained in Germany. By that time there was little doubt in any Jew's mind that survival could be counted in months rather than years.

The First Exodus

The drive toward the Belgian border had us skirting the city of Aachen in westernmost Germany. After about eighty kilometres we stopped in what appeared to be the middle of nowhere. This part of the trip lasted about an hour and a half and when the driver stopped the car the first time he told us that at the next stop, about ten minutes away, we'd have thirty seconds to get out of the car. He would start driving again whether we were in or out of the car. He instructed us to cross the road, hide in the bushes and wait there for a guide who would identify himself by calling out my father's name. He also suggested that we throw all of our jewellery out of the car now so that if we were stopped by the German patrol we would be less suspicious. This was obviously a clever ploy to get people to dispose of their valuables at that spot so the driver could easily retrieve them.

About ten minutes later, as he had said, he stopped the car at a desolate stretch of highway and we clambered out like scared rabbits, crossed the highway and entered the dark bushes to hide. For the next ten minutes, which seemed like hours, we stood in the darkness not knowing what to expect. Would anybody be there or would we be left to our own devices? If so, the Germans would undoubtedly find us and we would suffer dire consequences. My thoughts strayed to the possibility that the smugglers would abandon us and what we would do if that happened. We could find our own way – after all, I was a Boy Scout trained to always find my way whatever the surroundings.

None of us said a word for fear of attracting unwanted attention or missing the smuggler's approach. It was pitch dark. The smugglers opted for moonless nights for these "excursions" to reduce the risk of detection by border guards. We were standing about five metres from the highway, with the trees and bushes obstructing our view. Only one car went by, which we assumed was our driver returning to Cologne. It was one of the eeriest feelings I ever remember experiencing, almost like being in a ghost house and not knowing what to expect, not knowing where the danger might come from or what form it might take. A poem came to mind that we had learned in school. In Goethe's *Erlkoenig* are the lines, "Wer reitet so spät durch Nacht und Wind, es ist der Vater mit seinem Kind" (Who rides so late through the night and wind, it is the father with his child).[1] My father was taking this heavy responsibility on his shoulders, obligated to trust people he had never met and whose intentions he was not sure of, riding not only with his child but his wife and sister-in-law.

The waiting was endless. Then, the sound coming like a shot, a man called out my father's name and without further ado instructed us to follow him. We were so relieved to see him that we unhesitatingly followed him into the heart of the forest. We proceeded through the trees, occasionally along a path but always in the shadow of the darkness, holding hands so that we wouldn't be separated from each other. After ten minutes or so, our guide stopped and told us that we were not to carry more than two suitcases. We transferred whatever we could into the two bags and left the rest lying on the ground. The guide carried one suitcase and my father and I took turns carrying the other. My mother's handbag contained all the necessary shaving

---

1   Goethe's 1782 ballad *Der Erlkoenig* (The Elf King) was firmly anchored in the German school curriculum. It is still sung today, often in the version by Schubert.

do if that happened. We could find our own way – after all, I was a Boy Scout trained to always find my way whatever the surroundings.

None of us said a word for fear of attracting unwanted attention or missing the smuggler's approach. It was pitch dark. The smugglers opted for moonless nights for these "excursions" to reduce the risk of detection by border guards. We were standing about five metres from the highway, with the trees and bushes obstructing our view. Only one car went by, which we assumed was our driver returning to Cologne. It was one of the eeriest feelings I ever remember experiencing, almost like being in a ghost house and not knowing what to expect, not knowing where the danger might come from or what form it might take. A poem came to mind that we had learned in school. In Goethe's *Erlkoenig* are the lines, "Wer reitet so spät durch Nacht und Wind, es ist der Vater mit seinem Kind" (Who rides so late through the night and wind, it is the father with his child).[1] My father was taking this heavy responsibility on his shoulders, obligated to trust people he had never met and whose intentions he was not sure of, riding not only with his child but his wife and sister-in-law.

The waiting was endless. Then, the sound coming like a shot, a man called out my father's name and without further ado instructed us to follow him. We were so relieved to see him that we unhesitatingly followed him into the heart of the forest. We proceeded through the trees, occasionally along a path but always in the shadow of the darkness, holding hands so that we wouldn't be separated from each other. After ten minutes or so, our guide stopped and told us that we were not to carry more than two suitcases. We transferred whatever we could into the two bags and left the rest lying on the ground. The guide carried one suitcase and my father and I took turns carrying the other. My mother's handbag contained all the necessary shaving

---

1   Goethe's 1782 ballad *Der Erlkoenig* (The Elf King) was firmly anchored in the German school curriculum. It is still sung today, often in the version by Schubert.

covered us in the barn. No blame would fall on them and they would be declared good Nazis for having exposed some Jews and preventing them from fleeing the country. The day went quietly, but we passed the time in constant fear.

A few hours after the German border patrol had left the farmhouse, nothing untoward had occurred, and so we rested a bit easier. To perform the most intimate bodily functions under these circumstances was not easy – we had almost no privacy. My father rigged up a blanket in the corner of the ground floor of the barn so that the ladies would feel more comfortable performing their natural functions. At least it was summer and we didn't have to suffer from the cold. A hose connected to the water faucet on the inside of the barn served as our sole water supply for drinking and washing. We spent the day walking around in the barn and sleeping, aware that we needed to be rested for what we might face when we resumed our journey that evening. We were served a cold meat plate dinner that was quite adequate and tasty. It looked as if the farmer's family made most of their food and even the bread appeared to be baked at home. I always wondered what the farmer was paid for offering us shelter and hiding us from the Germans for that one day. I doubt that they did it out of the goodness of their hearts, much as I would like to believe so. At dinner we were told that we would be leaving at midnight to walk across the border into Belgium.

The hours leading up to midnight passed slowly and we couldn't suppress our fears of being either betrayed or detected. The barn was in a total blackout, greatly restricting our movements. Finding our way to the toilet facilities, such as they were, was difficult, with much stumbling and running into posts. Since it was summer, we did enjoy the maximum number of daylight hours, but darkness descended on us all too soon. Fear is a more ferocious companion in darkness than daylight. We sat huddled together, drawing courage from each other and making every attempt to sound cheerful. When the smuggler appeared and told us to get ready to leave, it was none too soon for us.

We left the barn through a small side door and were very soon engulfed by a forest again. Only holding hands kept us from either falling behind or being separated as we snaked through the woods. After about an hour of brisk walking, we reached a large open field. Our guide, who hadn't spoken a word all this time, told us that we would have to run across the field and assemble in the bushes on the other side. The field was about 250 metres wide and, as we soon discovered, there was a barbed-wire fence across the middle of it. Fortunately, we were able to crawl and slink underneath the lowest strand of wire. It had apparently never occurred to our guide to mention the fence to us or tell us how we were to navigate past it. I have often wondered why he didn't draw our attention to the fence and whether it was out of maliciousness or fear. We later learned that this area was no-man's land between Germany and Belgium. Could the guide have wanted to be sure that if we were caught he was nowhere near us and could not be implicated? Crawling under the wire fence on their stomachs wasn't easy for my mother and aunt, who were hardly dressed for this type of exercise – they were both wearing high-heeled shoes and silk stockings. My father wasn't dressed for the occasion either – he was wearing a shirt and tie and a regular suit. None of us had given any thought to what we would be facing on this journey and how to dress for it.

After clearing the fence we ran to the other side and reached the safety of the bushes, where we were met by a Belgian guide who told us to hurry up and leave the area as quickly as possible. He told us in no uncertain terms that if the Belgian border police caught us, we would be unceremoniously escorted back across the border and delivered into the hands of the Germans. Consequently, in his determination to put as much distance between us and the border area, he set a pace that my parents and aunt had difficulty meeting. The terrain we were traversing was hilly with some inclines rather steep to climb. It wasn't too long before both the heels on my mother's and aunt's shoes broke off, which, of course, was a blessing in disguise.

Their silk stockings were already in tatters and their outfits looked much the worse for wear.

The guide was relentless in his speed for at least the first half-hour. After that point, he suggested that we take a rest since we were now deeper into Belgian territory and, I presume, further from the dangers of the patrolling Belgian border officers. He told us we would have another hour of walking before meeting yet another guide and that we had to make the rendezvous on time. We felt relieved knowing that we were now on Belgian soil and more secure having left the Siegfried line behind us.[2] Our new guide spoke German with a noticeable accent that was music to our ears. The fact that we were no longer in the hands of a German guide gave us a feeling of confidence and security.

Who can describe the feeling that comes from the very deepest awareness of having cheated death? We all knew about the concentration camps and the treatment of the Jews who were there, even though the rest of the world was in a constant state of denial. Even though there were no death camps as yet, my parents had many friends and acquaintances who had died in Dachau and Buchenwald of "unknown" causes. At least we were now free agents, no longer subject to the constant antisemitic harassment that had become part of everyday life in Leipzig. As a child, one of the most significant features of that antisemitism for me was that our non-Jewish neighbours had prohibited their children from socializing with us, making us pariahs in their eyes. Boys who had been my schoolmates before I was forced to study at the Jewish high school ignored me and, when they weren't ganging up on me, would walk away, not wanting to associate with me. It was an odd feeling for a young boy to be so isolated, par-

---

2 The original Siegfried Line to which the author refers was a line of World War I defensive forts and tank defences built by Germany in 1916 in northern France and Belgium. It is not to be confused with the Siegfried Line that the Germans built in the late 1930s for much the same purpose.

ticularly when there weren't many Jews in our neighbourhood. I was really looking forward to entering a new school in Brussels and gave little thought to the language difference. As we walked further along the path of freedom, our feelings of euphoria rose like the mercury in a thermometer.

About an hour and a half later, when we clambered up the side of the road, having just completed an endless series of climbs up elevations and bluffs, we saw a man standing beside a waiting automobile. When our guide and this man exchanged a friendly greeting, we knew that this was our transportation into Brussels. Never has a car looked so good to me as this one did on that fateful day, July 20, 1939. The driver came well equipped with the necessities required by people who had just walked through hell to reach him. He produced silk stockings for the ladies, a razor and shaving cream for my father and candies for me. He also gave us milk and sandwiches, which we devoured. At this point my father realized with relief that he had managed our exodus in the best manner possible and that, despite his earlier misgivings, he had chosen the right people to help us escape. We were safe and only a car ride away from the life of a "normal" displaced person. The driver made sure that we cleaned up well and erased all the signs of our nocturnal excursion before setting off for Brussels. He had a cloth brush to wipe away the dust and dirt, a needle and thread to repair the obvious tears in our clothes and even a bucket of water and a wash basin to clean off our hands and faces.

I really don't remember how long the trip to Brussels took since our exhaustion overcame our exhilaration and we all fell asleep soon as the drive began. It was only a little while before we entered the city of Brussels and the driver woke us, telling us that we had arrived and he would drive us to the boarding house where we would spend the next few days.

We couldn't register at a hotel since we were illegals in Belgium. Our first step in establishing a legal footing was to report to the police station to obtain refugee status. The Belgian authorities were very lenient as long as they could be assured that those applying for refugee status were indeed "stateless." While my parents still had their recently acquired Polish passports, they didn't want to show them in case we would be sent to Poland. Since my father was born in Vienna, the Belgian authorities took it for granted that after the Austrian annexation he was German and, as a Jew, they couldn't send him back to Germany. This, of course, also applied to his immediate family. The owners of the boarding house told my parents how to manage our registration at the police station, accompanied them there and acted as interpreters. We were granted residence status in Belgium and were then free to move anywhere in the country.

My parents elected to remain in Brussels even though the larger Jewish community was in Antwerp, the famous diamond centre of Europe.[3] Our next task was to find living quarters because our lodgings at the boarding house were only temporary. We needed a three-bedroom unit since my parents, my aunt and I each required a bedroom. We found an apartment in Laaken, a suburb of Brussels and the location of the official residence of the Belgian royal family. The palace was on a huge estate and the Japanese tower and China pavilion could be seen from the fence. The following May, just before we left Brussels, I had an opportunity to visit the gardens and the "Glass City" that housed thousands of rare tropical plants, including the first orange tree I had ever seen.

Our new apartment was unfurnished, so we stayed at the boarding house until the lift with our belongings arrived from Germany. When the lift did arrive, my father discovered to his dismay that the only way to avoid paying customs duties on all the contents was to

---

3 An internationally renowned hub for the diamond trade from the early 1500s, in 1939 Antwerp was one of the largest diamond-cutting and diamond-dealing centres of the world. From the mid-nineteenth century to the beginning of World War II, many of the city's Jewish residents were involved in the diamond trades.

wait a year to remove them. Fortunately, the customs authorities allowed us to remove absolute essentials such as clothing, basic furniture and kitchen utensils. Persian rugs, paintings, electrical equipment and dining room furniture didn't fall into that category and couldn't be removed. We retrieved what we could of our belongings and the balance was sealed in the container and remained in storage at the bonded warehouse of the Belgian Cartage Company.

Our new apartment was considerably smaller than the one we had had in Leipzig, which, of course, required us to spend less money to furnish it with what we couldn't retrieve from storage. We had parquet floors without any rugs and almost kitchen-like furniture to decorate the dining room. The resulting decor was sparse and I'm sure that my mother longed for the comfort of the surroundings she had left behind. None of us spoke French or Flemish Dutch – the main languages spoken in Belgium – and communication was difficult.

After a week, my father selected a French-language school for me and bravely went there to discuss my enrolment for the coming school year. I found out later that the headmaster spoke German, so my father was able to discuss my curriculum with him. Belgium is an officially bilingual country, with the majority of Belgians speaking one of the Flemish dialects, which are similar to Dutch, and living mainly in the northern part of the country. The long-standing friction between the Flemish-speaking Flamands and French-speaking Walloons extended into Brussels, where certain parts of the city were predominantly French and other Flamand.

The district where we lived, Laaken, was sort of a mixture of the two cultures, which meant there were both French and Flemish-speaking schools. The headmaster suggested that I enter the Flemish-speaking school since the language was closer to German than French and would be easier for me to learn. Because of the similarity to German, there would also be a number of words that I would understand, which would make it easier for me to understand the teachers. My father disagreed, however, and said that he wanted me to be placed in the French school – he most emphatically didn't want to preserve my knowledge of the German language. He felt confident that I could learn French quickly and thought that fluency in French would be of more use to me in my later life than Flemish. When I started school in September, I was registered in the French-speaking school and had already acquired some French vocabulary and grammar over the course of the school holiday. My father hired a private tutor who came to the apartment three times a week for about four weeks for what was really the closest thing to what we would define today as an immersion language course.

~

We hadn't been in Belgium very long before our world suddenly went topsy-turvy. The events causing this upset didn't take place in our immediate neighbourhood, but we felt the breath of disaster blowing in our direction nonetheless. When Hitler had seized the whole of Czechoslovakia in March 1939, the world didn't say, "Enough," and he clearly wasn't satisfied with his conquest of Poland. The unscrupulous bombing of Polish cities in September of that year should have served as a warning to the countries of Europe of what else they could expect from the Nazis, but even after war had been declared, all parties seemed to be waiting patiently for his next move.

Even more disquieting was listening to Hitler's speech to the German parliament on September 1, 1939, when the full force of his oratory came into play. On September 3, 1939, the Brussels newspapers quoted French prime minister Edouard Daladier's September 2 speech before the Chamber of Deputies in Paris that laid bare Hitler's lies and nefarious schemes. To us it spelled doom and instilled renewed fear for our lives. We had little doubt that the Germans would attack Belgium as soon as an outright war began.

That came to pass on September 3 when France and Britain declared war on Germany and within a few weeks, on September 27, 1939, Warsaw had surrendered.[4]

Our life in Brussels continued with the possibility of a German invasion hanging over our heads like the sword of Damocles. We weren't sure when it would descend. We were, at best, living in a precarious existence with a suitcase mentality. Our landlord assured us that the Belgian fortifications were impenetrable, that the dykes, in particular, would repel any German access into Belgium. He magnanimously extended this bit of military theory to Holland, but didn't even bother to mention the famous Maginot Line of France since he was sure that the Germans would never get through the Belgian and Dutch defences.[5]

It was in this atmosphere that I first entered my new school at the beginning of September 1939. I soon discovered that my situation had changed dramatically. I was no longer the "dirty Jew" ostracized and threatened by my school friends as I had been in Leipzig – now I was the *sale boche*, the "dirty German." What a transformation for a boy of thirteen and a half! I remember asking myself how was it possible that even though we all hated the Germans, I was maligned as one. It no longer mattered in this Brussels school that I was Jewish, but the fact that I was born in Germany seemed more important than the fact that I had fled Germany to stay alive.

Under these circumstances I found it difficult to concentrate on my studies – even more so when the subjects were taught in a language I had yet to master. My comprehension was most challenged in the sciences. Fortunately, I found French relatively easy to learn and by

---

4 Germany invaded Poland on September 1, 1939, and was met with fierce Polish resistance. Two weeks later, the Soviet Union invaded Poland from the East. Faced with a two-front war, Poland was unable to repel the invaders and the capital, Warsaw, was captured by the Germans by the end of the month.

5 The Maginot Line was a series of massive border fortifications built by the French after World War I to prevent another German invasion.

Christmas the headmaster called my father in to discuss my progress. When I was first enrolled in the school, it was decided that because of my need to learn a new language I should repeat the school year I had just completed in Leipzig. The headmaster had thought that while this would slow down my academic advancement, it would significantly lessen the psychological effect of failing my year. At Christmas, though, the headmaster told my father that my French had improved enough for me to move into the class commensurate with my age. I wouldn't end up losing any time whatsoever. All I needed to do during the Christmas holiday was catch up on the work that the class had already studied. By Easter my school grades were up to par, although due to subsequent events, I never did find out what the end result of this switch at Christmas would have been.

My upgrade did bring about a change in my classmates' approach, though. Because I was with a whole new crowd in my new class and my French was now good enough to explain who I was and where I came from, I was no longer considered to be the "dirty German" but was accepted as one of their own. They introduced me to some of the interesting sites of Brussels, including "Manneken Pis," a statue that has caused a lot of controversy but in Brussels is highly revered.[6] It is a bronze statue of a little boy standing at a corner urinating that is draped in different clothes appropriate for the season or ceremonial occasions. There are always fresh flowers at the foot of the tall pedestal. My classmates also showed me the magnificent Grand Place and the town hall with its statues of Belgian royalty and prophets on the bell tower crowned by St. Michael, the city's patron saint. The inside of the building, with its tapestries, is something to behold.[7]

---

6   The famous Brussels landmark statue "Manneken Pis" (Dutch for "little peeing man"), also known in French as the "petit Julien," was created by Belgian sculptor Jerome Duquesnoy in 1619.

7   The Brussels town hall, built in 1404, is a classic example of late Flemish Gothic style of architecture. The building been furnished over the years with tapestries,

I was most grateful to my schoolmates for this exposure to Brussels history. I was now invited to their homes and parties, I went skating with them, and they in turn came to our apartment. They no longer looked upon my parents as Germans to be avoided but as people who had fled from the Nazis and suffered at their hands. There was still not much interaction between their parents and mine, but this may have been due to the language barrier. My parents found it difficult to learn French, even though my father did acquire a smattering of the language.

I remember two very funny incidents concerning my father's lack of French. One day when he left to go to a meeting, my mother asked him to get a dozen eggs from a store on his way home. In those days men like my father did not go grocery shopping. When he arrived home he told us that he had had great deal of difficulty getting the grocery store clerk to understand what he wanted since the man didn't speak any Flemish. In desperation my father crowed like a cock and reached behind him with his hand, bringing the open hand forward to show that he had just laid an egg. The clerk got the message and, using his fingers, asked my father how many eggs he wanted. Another time, my father came home and declared that he wanted to meet Mr. "A. Louer" since he clearly owned a lot of real estate in Brussels and he could possibly do some business with him. He was not aware that "A Louer" means "For Rent" in French.

My parents settled into a circle of German-speaking friends, mostly people who, like us, had fled Germany. They met at the Café Royal at the Hotel Royal on the Place du Midi with their emigrant friends on Saturday afternoons and one could almost believe that they had been transplanted from Café Felsche in Leipzig to Café Royal in Brussels. What a wondrous generation of people who, despite the hardships,

---

paintings and sculptures that largely represent subjects of importance in local and regional history. It dominates the city's main square.

attempted to conduct as normal a life as they could. Uncle Dadek had left Leipzig for Brussels three years ahead of us and established a small business, so he was able to employ my Aunt Rena. Her fiancé, Kurt Berliner, had also come to Brussels from Berlin and, for a few months, life did take on some degree of normalcy.

We started to appreciate Belgian food and my aunt and I both especially loved the famous Belgian *pommes frites* that sold at street stands wrapped in newspaper. It was surprising that the fat-laden and steaming French fries didn't melt the newsprint, but even if it had, it would probably have only added to the incredible taste. The secret to making Belgian *pommes frites* is that they are fried twice. There were other stands that served Belgian waffles covered with powdered sugar and whipped cream, and stands that sold the most delicious chocolates Belgium is so famous for. But best of all were the fresh oysters. The fish boats anchored below the bridge that spanned one of the canals between Brussels and Laaken. We would put money into one of the baskets attached to the bridge with long cords and lower it to the fisherman. He would then load the basket with the number of oysters, already pried open, that we had paid for and we would hoist the basket up. What a feast to eat these fresh oysters just few hours after they had been harvested!

There were lots of new things for me to experience in Brussels – museums to visit, movies to see, parks to walk in and outdoor concerts to listen to. These were the things that I had not been allowed to do in Germany for the last three years of my residency there. It is only when you are not permitted to do something that you begin to realize the pleasure of experiencing it again. Freedom of movement can only be really appreciated by those who have been deprived of it.

~

After September, discussions about the state of war between Germany on the one side and France and England on the other seemed to fade into the background. My parents and their friends talked about it when they met at the coffee house, but in school we paid little attention. The Belgians really believed that their dyke system was a powerful deterrent to a potential Germans invasion.

We felt deeply for the people who were still under the German yoke. The news emanating from Germany and Poland sounded ominous for the Jews. The first *Judenräte* (Jewish Councils) had been established in September 1939, almost immediately after Poland's surrender.[8] In October the Nazis established the first ghetto in Piotrków, Poland as an unguarded and unfenced forced residence.[9] There was no world reaction and it came as no surprise when we learned about it in Brussels since there have been many instances of such enclaves for Jews throughout history. In November 1939 the Germans introduced a decree that all Jews in Poland over the age of ten had to wear white armbands with a blue Star of David prominently displayed on the outside of their clothing. Forced labour for Jews had commenced and the first deportations of Jews from Austria and the Protectorates to the Polish ghettos started.[10]

A boy's bar mitzvah is scheduled to take place on his thirteenth birthday and parents make arrangements for this event long in ad-

---

8 Jewish Councils were established by the Nazis throughout the territories they occupied to facilitate the implementation of their orders. Faced with difficult moral choices, these councils frequently tried to help community members but in fact had no power or independence of action. For more information, see Judenrat in the glossary.

9 Jews from surrounding towns and villages were brought to and segregated in Piotrków from early in September 1939.

10 The Nazis established the Protectorate of Bohemia and Moravia in western Czechoslovakia in March 1939. Unlike the *Generalgouvernement* – the occupation regime in central Poland – Bohemia and Moravia were declared semi-autonomous Nazi-administered territories within "Greater Germany." Deportations from the Protectorate of Bohemia and Moravia to the ghettos of the *Generalgouvernement* began in October 1939.

vance. The Torah portion that the young man is to read must be determined so that he can practice, but his recital includes various prayers, blessings and chants that must also be learned. When my thirteenth birthday approached in February 1939, we were still in Germany and the Germans had destroyed many of the synagogues during Kristallnacht. While some Jewish Orthodox services were held in secret, it was difficult for us to adjust to these services since we were members of the Reform movement of Judaism.[11] Part of our religious service was conducted in German, but the Orthodox did all their traditional singing and conducted all their services in Hebrew. As a result, I couldn't be presented to "manhood" on my scheduled day.

One of the first tasks my father undertook when we arrived in Brussels was to look for a Reform congregation where my bar mitzvah could take place. Reform Judaism was practiced in the Grand Synagogue in Brussels, making it easier for me to be called to the Torah. It was a sad sort of affair that took place on March 2, 1940, shortly after my fourteenth birthday. Only my parents, Aunt Rena and her fiancé, Kurt Berliner, and Uncle Dadek attended. I had no Jewish friends and certainly no childhood friends. There was really nothing of the joyous feeling we experienced when my brother had his bar mitzvah. Our present fate of running for our lives and being in strange surroundings was really highlighted during the event.

While the Saturday service was fairly well attended, most of the people present were there to witness the bar mitzvah of another boy on the same day. The rabbi had consented to let me attend as well on that Saturday, even though the other bar mitzvah had been scheduled a long time ago. The reading of the Torah was split between us and we both recited the "Baruch Sheptarani" blessing. After the service, the family of the other boy had their kiddush in the community hall

---

11 Reform, or Progressive Judaism, emerged in nineteenth-century Germany. For more information, see the glossary.

of the synagogue. From the synagogue we proceeded to our small apartment to have lunch, but the spirit of celebration was not with us. My parents were very aware of being in a foreign land where they encountered language problems daily and where the future was uncertain. Within two months, their trepidation was confirmed.

~

Beginning on April 9, 1940, several events occurred that caused us great distress. The first was the invasion of Denmark and Norway. We also heard that a ghetto had been established in Lodz, where my mother's sister lived, and sealed off with more than 200,000 people locked inside.[12] In January 1940 Heinrich Himmler issued a directive that created the concentration camp in the Polish town of Oświęcim, known more commonly by its Germanized name, Auschwitz.

But our worst fears faced us a month after the Norway invasion. On Friday, May 10, 1940, by the time I awoke to prepare for school, Hitler's blitzkrieg had started.[13] What alerted us first were the Stuka planes attacking Brussels. The Ju 87 or Stuka – short for *Sturtzkampfflugzeug*, or dive bomber – started its dive from 15,000 feet and reached a maximum speed of 350 mph at an 80-degree angle. Within thirty seconds, the pilot pressed a button initiating the automatic pullout system and with machine guns blazing, the Stuka strafed indiscriminately. The whirring noise created during that dive gave the Stuka its reputation for being an instrument of deliberate destruction.

---

12 The Germans ordered plans for the Lodz ghetto to proceed in February 1940 and on May 1, 1940, only eight months after the German invasion, the Lodz ghetto was officially sealed.

13 Literally meaning "lightning war," blitzkrieg is the term for a new style of warfare that characterized Germany's offensive in the West in 1940. On May 10, 1940, the Germans simultaneously invaded the Netherlands, France, Luxemburg and Belgium. For more information, see the glossary.

The Germans showed no compassion for enemy civilians and strafed and bombed the city mercilessly. We hadn't heard the announcement that schools were closed for the day, so I proceeded there as usual. When I arrived I found a number of kids milling about and we were all at a loss as to what to do next. Normally school being out was a cause for celebration, but we sensed the seriousness of the situation and were all in a sombre mood. As a Jew, the attack was even more tragic for me than for the others because I felt the futility of trying to escape the Germans. The other kids talked about the stories they had learned from their parents of the cruelty practiced by the Germans during the occupation of Belgium during World War I. My complete acceptance by the other students was demonstrated by the way they included me in their conversations and freely berated the Germans without looking at me. It hadn't been easy to get to this point; I had worked at it solidly for the first six months I was in school in Brussels. Learning the French language came easily to me and after six months I was fairly fluent without much trace of an accent. The absence of a "German" guttural accent assisted in my assimilation and acceptance by my peers.

Before too long one of the teachers told us to go home. On my way I crossed the bridge where I had enjoyed the oysters so many times only to witness an event that has remained with me forever. Just when I was about halfway across the bridge, there was another German aerial attack and the anti-aircraft guns were blazing. People were milling about on the walkway of the canal below the bridge and the oyster boats were anchored as usual. As I looked down I saw a woman who was looking up at the sky suddenly fall into the canal, the water around her turning red. I later learned the woman had been hit by a piece of shrapnel in her throat and had died shortly after she hit the water. Little did I know that this was only the beginning of the dying I would witness over the next few weeks. A fourteen-year-old boy is forced to mature much too quickly when he has these kinds of experiences. It doesn't allow him to hold onto much of childhood. It is not – nor should it be – normal for a fourteen-year-old to fear for his life and the lives of his family.

Germany's intention of conquering not only Belgium and Holland but also France limited the escape routes open to us. We had to try to assess when we should leave because there was always the possibility that the Germans might not succeed in their invasion attempt. The Germans continued their bombing of Brussels and the Stukas had a field day diving toward the civilian population with their machine guns firing. We would run for shelter whenever we heard the dreadful whirring sound of those planes. We feared them more than the bombers because of their indiscriminate attacks on civilians.

We knew that any decision to stay or leave would have to weigh the emotional impact of fleeing for a second time in less than a year against the potentially dire consequences of failing to escape the advancing Germans. While the gas chambers were not yet in existence, many Jews were being shot or starved or worked to death in the concentration camps in Germany. The very few who had been released from Dachau or Buchenwald attested to these atrocities and, while the world at large ignored these charges, the full extent of these events had a terrifying impact on those who were directly in the path of the advancing Germans.

My father relied on information gleaned from other German-speaking refugees, but our landlord, who spoke some German, almost convinced my father that the Germans would never be able to break through the Belgian defences once the dykes were opened. By Saturday night my father had decided to wait for further developments. On Sunday the Belgian authorities announced that all adult men born in Germany or Austria had to register at the sports stadium on Monday morning. The rumour mill was full of speculation as to why this registration was required – the rumours covered the spectrum from the need to ferret out fifth columnists to the unfolding of a nefarious scheme to round up German-born Jews and send them back to appease the Germans.[14]

The registration call had the immediate effect of prompting a number of people to board trains and buses leaving Belgium for France. We heard that some, in desperation and despondency, even returned to Germany rather than face the uncertainty of flight. It's hard to imagine what would make people opt for almost certain death rather than face the unknown. They knew that a return to Germany would seal their fate, but they were even more afraid of the trials and tribulations they would confront during an escape. For some, it was a decision based on their financial situation. These considerations were very powerful and juxtaposed the fear of uncertainty against the security of a previous existence. Who can judge human emotions in a time of crisis under circumstances so bizarre, circumstances never before encountered by civilization? People also refused to believe the rumours of impending annihilation that circulated among the refugees. Nobody would accept that such alleged barbarity was possible in twentieth-century civilization.

On Monday morning, May 13, 1940, my father proceeded to the sports stadium to register. He had brought his Polish passport with him as a precaution and it turned out to be one of the wisest decisions of his life. Monday afternoon brought the announcement that all men who registered would be deported to France immediately under the auspices of the Belgian and French governments. France was said to be preparing an internment camp, but no locations were mentioned. My mother, aunt and I were devastated since we didn't know what to do now that my father was no longer there to make decisions. No visitors were allowed into the sports stadium and we didn't even know whether my father had already been transported to France.

---

14 Fifth columnist is a term used to designate a person who is clandestinely collaborating with an invading enemy. For more information, see the glossary.

On Tuesday morning I arose around 6 AM and took down the prayer book, my *tallis* (prayer shawl) and my *tefillin* (phylacteries) and proceeded to pray and wind the *tefillin* around my arm and head as I had been taught to do during my bar mitzvah training. Tears were running down my cheeks as I prayed to God, asking for the release and safe return of my father. I promised God nothing in return, pleading only for compassion. At breakfast I told my mother that my father would be home shortly and my mother tried her best to hide her disbelief. Somehow I felt as if a load had been lifted off my shoulders and a sixth sense told me that my father would return home before the day was out.

Late that afternoon my father appeared at our door, a little worse for wear because he had slept in his clothes and hadn't been able to bathe or shave during his detention. He told us that when he learned that all the detainees would be shipped to France and not released as they had thought, he demanded to see the commandant of the military guards. After yelling at the soldier in what he made sound like Polish, he was escorted to the commandant's office. There my father asked the commandant if he spoke Polish and hearing, as expected, that he didn't, he suggested that they speak German. He produced his Polish passport and stated that while he had been born in Austria, he was a Polish citizen and was at war with Germany. Then he demanded to see the Polish ambassador. My father told the commandant that he had pointed out this fact when he registered, but that he had been detained anyway. The commandant could see a problem arising out of having arrested an "ally" and rather than face a possible international incident by calling for someone from the Polish embassy, he apologized and told my father to go home. Unfortunately, he couldn't do anything for my aunt's fiancé, who was German-born and of German nationality. We found out later that all the detainees were sent by train to southern France and ended up in an internment camp in Perpignan. My Uncle Dadek, who was born in Poland, didn't have to register and had decided to leave Brussels for France on Sunday. We never heard from him again and his fate remained a mystery.

It had been only ten months since we had gained our freedom from the Germans and we were again facing the prospect of persecution and death. Despite the self-assurance of the Belgians and the support of Britain and France, my father didn't wish to gamble with his family's lives. He reasoned that if the war ended with the defeat of Germany we could always return to Belgium, whereas the risk of staying and awaiting our fate was not the best solution.

The only deterrent at the time was that my mother had been quite ill and was still weak, making travel difficult for her. She had just suffered a severe gall bladder inflammation that had nearly killed her because she had received the wrong treatment. The Belgian doctor had ordered heat application and when her condition worsened, a friend recommended calling in a refugee doctor for a second opinion. Dr. Hermann was an elderly lady who had been a prominent surgeon prior to her flight from Germany. After examining my mother she immediately ordered ice packs and medication to reduce the inflammation. A problem arose in getting the medication because she was not licensed in Belgium and couldn't write a prescription. However, she had an agreement with one of the pharmacies at the other end of town where they were willing to dispense medicine at her bidding. When the Germans invaded Belgium my mother was just recuperating and was slowly regaining her strength.

Another problem was deciding what we would carry with us on the impending journey. We knew that we couldn't carry too much luggage and had to select very carefully what we would need to see us through an undetermined period of time. While we knew that we were going to go to Paris to stay with Uncle Willy, we had no idea how long the journey would take because troop-train movements were causing delays. We decided that each one of us would pack reasonable amounts of clothing changes and toiletries and we ended up with three small suitcases. Unfortunately, most of our family memorabilia was left behind. My father paid the rent six months in advance, being somewhat optimistic that we would return within that time. The landlord kept on assuring us that the Germans wouldn't enter Brussels because the Belgians and Dutch would halt their advances by opening the dykes and flooding the land. But the Belgians and Dutch had overlooked the possibility of the Germans coming equipped with rubber rafts in anticipation of this defence strategy. In reality, the fall of Eben-Emael, Belgium's main line of defence against a German attack, crumbled quickly and this alone should have been an indicator to the native Belgians that their defences were being overrun.[15]

Our landlord's cousin was a soldier at Eben Emael who had been wounded and evacuated from there. He reported that the Germans had arrived in the centre of the fort by parachute and had immediately occupied one portion of it. The Germans' greatest strength was the element of surprise. In order to confuse the Belgians, the Germans dropped a great number of rubber dummies from the planes so that the Belgian army command would believe that the number of troops was much greater than actually was, while other German soldiers came in by glider and landed in the fort. This was part of their famous blitzkrieg strategy that not only consisted of tank movements, but also encompassed a multi-faceted strategy of surprise. On May 15, 1940, the Dutch army surrendered in order to stop the indiscriminate German bombing attacks that had killed a great number of the Dutch people. The defeat of the Dutch left the Germans in a position to concentrate on Belgium, France and England. This calamity undoubtedly influenced my father's decision to leave Brussels immediately – it was becoming obvious that Brussels would fall and that we would be back under German rule.

---

15 Fort Eben-Emael was a Belgian underground fortress located between Liège and Maastricht, near the Albert Canal. Constructed in 1931–1935, it was considered impregnable.

The Second Exodus

We left our apartment in Brussels on May 15, 1940, proceeded to the railroad station and boarded a train for Paris. My father had selected Paris as our destination because his brother Willy was there; it never really occurred to him that we wouldn't soon be back in Brussels. My father reasoned that we could stay with Uncle Willy while the Allied armies defeated the Germans. We had first-class tickets, but still had to fight for seats on the train. There was a great deal of public resentment toward anything German and I was the only one who spoke French, so my parents and aunt needed to be quiet when we boarded the train. We managed to find an empty compartment with four seats facing each other and settled in. This meant that my mother could lie down on two of the seats and the three of us could share the other two. While everybody was looking for seats, the other people on the train did respect a sick person's need to lie down. I told anyone asking for space that my mother had just been released from the hospital three weeks earlier than recommended in order to flee. We placed our three suitcases in the luggage rack and kept a close eye on them – they now contained all our worldly belongings.

The train finally left the station after sitting there for about two hours. The waiting intensified our anxiety since we didn't know how close the Germans were to entering Brussels and if their arrival would prevent the train from pulling out. Most of the passengers on the train weren't Jewish, so they didn't endure the same phobia that we did. Their fears were based on the stories they had heard about atrocities committed on the civilian Belgian population by German troops during the occupation in World War I. Little did they know that this time around it would be much worse as the Germans sought revenge for the activities of the Belgian resistance movement.

Whenever we were close to the road as the train wound its way through the Belgian countryside, we could see troop movements toward Brussels. Convoys of trucks loaded with soldiers and pulling cannons were proceeding toward the front and some of the equipment not only looked but was in fact antiquated. Little did these soldiers realize that they were fighting a losing battle against a well-equipped army famous for its blitzkrieg tactics. The mood on the train was one of hope that the Maginot line, if not the dykes, would stop the Germans from advancing into France. The train moved slowly with many stops, and it took us more than four hours to reach Mons, a city about a hundred kilometres southwest of Brussels. For some reason the train didn't stop there, but merely slowed down as it moved through the station. Shortly after we left Mons behind, we arrived at the French border, where immigration officers boarded the train. There was such chaos that checking passengers was almost impossible – most of them didn't have passports or other supporting identification. By the time the officers got to our cubicle I had gathered that the best thing to say was that we were from Brussels. I observed that when other passengers said this, the immigration officials just walked away. We didn't know if Belgians required visas to enter France, but we did know that Poles did. Producing the Polish passports would only cause problems since the officers assumed we were Belgians. So it was far wiser to let them believe we were Belgians. We didn't encounter any language problems since the French officers believed me when I told them that we were Flemish and consequently my parents and aunt didn't speak French. Fortunately, the French officers didn't speak Flemish. Once we were safely in France we thought that our problems would be over. We knew that the distance from the border to Paris was about two hundred kilometres and we would arrive in Paris in about six to eight hours; based on the length of time it took to reach the French border, we would arrive in Paris in the early morning.

When daylight came, however, we saw that we were only just entering Reims, a city about 130 kilometres northeast of Paris. Somebody said that the train had been shunted during the night and had started to proceed east instead of south. Being under the impression that trains always offered food and drink, none of us had given any thought to bringing our own food. We had had lunch before leaving for the station so the subject didn't arise until some time later. When it did, however, we found out that the train didn't have a dining car, but it stopped long enough in the station at Reims for us to run out and buy some food. The food sellers in the railway station were gracious enough to accept Belgian currency as almost none of us had any French currency. I managed to buy some sandwiches and a few bottles of water before the supply ran out. Rumours about the surrender of the Netherlands were flying around and aroused considerable anxiety amongst the passengers. This was the first news of a German battle victory since the surrender of Poland in September 1939. Everybody grew increasingly pessimistic about the future and about our own fate.

Shortly after leaving Reims we heard the awful ear-piercing sound of German Stukas diving toward us. Two planes were coming straight at us and made about three passes each with their machine guns blazing. Miraculously, our car wasn't hit, but the car behind us was strafed and a few people were injured; two people were killed. As I've said, the train was heading south and there was no reason to assume that it was anything other than a civilian train. The attack was clearly intended to maim and kill innocent people. Shortly after the air attack we saw a train moving north filled with British soldiers and *matériel*. They waved cheerfully as the trains passed each other and we returned their waves, thinking of them as the fighting men who would stop the German advance. It was a comfort to believe that the Germans would be defeated through the combined efforts of the Allies. The fact that the British were participating in this campaign made a lot of people think twice about the old adage of World War I that "the British will fight to the last Frenchman."[1]

The train kept moving and stopping all day and when we reached Orléans – about 130 kilometres south of Paris – late in the evening, women at the station were handing out sandwiches and water to all the passengers. We couldn't get any supplies for my mother because she was too weak to leave the train and people had to present themselves in person to receive their allotment. By now we had covered about five hundred kilometres in a day and a half and we had become painfully aware that Paris was northeast of us and that we somehow bypassed it. When we left Orléans around midnight, we didn't know our destination nor could we get any information. Our feelings of uncertainty were only alleviated by the comfort of knowing that travelling south placed more distance between us and the Germans.

We gathered what news we could at the frequent stops the train made through the French countryside whenever we were able to leave the train and speak to farmers. The information we gleaned didn't sound very encouraging; we got confirmation that the advancing Germans had conquered the Netherlands. According to the people we spoke to, the radio reported that the Germans had occupied Brussels and the fate of King Leopold III was unknown. He was a much-liked monarch whose popularity was greatly enhanced by the love the Belgians had for his late wife, Queen Astrid. The radio an-

---

1   The phrase that "the British will fight to the last Frenchman" was a piece of World War I propaganda disseminated by the Germans to suggest that the British were using French forces to bear the brunt of the engagement in the Battle of France. The Germans used it to discourage the French from assisting the British as British troops became increasingly cornered near Dunkirk.

nouncers apparently still avowed that the Maginot Line would stop the onslaught and that the French and British troops would push the Germans back.

Every time the train stopped we scrambled out for food and drink since hours had passed since we had pulled out of Orléans. The train passed through a number of small centres without stopping, presumably to minimize the possibility of people getting off. Our stops were mainly in the countryside and at one of them many of us saw a water pump in the field and I decided to refill our three empty bottles. It was one of those pumps where you had to manipulate the handle up and down and hold the container under the spout, which usually takes two people. There was no one I could ask for help. Everyone was pushing and jostling to be able to get to the pump before the train started up again. I was also worried that if I asked anyone for assistance, I might lose the bottles. I clamped both filled bottles between my knees and when I had filled the last one, the person standing behind didn't even give me a chance to turn away before starting to pump the handle. The cast-iron handle hit my third bottle and it broke in half. Half of the glass hit my knee and tore a good-sized gash into my skin. Despite the severe bleeding I managed to get back to the train just as it started to move, all the while holding onto the two remaining bottles for dear life. My father, who had been watching from the steps of the train, helped me in. We didn't have any bandages and there was very little we could do to stop the blood flow. I elevated my leg by placing my heel on the opposite seat until the blood had coagulated. The scar of that cut stayed with me for the rest of my life as a vivid reminder of that awful train ride.

Our next stop was about thirteen hours after we had left Orléans, at around 1 PM on May 18, 1940, in Limoges, about 240 kilometres south of Orléans. At one of the stops before Limoges, our locomotive had been uncoupled and left for parts unknown. It took a few hours for a replacement engine to arrive and we could see that it was a considerably older model. During this part of the journey we were frequently shunted onto switch tracks to allow northbound trains to pass. Many of them were loaded with war *matériel* such as tanks, cannons, trucks and ambulances. A few carried French soldiers who appeared to have been brought north from their central base camps. They didn't look battle-worn. We didn't know at the time that many of the soldiers weren't given any ammunition beyond what they carried with them. Had we been aware of this shortcoming, our view of our chances for survival would have dimmed even more.

By now we knew that we were too far south to ever see Paris – it was at least eight hundred kilometres north of us. Again, the benevolent citizens of Limoges were out in force to supply us with food and drink. They informed us that in the past four hours two trains carrying refugees from Belgium had preceded us. But, as in Orléans, we couldn't obtain any information that would give us any indication of where we were headed. We each received sandwiches and a bottle of water – again I had a hard time getting the person handing out the supplies to believe that my mother was too sick to leave the train and give me her ration. My mother has missed out on the food ration in Orléans and I wanted to be sure that it didn't happen again. When I told the woman that she could personally deliver the food and drink to my mother in the train she relented and gave it to me.

The train stayed in the station in Limoges for about four hours, which gave us a chance to catch up on the latest news – it wasn't too encouraging. We received confirmation that Brussels had indeed surrendered to the Germans and that the Belgians were talking about an armistice.[2] It was impossible to walk around inside the train cars because there were so many people blocking the passageways and corridors. Each train car contained many more passengers than it would normally accommodate. Everybody had carved out a place

---

2 On May 27, 1940, with little notice to his French or British allies, King Leopold III of Belgium took the decision regarding surrender out of the hands of his government and spontaneously surrendered Belgian forces to the Germans.

wherever they could – including in the passageways – and jealously guarded their space. Again the stop was long enough to allow us to stretch our legs at the station without fear that the train would suddenly pull out.

When the train finally did leave the station at Limoges at around 5 PM, everyone tried to guess where our next stop would be and when we would get our next meal. People ate very sparingly, making the sandwiches last as long as possible since no one knew when and where we would be getting our next meal. By this time we had been on the train for three days – at least seventy-two hours – and experience had taught us that we couldn't count on a regular supply of food. We had to economize and plan ahead. This was one time when money couldn't buy anything; we were totally dependent on the good will of the citizens in the towns where we stopped. Everywhere we went the food kiosks in the railway stations were shuttered by order of the stationmaster to avoid chaos. The townspeople were obviously prepared for what was happening – ours was not the first train of refugees to come through the area and they gave us provisions most willingly and with a smile. We were all in the same boat – afraid of the Germans – and that created a common bond between the residents and train passengers. We all knew that the Netherlands had surrendered and that Brussels had fallen to the Germans. The hope of stopping the German advance by flooding the dykes had completely evaporated and the next real line of defence was France's Maginot Line.

By the time we pulled out of Limoges station to continue our odyssey into the unknown, we had become acquainted with some of the neighbours in the adjoining seats. We all bemoaned our fate, albeit for different reasons. As far as we could tell, we were the only Jews in that car; in fact, if there were other Jews on the train we hadn't met them. Our travelling companions were aware of my mother's ill health and her physical weakness, but as far as they were concerned – and painfully so – we were Germans. My explanation that we had escaped from Germany because of Hitler's sworn intention to murder all the

Jews did lessen their tendency to direct their hatred of the Germans at us a little; some of them even tried to speak German to my parents and aunt. The fact that we were all trying to escape from the German onslaught established some degree of mutual understanding.

Our train continued in a southerly direction, putting more distance between us and the front, but the question of our destination continued to prey on our minds. Fortunately, however, my mother was beginning to show signs of regaining her physical strength, which was most surprising given her lack of proper nutrition. Presumably the extended periods of rest had enabled her to get better and her improved condition made it a little easier for us to face the unknown future. The only time my mother got up was to go to the restroom. By now both restrooms in the car were in a deplorable condition and we had run out of paper long ago. During our stops we searched for newspaper that we could cut up and use as toilet paper. Even worse was the lack of soap and any other toiletries. My father had had to give up shaving because he had run out of razor blades. During our long trek, the restrooms frequently didn't have any fresh water for flushing or washing, a situation that was exacerbated by passengers using what water there was to wash their clothes. The sanitary conditions deteriorated daily and the only saving grace was that the outside temperature remained cool, keeping the odours down.

Fights broke out in some of the cars, which was really not surprising considering that a large number of total strangers were being forced to stay together in close quarters for days under less than acceptable conditions. Tempers flared quickly, particularly when ignited by fear and anxiety. We were all only too aware that we had no control over our destiny and no say in our final destination. The authorities were likely debating how to handle this great influx of refugees and where to route us – they just kept us moving on the trains until they could come up with a plan.

No doubt the rail system was also already overloaded by the troop movements and the civilian trains were being shunted onto any available open tracks. We travelled throughout night and because we stopped so often it became impossible to judge how far we had come and in what direction we were headed. The countryside looks amazingly similar from a train window, but speaking to people at some of the stops during the night gave us some indication that we were heading further south in France, toward the Mediterranean.

By May 19 we had spent four days on the train, forced to sleep sitting up. My knee was throbbing with pain from the cut and whenever I suddenly jerked my knee in my sleep the wound opened up and started to bleed again. It was probably a much deeper cut than it looked and should have been treated with a few stitches. In the late morning we realized that we were approaching another town and looked forward to getting some food supplies. We had learned to watch for an increase in the number of houses to gauge when we were getting close to a town. Maybe here the stationmaster would not have ordered the kiosks to be shuttered and they would accept Belgian currency. Over the last four days we had survived on about six sandwiches each and plenty of water. We were all starved for a decent meal, but nobody spoke about food. The lack of a full night's sleep for so many days had also taken its toll on people and our senses were dulled. In a way this was a blessing because we weren't so conscious of the many of the hardships we had endured.

At around 9 A M we pulled into the railway station at Toulouse, a city in southern France about three hundred kilometres south of Limoges, halfway between the Atlantic Ocean and the Mediterranean Sea. By now we had travelled over one thousand kilometres. There were no people on the platform offering us food, but although the kiosks were open, the merchants wouldn't accept Belgian currency and there wasn't any place in the station to exchange money. We were told to stay in the cars because the train might pull out at any time, but at about noon there was an announcement instructing us to leave the train, take our belongings with us and register at a desk set up in the waiting room. The people who had been injured during the

German Stuka attack were taken to the hospital for treatment and the dead were removed. The rest of us were told that we could go to the station restaurant to receive one sandwich and one bottle of water each. Again, we had no idea what was going to happen after this registration procedure, but we weren't allowed to leave the station. Another announcement would be made by 4 PM to give us further information.

The registration process was lengthy – for the first time we realized how many people had been on the train. I walked around in the waiting room to try to find out what was going on and soon discovered that people who had documentation proving their Belgian nationality were being allowed to leave the station while those of other nationalities had to remain. I was terrified that we would be sent back and I went to tell my father what I had found out. We didn't want to upset my mother or my aunt, so he asked me to keep quiet about it. By now we were able to see that a number of the non-Belgians were Jews. My father spoke to a few of them about my observation, but they seemed resigned to whatever fate befall them and were prepared to accept it. Their apathy was astounding, although their sense of survival had no doubt been dulled by the trauma of the long train journey.

When our turn came to register, my father produced our Polish passports and the French policeman examined them very carefully. I translated the questions he asked – Where were we headed when we left Brussels? Did my father have sufficient funds to support himself and his family? Were we intending to stay in France or go elsewhere? Had any member of our family ever been in the German army? Did we have any family relations in France? What was their nationality? He also asked our religion, our ages and our marital status. One of the last questions I remember clearly because I thought it was so odd: How much luggage did we have with us? After the interview, the officer told us to return to the other waiting room that was now being used to accommodate the non-Belgians passengers. By the time the whole registration process had been completed, there were about 150 people in there. The atmosphere was fairly tense. About one-third of the people seemed to be Jewish and they decided to try send a message to the Jewish community in Toulouse about our situation.

At around 6 PM we were told to bring our luggage and board buses that were now standing outside the station. At least we knew that we weren't going to be sent back toward the German lines. That afforded us some degree of comfort – whatever we encountered wouldn't place us in immediate danger. The buses wound their way through Toulouse to another part of town and after a twenty-minute bus ride, we pulled into what appeared to be a veterinary school. We got out of the vehicles and saw a huge barn. The police officers told us to go into the building and find a place to sleep; the following day we would be told what was to happen. The ground inside the barn was covered with hay, some of it topped with fresh animal droppings. We weren't quite sure when they had moved the cows to make room for us, but the smell was overpowering. Nonetheless, we were all so tired after the arduous train ride that the surroundings didn't deter anybody from stretching out on the hay and going to sleep. Nobody really cared about anything other than sleep and nourishment; when the authorities brought in ample quantities of food and drink, our happiness was supreme.

When we got up the next morning, the authorities still hadn't decided what to do with us. Over the next few days, we were free to come and go as we pleased, but at night we had to stay at the veterinary school. Although there were some small children among the 150 people in our group, most were adults. Few of them spoke French and I was often called on to act as interpreter. My father decided that he and I should go into town and find out what was going on with the war and what we could learn from other refugees in Toulouse.

We learned quickly that there is a formula for finding where refugees gathered: head for the city and ask directions to the largest coffee house in the centre of town. The coffee house we were looking for in Toulouse was located on a square and after we found it we sat down and ordered coffee. It was full of people speaking various languages – German, Polish, Yiddish – but almost no French. We knew immediately that we were at the right place and my father looked around to see if he could spot any familiar faces. As it happened, my father recognized a gentleman from Leipzig sitting a few tables over and motioned to him to join us. After the usual exchange of niceties and information about the war the man asked my father if he had already seen his brother Willy. My father replied that he was more than perplexed by the question since, as far as he knew, his brother was still in Paris. No, the man informed him, Willy was indeed here in Toulouse. He gave us the name of the hotel where he was staying. My father told me to go there at once to let my uncle know that we were here in Toulouse.

The hotel wasn't too far from the coffee house and my father suggested that I bring Uncle Willy back with me. At about 11 AM I knocked on my uncle's hotel room door and a voice inside asked in French who was there. I asked if this was the room of Mr. Mann and the reply came back, "Komm herein, Fredie." (Come in, Fred.) I never did figure out how my uncle recognized my voice after not seeing me for four years, particularly since my voice changed.

The reunion between my father and his brother was most touching – neither had believed that they would ever see each other again. Uncle Willy knew that we had gone to Brussels and, I'm sure, thought that we'd been caught there when the Germans took the city. Seeing each other was a tremendous relief to both of them. Unfortunately, as time would tell, our time together wouldn't last very long. As a French resident, my uncle had no restrictions on his movements within France, whereas we were not allowed to move out of Toulouse or out of our forced residence. The French government had other plans for the refugees in the veterinary school.

As is usual when there is human misery, some people take advantage of the situation; this became apparent when my father was forced to sell some of my mother's jewellery. He didn't want to ask his brother for money, even though he had helped Willy financially many times in Leipzig. My father must have believed that as the eldest in the family – especially under the present circumstances – he had to be self-sufficient and not take any of my uncle's funds. Uncle Willy owned two lingerie stores in Paris, but he had closed them temporarily during this period of uncertainty. As it later turned out, taking care of his business ended up costing him his life.

There were a number of people in the coffee house who bought jewellery and my father made a deal with one of them. The lesson I learned then was loud and clear: A Jew must always have a suitcase mentality and possess assets that can be quickly converted to cash. Neither real estate nor corporate investments meet this qualification. Jewellery, however, is always readily negotiable for cash, even though it may not fetch anywhere near the original purchase price. The lack of ready cash often dictated the sad fate that befell so many Jewish refugees.

Toulouse had become the hub for Jews who had escaped from various European countries and the French were trying to find a way to deal with all of them. Not only were they concerned about the strain on the infrastructure – finding adequate housing and food – but they were also worried about the existence of so-called fifth columnists, spies that the Germans were believed to have so successfully planted among civilians during and after the blitzkrieg.

We continued to frequent the coffee house on the main square over the next few days. After a while the waiters got to know us and would automatically serve us our favourite drinks as soon as we sat down. Since our conversations were mainly in German, they had no way of knowing what we were saying and could be of no help to the French police in differentiating the real Jews from the German spies. We had the same problem distinguishing between legitimate refugees and fifth columnists. Many people in Toulouse claimed to have escaped from the Germans and I heard that the Gestapo had gone so far as to force the spies to be circumcised.[3] They even spouted a few words in Yiddish or Hebrew. The spies were primarily concerned about Jewish scientists who were escaping to safety and there were rumours of kidnapping and disappearances. We were certain that the people who had been detained with us in the veterinary school were Jewish because they had been on the train with us from Brussels; the others simply appeared from nowhere.

After we had been at the veterinary school for four days, we were moved out of the barn to the classrooms and cots were set up for us. The washrooms on the classroom floors didn't offer any bathing facilities, but we were fortunate to be able to use Uncle Willy's hotel room to bathe. The school was closed because most of the teachers had been conscripted into the army and the authorities claimed that these facilities were the only ones with sufficient security to house the multitude of "German" refugees. Three meals a day were served in the school dining room, but my parents, aunt and I ate most of our meals outside the building. The food in Toulouse was very good and I still remember the salted meats such as *saucisson*, *saucisse* and ham, and the duck cutlets. It was in Toulouse that I developed my taste for *chanterelles*, and they are still my favourite mushrooms. I also got my first taste of walnut liqueur, a Toulouse classic. Most of the time my uncle joined us and we were able to engage in some semblance of family life.

There were a few attractions for a young boy in Toulouse. The Capitole, rebuilt in the eighteenth century after a fire destroyed the original building, is a magnificent town hall. It is also the home of an

---

3 Circumcision of Jewish male infants is a traditional rite that marks their entry into the Covenant with God. It was not usual in non-Jewish males in Germany. The Nazis routinely checked whether boys and men were circumcised to determine if they were Jewish – they accordingly would have understood that this was something Jews might check to uncover Nazi spies posing as Jews.

opera company and symphony orchestra; but due to the war there were no performances there. There were also mansions built centuries ago that stood as a reminder of the prestigious past of Toulouse as a major metropolis. I admired the monastery buildings on the rue Lakanal and wondered why we couldn't be housed there instead of in the veterinary school. The city's water tower stood like a lighthouse at the entrance to the Pont Neuf.

Throughout our time in Toulouse Aunt Rena was most concerned about the whereabouts of her fiancé and had no way to trace him since the Red Cross had no information. She held out hope that he would communicate with Uncle Arno in London. We had sent him a telegram after we arrived in Toulouse so that he could tell my brother where we were. My uncle couldn't correspond with us because we didn't know how long we would be in Toulouse. As it happened, after some two weeks in Toulouse we were informed that we would soon be moved to a new location.

~

On May 28, 1940, Belgium officially surrendered to the Germans and King Leopold chose to stay in Brussels rather than form and head a government in exile. After Holland's surrender on May 15, 1940, Queen Wilhelmina had fled to London and established the Dutch government in exile there. By now the Poles and the Dutch governments in exile had created an official opposition to the Germans, supported by the Allies. Nonetheless, the war effort appeared to be favouring the Germans, and on June 4 we read about the evacuation of Dunkirk and the repatriation of the remainder of the British army.[4] It

---

4 Between May 26 and June 4, 1940, more than 300,000 British, French and Canadian troops hemmed in by the German army were evacuated from the beaches of Dunkirk, France by a hastily assembled fleet of some eight hundred boats – small fishing vessels, pleasure craft and commercial boats guided by navy

was not long before we also learned that the Norwegian army had surrendered to the Germans. Although this event was far enough removed from us geographically as to not to be considered drastic, it was still a terrible blow to our morale when we realized that the British would no longer be defending Continental Europe – only the French army stood between us and the Germans. The French continued to fight valiantly as Prime Minister Paul Reynaud tried to save the country from total German takeover.

The French authorities in Toulouse informed us that we would be moving to Rodez in the Department of Aveyron. We had spent more than three weeks in the veterinary school and at first were glad to be leaving our primitive living quarters. At the same time, Rodez was about 150 kilometres northeast of Toulouse and we weren't too thrilled about moving in a northerly direction, toward the fighting. News from the front indicated that the French troops were no match for the Germans, who were steadily advancing deeper into French territory. The Maginot Line had proved to be ineffective because the Germans had simply skirted it by coming through Belgium. According to the news reports, the French government in Paris was looking for someplace safe to relocate for the duration of the war. The questions at this point were how long it would be before the French capitulated and what would be our fate. We didn't have to wait long for an answer.

The French government moved to Tours – a city in central France about 240 kilometres southwest of Paris – on June 10, 1940, and on June 14 the Germans occupied Paris. Our fears of being captured were not assuaged when we knew Rodez would bring us closer to Paris rather than farther away from it. We could never understand

---

stroyers – and taken to safety in England. In his subsequent "We shall fight on the beaches" speech in the British House of Commons, Winston Churchill referred to the event as simultaneously one of Britain's greatest military defeats and a "miracle of deliverance."

why the French wouldn't let us stay in Toulouse or let us proceed on our own.

There were about one hundred of us left in the veterinary school and the authorities insisted on moving all of us together. A few days after the announcement of our proposed move from Toulouse, the supervisor told us at breakfast to pack all our belongings and be ready to leave early in the morning. We went into town that day to visit with Uncle Willy. He said it was just as well that we were leaving because now that Paris had fallen he intended to return there to liquidate his stores. He said that once his business was concluded, he would come back and join us in Rodez. We could stay in touch with him as he was returning to his apartment in the Hotel Papillion in the 16th District.

On the morning of June 16, 1940, we got ready to relocate to Rodez. I dressed in my Boy Scout uniform that I hadn't worn since we arrived in Toulouse. It was quite an impressive uniform with its hat, shirt, neckerchief, riding breeches, riding boots and a large cape with pockets on the inside. Worn over the neckerchief was the usual lanyard with a whistle stuffed into one of the shirt pockets. This was the uniform we had worn in Brussels and was unique to the English Boy Scout troop to which I belonged. I had advanced to assistant scoutmaster and on my uniform I displayed a number of merit badges that I had earned in Brussels. The reason that I was promoted to assistant scoutmaster at a rather young age was that during my days in Germany I had belonged to the Jewish Boy Scouts and we were quite advanced in our training.

Two days after the fall of Paris we boarded one of the four buses to Rodez. We still carried our three suitcases containing what clothes we had – that was the extent of our belongings. Unless we were able to return to Brussels our entire collection of family photographs would be lost forever. We hadn't packed any photo albums or other memorabilia that recorded our family's history. Suddenly, our present was also our past, with little hope for the future. None of us was in the best frame of mind as we rolled along the highway toward Rodez. There was very little conversation and the mood was rather sombre; everybody was preoccupied with thoughts about the oncoming events. Even the small children seemed to be affected by the adult feelings of uncertainty – there was no evidence of child-like exuberance or playfulness.

The countryside we drove through looked extremely peaceful and, were it not for the trucks loaded with wounded soldiers proceeding south, one could almost forget that there was a war raging up north. An uneventful four hours later we arrived on the outskirts of Rodez after passing through Albi, another larger town on our way. We mostly passed through villages and the buses made a number of stops for people to use toilet facilities and to get some snacks.

We were accompanied by officers from the gendarmerie – the division of the French military that performed policing duties – with one officer posted in each bus. Almost none of the people on the buses spoke enough French to converse with these officers and the officer on our bus carried on a conversation with me. When any of the officers wanted to communicate something to the passengers on the other buses they would call on me to interpret. During my conversation with the officer on our bus I found out that we were going to be lodged in huts that had been previously used for army training. The officer couldn't tell me very much about them since he hadn't seen them but only repeated what he'd been told by his superiors. What we mostly talked about was his concern for his son who was in an army division stationed in the subterranean caves of the Maginot Line. He said that he hoped that the soldiers had been issued more ammunition than they had been allocated just before the invasion of France. During one of his leaves, his son had told him that they had only been handed a few rounds of bullets for their rifles. The French army command was convinced that the Maginot Line was invincible and that maintaining its impenetrability would require very little effort.

Little did the French army command expect the assault to come from the rear of the line rather than as a frontal attack. Both the French and British had believed that the Germans would never get through the Dutch and Belgian defences and would be forced to retreat from the advanced positions they had gained in their blitzkrieg offensive. They thought that their situation was very different from that of Poland, where Russian cooperation had assisted the Germans in a fast victorious campaign.[5] Once again, their predictions would turn out to be wrong.

We arrived at our destination in the late afternoon. It didn't take long for us to realize that we were actually being quartered in what was then called a lunatic asylum. There were wards and some private rooms. Our group was composed of about thirty-five families and twenty individuals. There were separate wards for men and women and couples without children were given their own rooms. We were served meals in the main dining room where all the patients ate, but on a second-shift basis so that we never actually ate with the residents. The only place we encountered them was in the huge garden and none of them was belligerent or aggressive. They were housed in a different building and we assumed that the facilities we occupied were never fully utilized.

The war news continued to be grim and we expected the worst. On June 17, 1940, Maréchal Henri-Philippe Pétain asked for an armistice with Germany. It must have been difficult for the "Hero of Verdun" whose defiant slogan in the battle of Verdun against the Germans in World War I had been "Ils ne passeront pas" (They shall not pass), the battle cry of the French army at that time. The French

---

5 The Treaty of Non-Aggression between Germany and the USSR – colloquially known as the Molotov–Ribbentrop Pact – that was signed on August 24, 1939, stipulated that the two countries would not go to war with each other and divided Poland into Nazi and Soviet spheres of influence. By the time the Nazis breeched the pact and attacked the Soviet Union on June 22, 1941, Poland was fully under Nazi control.

signed the armistice on June 22, 1940. That was a hard blow for all of us because once again it brought us closer to the Germans and the possibility that they would exercise the controls included in the armistice treaty.[6]

The French authorities in Rodez told us that we would soon be moved from the asylum to a camp within the town itself. In the meantime, however, we weren't allowed to leave the grounds. After about a week, a French army captain arrived and informed us that all the men age eighteen and over would be moved to an internment camp in Albi, about seventy kilometres away, and that the women and children would be relocated to the camp in Rodez. The captain appointed me the official translator and asked me to translate his speech. A few days later, the men were given notice that they would be moved the following day. At least we knew my father was going to a place not too far from Rodez.

The day after my father left, the captain told me to report to the *sous-préfet* at the prefecture of the Department of Aveyron the following morning. I wondered why I had been singled out for this appearance and had considerable misgivings. I told my mother about it and we figured that they couldn't likely be sending me to Albi because if that were the case, they would have just picked me up and transported me there. After talking about it for a long time, we decided just to wait until the next day and see what happened.

The following day I walked to the prefecture wearing my Boy Scout uniform and went to see the *sous-préfet*. He told me that he was

---

6 The Franco-German armistice of June 22, 1940 divided France into two zones. The northern three-fifths were under German military occupation and the remaining "free" southern region – known as Vichy France after the location of its administrative centre – was under nominal French sovereignty. The Vichy government was led by Maréchal Philippe Pétain. One of the other provisions of the armistice was an agreement by France to turn over all German and Austrian refugees to the Germans.

putting me in charge of the camp to which we were being moved and that I was to report directly to him with any requests or requirements for the residents. I was to be given a separate room and would allocate rooms to the others. He also said I would be given a weekly stipend as pocket money for any purchases required. He called in his assistant and he and I went to visit the camp where we were to be quartered. I was being given a great deal of responsibility for a fourteen-year-old boy.

The camp was in a wide-open field surrounded by apartment buildings with stores and a movie theatre nearby. In other words, we would be living within the confines of the main part of the city of Rodez. A day later about fifty of us moved to the camp. There were four rectangular huts placed and another square hut at the entrance. This building turned out to be the commissary where we could have our meals. The whole area was surrounded by barbed wire with one front gate and two sentry boxes, each one manned by a soldier. The barracks had individual rooms and each room had two beds, a table with three chairs, a dresser with a mirror and a shaded lamp in the centre. It also had a sink with a cold-water faucet. I selected a room by the entrance for myself and my mother and aunt shared the room next to mine.

I continued to help the captain with translation when he instructed us about the rules and regulations and told the people that I was to be the camp commandant. The main restriction was that no one could leave the camp grounds without a special permit that had to be requested through my office. Our meals were to be brought in and served in the extra barracks. The captain told us that we could either eat in the barracks or take the meals to our rooms. All the cleaning as well as the kitchen duties were to be done by the inmates. The captain told us that a French army lieutenant would come to the camp every day at dinner time. Any consultation or complaints could be voiced at that time. For any outside needs, the inmates were to prepare a list of requirements and an representative from the *sous-préfet*'s office would make the purchases.

The meal service worked very smoothly and most people decided to eat in their rooms instead of in the barracks. The barracks had long picnic tables with benches that seated about five people on each side. At the end of each barracks were big laundry tubs and a double-cylinder wringer operated by a crank. The laundered item was squeezed between the two cylinders to remove the water. Some people were quite adept at this and could do a whole basket of laundry in a relatively short time by overlapping the pieces of clothing and never stopping the crank. For things that needed ironing, there was a stove on which cast-iron flatirons could be heated. The French military supplied sheets, pillowcases and towels weekly.

Also at the end of each barracks was a room outfitted as bathing quarters. There were sinks along the wall and six showers, and separate small rooms facing the outside with toilets. We set up a schedule for taking showers and in accordance with French custom, the toilets were in different rooms, accessible directly from the halls.

After about two weeks I suggested to the *sous-préfet* that they institute a morning roll call and allow the residents to leave the camp freely during the day. He acceded to this request, which removed some of the tension within the camp. We had very few troublemakers and the changes allowed for a relatively smooth co-existence among all the people. During the time that we lived in Rodez, harmony prevailed because everyone was aware that if we gave the French authorities any reason to do so, the rules would be tightened.

Rodez was a town of about 30,000 inhabitants, not counting the outlying areas of greater Rodez, which had about 45,000 inhabitants. The town was on the main railway line, which served me well when I had to travel later in our stay. The cathedral was built at the start of the thirteenth century and completed during the sixteenth. The view of the winding pedestrian streets and the green surroundings from its bell tower was magnificent. It was a most impressive structure, as were some of the old houses from that period. The lakes of the Levezou – the largest in southern France – were nearby.

The war news remained discouraging, and the usual boisterous celebrations of July 14, Bastille Day, were very sombre that year, with no parades or flag waving. The mayor of Rodez had published a very critical analysis of recent events in the local newspaper and military personnel in the town stayed in their barracks. People were in no mood to celebrate this day and undoubtedly there was even less desire to reflect on France's past glory in the occupied zone.

⁓

About a month after we settled into the new camp, the *sous-préfet* sent for me and introduced me to the chief scout of Rodez. He told me that Maréchal Pétain had created an organization known as the Jeunesse de Pétain in direct competition with the two existing scout organizations in France – the Scouts de France, the Catholic arm of the French Boy Scouts, and the Éclaireurs, the non-denominational scouts.[7] Once Pétain had started his youth group, the Scouts de France and the Éclaireurs had gotten together to fight against the inroads made by the Jeunesse. The two scout organizations moved their headquarters to Vichy, which had become the capital of unoccupied France.

The chief scout of Rodez told me that they would like me to travel within unoccupied France to speak to youth groups and convince them either to remain in or join with the Boy Scout movement instead of joining the Pétain group. He felt that there was no better emissary for their mission than a Boy Scout who had fled Germany and had been in a country where it was not only prohibited to be a Scout, but where the Hitler Youth organization was a forerunner of the Jeunesse de Pétain. He was fair enough to mention that the

---

7 In Vichy France, Pétain established the paramilitary youth organization Jeunesse de Pétain – formally called Chantiers de la Jeunesse Françaises – that closely paralleled the Hitler Youth. For more information, see the glossary.

assignment might not be without danger because, as a Jew and an opponent of the Jeunesse, I might be a target for retaliation. I was really too young to evaluate the consequences and therefore readily agreed to accept the task. The chief scout told me that for the first couple of weeks I would be addressing groups within the Department of Aveyron. Later I might be required to travel to other regions and that I would be paid a per diem allowance, plus free transportation and meal expenses.

My first meeting was with a group of about fifteen ten-year-old boys in a private home in Rodez. I suppose that my being fourteen years old and looking older made me a role model for them. I proudly displayed the badges I had earned in Brussels on my uniform, which undoubtedly impressed my audience. Their questions centred mainly on my flight from the Germans and their camping prospects if they joined the Boy Scouts. Apparently the Jeunesse de Pétain was making all kind of promises to attract members. Nobody brought up the subject of my being Jewish, which made me realize that these kids had no racial prejudice. Their main concern was the German occupation of France because their parents talked about the brutalities committed in German-occupied France in World War I.

Most of the boys in the room couldn't believe that Pétain would cooperate with the Germans and their interest in his youth group was minimal. They told me that their teachers made disparaging remarks on the subject. The overall school system tried to stay neutral, but the resentment permeated through the system. While German was to be taught as a second language, a number of the school administrators refused to place it on the curriculum for the 1940-1941 school year, arguing that it was too late to hire German-language teachers.

In the meantime, we closely watched the events shaping the outcome of this first phase of World War II, aware that the Germans could take over all of France, or at the very least, could exercise the victors' prerogative of control over the Vichy government. It was well known that Pierre Laval, the prime minister, was a German sympathizer and would accede to any and all German requests. This meant that Jews were not safe in unoccupied France and my mother, aunt and I started thinking about how best to escape to safer surroundings. It was difficult to plan since my father was in the camp in Albi and we didn't know what was happening to him or if we could obtain his release. My mother and I did realize, however, that he was in greater danger of being deported while he was in Albi with the other men than if he were in Rodez with us. I started thinking about how I could get assigned to speak in Albi so that I could investigate the chances of getting my father released.

The newspapers reported the German attack on Britain and the so-called Battle of Britain was in full swing.[8] The Italians had also taken advantage of the weakened British position by invading British Somaliland and had fully occupied it by the middle of August 1940. The attack on Britain caused us anxious moments since both my brother and uncle and his family lived there and we were totally ignorant of their fate. We had had no news from England since leaving Toulouse, as there was no longer any postal service after the German-French armistice was signed.

~

During a report session at the *sous-préfet*'s office in the middle of August, we were advised that we would be moving to Naucelle, a small village about thirty kilometres southwest of Rodez, as the army required the camp we were using. We would be quartered with local families whose draft-age sons and husbands had been conscripted. The families needed financial assistance and our stay would give them additional income. We worked out a lodging plan with the *sous-*

8 Germany's campaign to achieve air superiority over Great Britain before launching a land invasion, known as the Battle of Britain, lasted from July through September 1940. For more information, see the glossary.

préfet's assistant and I took advantage of my position to house my mother, my aunt and myself at the mayor's residence. I sent a letter to my father in Albi and informed him of our move and our new address. Naucelle was closer to Albi – it was only about forty kilometres away – and I told my father that I would try to visit him shortly after our move.

A few days later the *sous-préfet* advised me that he was sending a former Belgian police inspector from Schaerbeek, a suburb of Brussels, to accompany us and that he and I would share supervision responsibilities. He would live in the hotel and coordinate activities, and would share meals with us in the communal dining room. He apparently had no income since fleeing Brussels and this was a way to assist him. I wasn't too happy about this development since the police inspector was of Flemish origin and as far as I knew they were notorious antisemites. Before the war there had been a number of unpleasant incidents in Antwerp, which is a Flemish stronghold and the centre of the diamond industry in Europe. Most of the dealers, cutters and graders were Jewish and there were a number of attacks on them.[9] My paternal grandfather's brother had moved to Antwerp from Poland and was a member of the Antwerp diamond exchange.[10] During our brief stay in Brussels, my father had gone to Antwerp but was not too taken by that branch of the family and never suggested a meeting between us. I hoped that the police inspector would not turn out to be racist.

I would now have to resolve a few logistic problems if I was to continue my work for the Boy Scout group. While I was in Rodez

---

9 The particular victimization of Jews in Antwerp during World War II had its roots in pre-war Flemish nationalism that combined antisemitism with sympathy for Hitler's National Socialist ideology.

10 As the trading centre for Antwerp's diamond industry, the Antwerp diamond exchange controlled the flow of diamonds throughout the world.

I could obtain a *titre de voyage*, travel orders, from the *sous-préfet* that entitled me to obtain railway tickets and hotel accommodation. In Naucelle I wouldn't be able to get the tickets without telephoning Rodez and then waiting for the documents to be delivered. The *sous-préfet* decided to give me one blank signed travel order at a time that I could fill myself. In most cases I would have to change trains in Rodez on my way to and from Naucelle, which wouldn't make it difficult for me to continue my activities.

My next trip was to Vichy where I was to address high school students who were still on summer vacation. I would not have chosen to do this because it placed me right in the lion's den – Vichy was the capital city of unoccupied France and Pétain's government. The idea was to approach these boys before they returned to school where they would be subjected to the propaganda of the Jeunesse de Pétain. To accommodate the Germans, Prime Minister Laval exerted strong pressure on Pétain to cooperate with them. It was regrettable that the hero of the Battle of Verdun was now a pawn of the Germans.

I was quartered in the apartment of one of the scoutmasters and he and his wife took me to the hall where I was to address the assembled boys. There were a number of other speakers ahead of me and I was quite nervous because this was my first time addressing a large crowd. When it came to my turn, I was introduced as an assistant scoutmaster from Brussels who had fled ahead of the German occupation of that city. Since nobody specified whether I was Walloon or Flemish, my slight accent could be interpreted as Flemish. There was no mention of my being Jewish or of German origin. This limited the content of my speech since I didn't want to broach the subject of my German background. In order to get across what the Germans had done to the Boy Scout movement in that country, I created an imaginary friend, a refugee from Germany who had gone to school with me in Brussels. After that presentation I had no problem speaking to larger audiences and employed the story of my "German friend" many times. It was hard to tell if these meetings were effective, but there was little doubt that the Jeunesse movement was not very successful and its membership remained small. My presentations were well received and the organizers invited me to appear again in Vichy at a later date.

On the second day of my stay, I visited the famous Vichy water fountain.[11] The water is claimed to cure or alleviate symptoms for people with stomach trouble and/or rheumatism. I was directed to the Halles des Sources, an enormous iron-framed greenhouse in which the various waters emerge from their spouts. People were lined up to get their cupful of the therapeutic water and many of them were speaking German.

Since the French government had established its operations in the city of Vichy, it had requisitioned a number of hotels and office spaces to accommodate the civil service employees, and the town now had a larger population than it had ever had before, even during the tourist season. Maréchal Pétain had his own offices at the pavilion and many of the ministries were located on the rue du Parc. Even more disconcerting was finding out that the Gestapo had its headquarters at the Hôtel du Portugal. Before going to the railway station to catch a train for Rodez, I stopped at the ministry of the interior to ask what was involved in getting an exit permit from France. I was told that it would only be approved if one could produce proof of acceptance by a country granting permanent residence. I picked up a number of application forms that required signatures by each applicant. While we knew we had to make every effort to leave France, we neither had a destination nor had we even given much thought to a possible route out of France. However, this information about a residence destination inspired us to focus on availability over preference. We were too isolated to garner this type of information in Rodez, and would cer-

---

11 Vichy has been famous as a spa town since Roman times – the waters there are thought to promote improved health.

tainly be more so in Naucelle, so I decided to contact Jewish groups for information.

In order to appear older, I started to smoke and carried cigarettes with me on me on this trip. My mother and aunt had never seen me smoke, although they were both occasional smokers. My mother would undoubtedly not have approved of my smoking at such a young age and I knew my father would downright forbid it. To cover the fact that I was smoking, I told them that I had to carry cigarettes in order to offer them to people or to give away as presents.

~

We were transported by bus to Naucelle at the end of August, about a week after I had returned from Vichy, and the *sous-préfet* sent his assistant to ensure our safe journey and relocation. He and I had laid out the plan for housing, so each family knew where they would be quartered and could go straight there. The bus stopped in the village square. The mayor must have notified his people because when the bus pulled into the village square, those who were to receive "guests" had assembled in the square and took charge of their new tenants. The mayor escorted my mother, Aunt Rena and me to his house, which was located on a side street leading off the square. He showed us to our two rooms on the second floor and told us that the rest of the house was also at our disposal, that we should feel like family. Once again my mother and her sister shared one bedroom and I occupied the other. The mayor and his family were very hospitable and they immediately took to my mother and aunt despite the language barrier.

The mayor then showed me to the barn where the communal meals would be served, about a five-minute walk from his house. The building was empty except for picnic tables and benches – since there were no kitchen facilities, the food would be prepared in the community hall that was only a few yards away. Needless to say, the structure wasn't heated and I assumed that different arrangements would have to be made when the temperature dropped. For the moment, though, we would only eat the midday meal – always the main meal of the day – communally; the other meals would be arranged in each home. The mayor showed me around the rest of the town, telling me proudly that the Cistercian Church had been constructed in the thirteenth century. He also took me to the Château du Bosc, the childhood residence of painter Toulouse-Lautrec.[12] On our way we passed by the place where the Belgian police inspector would be staying when he arrived the next day – it was the only hotel on the square.

Naucelle had a population of about two thousand and our arrival was a major event for the villagers. The inhabitants had never seen so many foreigners at one time and I was wondering whether they would be suspicious or accept us. The hotel, as I found out, had the only bistro in town, and the male population gathered there for their usual imbibing. France had no age restriction on drinking alcohol and since I looked older than I was, nobody suspected that I was only fourteen years old. On the first day of our stay, the mayor took me along to the bistro and introduced me to his friends. I didn't know what to order, so I said that I would have whatever the mayor was drinking. The waiter brought me a thick green liquid that tasted like liquorice. It was some time before I discovered that it was Pernod Fils, a favourite anise-based drink of the French. The sustained indulgence of this absinthe was rumoured to affect the brain – the French government was so concerned about its effects on the French troops in World War I that they banned it.

The next morning the mayor's wife served us a breakfast of delicious French breads – baguettes, brioche and croissants. The milk was still lukewarm since it had come directly from the mayor's own cows and the coffee was strong enough to clean rusty pipes. The break-

---

12 Henri Raymond de Toulouse-Lautrec was a noted French post-impressionist painter.

fasts served during our stay were absolutely incredible and always incorporated such homemade food as bacon, blood sausage, eggs and jams. For dinner we bought cold cuts at the local butcher and got bread from the mayor's wife, who was a marvellous baker. There was always plenty to eat and while we were probably best off at the mayor's house, we didn't hear any complaints from any of the other people.

Our first noon meal at the barn passed uneventfully and everybody was satisfied with the food prepared by the village women. After lunch I appointed three women to be in charge of washing and stacking the dishes and cutlery. To prevent any disputes over seating, I announced that everybody was to sit at the same place they had sat for this first meal. I told the rest of our group about the police inspector's imminent arrival and warned them to be careful what they said to him until we knew that we could trust him. The *sous-préfet* advised the mayor of my position as liaison officer between him and the people formerly in my charge, which also applied to any personal matters regarding our stay that needed the mayor or the *sous-préfet*'s attention. This of course opened up the question as to what the Belgian police inspector's responsibilities would be.

On the afternoon of the first full day of our stay in Naucelle I proceeded to the hotel to meet the new addition to our community. I thought that he looked more German than Belgian, being tall and blond with blue eyes. He questioned me about my background and that of my parents. As soon as he found out that we had lived in Brussels he suggested that he could help us if we returned there after the war. He said that he would visit the barn the next day to introduce himself. I asked how he would communicate with the residents and he told me that, being Flemish, he could speak some German and didn't expect to encounter any language problems. I suggested that he join us for the midday meal in the barn, and he said that he would think about it. We spoke about the demographics of the group – the number of mothers with children, single women, the ages of the children, whose husband was in camp in Albi or other camps, people's nationalities and so on. I had the distinct feeling that he resented my position and my youth and neither of us made any discernible effort to be cooperative with each other. At the end of the meeting he advised me that he was now in charge and that I was no longer to communicate directly with the *sous-préfet* in Rodez, that from this point on, all requests should be routed through him. I replied that this was not my understanding and I would check with the *sous-préfet* and keep him advised. Not long after that, we clashed publicly.

During the second week of September I managed to get an assignment to go to Albi to address a number of boys who were members of the Scouts de France. I filled in my travel documents for Naucelle–Albi–Rodez–Naucelle and took the train directly from Naucelle to Albi, but routed myself to return via Rodez to pick up a new travel document from the *sous-préfet*. The travel document also covered my hotel stay in Albi since I intended to stay at least one night in the hope of visiting my father. There was no telling how difficult it would be to enter the internment camp where he was lodged or how I would manage it. I had observed in the past that my unusual uniform seemed to give me some official standing and I had taken advantage of it a few times. I counted on the possibility of bamboozling the guards in the Albi camp into letting me in.

The day before I left the police inspector announced after lunch that my mother and aunt were being assigned to dishwashing duty. I had previously informed him that my mother and aunt were never to be called for dishwashing duties as a concession to me for my services in the camp. He had grudgingly agreed but it was clear the fact that I had informed him that morning that I would be leaving the next day didn't sit well with him because I hadn't asked for his permission. This was his revenge. There is a little background to this: I was up against the envious Mrs. Berg who could never understand why her son, who was slightly older than me, didn't share in my responsibilities. This was a question that had first surfaced during our stay in

Rodez and continued to fester in Naucelle. The situation had gotten more complicated, however, because Mrs. Berg was now having an affair with the inspector. Nobody knew where her husband was and some of us questioned if she was really Jewish. She used her bed-sharing position as a tool to instigate trouble between me and the inspector, which only served to fan the flames. Once I knew about their intimate relationship, I expected problems, but I also knew I could neutralize it quickly since *sous-préfet* would definitely not approve of their intimacy.

We were just leaving the barn when the inspector made the announcement and I stopped dead in my tracks. My mother and aunt made a move to turn and walk toward the cleaning facilities when I stopped them. Taking them both by their elbows, I ushered them toward the exit door where I turned around and called back to the inspector that neither my mother nor my aunt would be doing any cleanup duties. Then the three of us walked out, leaving him standing powerless in front of everyone. Out of the corner of my eye I could see his face getting beet red and he began yelling something that I couldn't hear. I knew that there would be repercussions during my absence, that he would take his anger out on my relatives while I was away. In order to avoid this I asked my mother and aunt to forego the communal lunches for the two days that I would be gone and eat at the house. I was even more concerned because I knew that my aunt had rejected the inspector's advances.

I left for Albi the next morning. My meeting was scheduled for late morning and lasted about two hours. The French Boy Scouts were fighting for their existence since they were losing members to the Jeunesse de Pétain and the Church wasn't supporting them. The Church had never been an ardent supporter of the Boy Scout movement because it competed with the Church's own youth programs – many of the acolytes actually preferred the Scouts to Church activities. And the fact that many excursions took place on Sundays didn't sit well with the priests. By now I was well versed in what I was expected to say to encourage the kids to keep on pushing their friends into the Scout movement.

Due to the split in the French Scout movement, it was important to stress that Scouts are Scouts and that religion shouldn't play a part. I impressed on them that when they met a non-Catholic boy, rather than walking away from him, they should direct his attention toward the Boy Scouts. I also brought up the point that the Scouts had existed prior to and would exist after the Jeunesse de Pétain. This was about as far as I permitted myself to go toward in suggesting that the Jeunesse de Pétain might not remain in existence for much longer. At the end of the meeting one of the boys came up to me and asked me if I would consider swapping belts with him. Mine had the buckle of the Belgian Boy Scouts and his had a cross interwoven with the Scout emblem. Because one does not usually deny such a request between Scouts, I consented and we exchanged belts.

The group offered to escort me back to the railway station but I told them that I wanted to walk around Albi a bit – I didn't want them to know that I wanted to get to the camp. I had some idea where to go because my father had written us that the camp wasn't far from the centre of town and that he could see the town hall clock from there. He also told us that the camp was managed by the French military, with a colonel in charge. After walking a few blocks I found a taxi and after a short ride we arrived at a camp gate guarded by a soldier with rifle and bayonet. I got out of the taxi, walked right up to the soldier and told him that I wished to see the colonel. My uniform clearly impressed him and I sensed that I had a momentary advantage. When he asked me why I wanted to see the colonel, I told him that I was a member of the Swiss Red Cross. He waved me in and told me to follow the road leading to the headquarters.

There were barracks on both sides of the road and I noticed people milling about. Once I was out of view of the soldier, I walked over to one of the barracks and asked if anyone knew my father. One of the men did and directed me to his barracks. As I got closer I recognized my father sitting at a table playing cards with some other men. When he saw me, it took a few moments for it to sink in that it was really me walking toward him. He jumped up and we ran toward each other; we clasped each other in a long embrace, exchanging kisses.

My father thought that I had been shipped to Albi and was now an internee. I told him how I had managed to come and that I would be returning to Naucelle. After we established that visitors were permitted, we thought it would be better if I went to the office to get official approval for my visit. At the office I was given a pass that was good for two days. I returned to my father's barracks and he suggested that we go into town for coffee. I was astounded – I had never heard of anyone leaving an internment camp for a visit to town. I soon learned, however, that the exit from the camp was through a cut in the barbed-wire fence at the rear of the camp. Everybody used it – probably even with the knowledge of the military guards.[13] The camp held about 250 inmates who were all of nationalities other than French and some stateless people. The majority were Jews fleeing from various countries and from the occupied zone of France.

We walked to a coffee house close to the campground and by the way that the waiter greeted my father, I realized that he must be a regular. There were some other camp inmates there too. I wondered if the waiter or the owner of the coffee house knew where these people were housed and if it made any difference to them. The conversation centred on the news that the Italians had successfully invaded Egypt. Nobody had much use for the Italians because of the sneaky way they

---

13 Over the course or World War II, there were various levels of camps in Vichy France that were successively called *camps d'accueil* (reception camps), *camps d'internement* (internment camps), *camps de séjour* (sojourn camps), *camps de séjour surveillés* (guarded sojourn camps), *camps de prisonniers* (prison camps), and, finally, *camps de transit* (transit camps). The fact that Emanuel Mann was being housed in a French-run refugee or reception camp rather than a Nazi-run concentration camp may explain the lax security.

entered the war against France and insisted on signing an armistice with France before the fighting could stop.[14]

We had pastry with our coffee and discussed how we could arrange father's release. It was common knowledge that if an internee could prove financial independence and had an invitation for residency from the mayor where he wished to reside, then the colonel would sign release papers. Both requirements were within our grasp and we decided that I would set to work on this as soon as I returned to Naucelle. By the time that we got back to the camp, some of the men whose wives were with us in Naucelle had heard of my arrival and came to inquire about their families. I told them what I could about our circumstances and the way the camp was set up. Since I hadn't told anybody in Naucelle that I intended to visit the camp, I hadn't brought any greetings or letters from their wives and children. My father and I discussed how his fellow internees might react if my father were to be released while they had to remain. The regrettable fact was that no one else there could meet the financial requirement for the release order.

Dinner was served in the mess hall at about 7 P M. My father asked a man passing by if he could bring us dinner for two. I later learned my father paid this man to fetch his meals, wash his clothes and generally look after his welfare. I had intended to check into a hotel for the night but my father told me that I could sleep next to him in the barracks. There was only one roll call per day that took place in the morning and as long as I stayed in the barracks, no one would know that I had spent the night there. And since I already had a visitor's pass, no one could accuse me of entering the camp illegally.

---

14 When the French government fled from the German invasion on June 10, 1940, leaving Paris open, Italian leader Benito Mussolini decided that the conflict would soon be over and quickly declared war on Britain and France so that Italy could be on what he thought would be the winning side. He signed an armistice with France on June 22, 1940, and on September 13, 1940, the Italians crossed the Libyan border into Egypt, challenging British positions there.

The next morning I returned to the headquarters and asked to see the colonel. I showed him my visitor's card with my name and title in the Boy Scouts. He agreed to talk to me and verified the release requirements I would need to get my father out. I told him that it would take me about two weeks to assemble the necessary documents and asked if my father would be allowed to leave with me at that time, as long as everything was in order. He said yes and I prayed that the same man would still be there on my next visit. When I returned to my father's barracks, a number of the men whose wives were in Naucelle pressed letters into my hands to deliver to their families. I was a little wary of accepting them – I was afraid that if I was searched when I left the camp, I might be accused of smuggling the letters out. As a precaution I asked one of the husbands to gather all the letters and give them to me outside the camp.

The day after my return to Naucelle I distributed the letters at lunchtime and was swamped with questions. They found it difficult to believe that the security at the camp was so lax that people could just walk out through the back fence, but the women were glad to know their husbands were not being treated badly. I told the them about the conditions of release, but the only condition they could meet was the residency requirement. I mentioned the matter to the mayor at breakfast and he agreed to issue letters of acceptance for residency to anybody who wanted one. I found the mayor to be very cooperative and sympathetic and it was really only the Belgian inspector who caused us any trouble. The mayor didn't care if anybody went away for a few days, but the Belgian insisted that anybody leaving Naucelle for more than a few hours must register with him. He questioned people about where they were going and why, and whom they were going to see.

My mother and I thought about how best to arrange for the affidavit of financial independence, which had to be issued by a bank or a notary. There weren't any banks in Naucelle, but the notary was somebody I knew well and was sure that something could be worked out with him. During our first visit I asked what proof he required and convinced him that jewellery was as good as cash since it could always be sold. The wording of the affidavit was very important if it was to convince the colonel to sign my father's release documents. I told the notary that my mother had about two thousand dollars in cash and my father had about five hundred dollars. I also told him that he would receive one hundred dollars for preparing and signing the affidavit. He balked at including my father's five hundred dollars as ready cash and insisted that I had to produce the two thousand dollars my mother held. The next item was the appraisal of the jewellery. There was one store in Naucelle that sold watches and other trinkets, but the owner had been drafted and his wife was running the store while he was in the army. I went to see her and persuaded her to give me an appraisal of my mother's jewellery that would be considerably higher than real value. All this took a few days to arrange since a lot of coaxing was involved to get the various people to agree to what I needed. The notary finally signed an affidavit stating that he had seen two thousand dollars in cash and that my mother had access to another roughly 25,000 dollars if it were required. The latter was the outcome of my convincing the notary that diamonds were as good as cash. I told him about my father selling one of my mother's diamond rings in Toulouse and how easy it was to do.

The opportunity to return to Albi with the documents presented itself when the Boy Scouts in Toulouse decided to mount a propaganda campaign and I was part of the team assigned to assist them. Albi was on the way to Toulouse and I could easily make a stopover on my way back.

The fact that the war was not going well for the Allies presented a problem for us. Even before the defeat of the British and Free French Forces in Dakar on September 25, 1940, the Vichy government had begun instituting more repressive laws against Jews and we were worried about how these developments would affect us. So it became imperative that our family reunite and meet any adversities together.

Thus it was that I left for Toulouse. On my way to the railway station I met the police inspector. When he saw that I was carrying a small suitcase, he demanded to know where I was going. When I told him, he insisted that since I hadn't asked for his permission, I couldn't go. I told him that I didn't need his consent and would prove it to him. I went into the hotel and telephoned the *sous-préfet* and explained the encounter I had just had with the inspector. The *sous-préfet* instructed me to leave on the train as planned and he would notify the inspector that he had no jurisdiction over my comings and goings. As I passed the inspector I told him I was leaving and he would hear from the *sous-préfet*, who would once and for all clarify my position. He again maintained that I couldn't leave. I told him that I didn't care what he said and proceeded to the station. I knew that this was a tremendous blow to his ego and that he would try to get even. He was a spiteful person and, goaded on by Mrs. Berg, he tried to show that he was boss. When I ignored his instructions he felt that he was losing power over the refugees in Naucelle and that I was undermining his authority. Whenever I was there people in the camp came to me to talk about their problems – they really didn't trust him and were wary of telling him anything important.

When I arrived in Toulouse I went straight to the Boy Scout office. One of the boys there told me that I would be spending the night at his house. His father, a school teacher, was away in the army and they were anxiously awaiting his demobilization. Dinner was comprised of a variety of breads and a selection of well-known Toulouse hot and cold sausages. After dinner we went to a movie and smoked. He was a few years older than me but didn't know it.

My meeting the next morning was at a high school gymnasium where about fifty kids were assembled. The senior scoutmaster spoke first and I was about the third of five speakers. Even the school headmaster took part in the presentation and urged the boys to remain with the traditional Boy Scouts. During the whole presentation the dreaded Jeunesse de Pétain was not mentioned by name even once, yet everybody knew against whom the presentation was directed. In the afternoon I attended a meeting of my host's Boy Scout troop where the usual training took place.

After the meeting I went to the coffee house where the Jewish refugees had congregated when we were living in Toulouse. I went because I wanted to see if I encountered anybody I knew and to get information on how to leave France and where to go. One gentleman I recognized had been an acquaintance of my Uncle Willy. After identifying myself and answering his questions about my uncle's whereabouts, I asked him what he could tell me. He was an Austrian-born resident of France who had never become a citizen. He told me that the best way to leave was to obtain a visa for an end destination such as Cuba, Siam (as Thailand was then called) or the Dominican Republic, and then apply for transit visas to travel through Spain and Portugal. As far as he knew, Spain wouldn't allow people to stay while waiting for passage to the end destination, but Portugal would. Making suitable transportation arrangements could take a while because of the shortage of ships crossing the Atlantic. The man pointed out that one of the greatest difficulties would be getting an exit permit out of France because they were available only from the ministry of the interior in Vichy. Transit visa applications for Spain and Portugal had to be made at their respective consulates in Marseille. The Spanish consulate also frequently demanded proof that the applicant wasn't Jewish and each applicant had to be there to present his or her own passport. I was rather dejected after he had given me all these details because I recognized the enormity of the task ahead of me. I had no train connection to return to Naucelle that evening so I stayed another night in Toulouse.

I was not in the best of moods when I returned to my host's apartment to spend my last night before returning to Naucelle via Albi. It took a lot not to display my emotions and my concerns about how to leave France. It was certainly not a subject that I cared to discuss with my host or his mother, and yet I was anxious to open up to somebody about my problems. It was too late in the day to try and meet any of my co-religionists and I was leaving early next morning so that I could stop over in Albi. So my feelings and misgivings just had to stay bottled up.

I rose early the next morning, ate breakfast, thanked my host and his mother for their hospitality and made my way to the railway station. The train ride from Toulouse to Albi took about two hours and I expected to be in Albi by 10 AM, which would give me plenty of time to see the colonel. I hoped that he would sign my father's release after examining the documents so we could make the late train to Naucelle.

When I arrived at the camp gate, the soldier on duty at first refused permission for me to enter. Again, I used the ruse that I was from the Swiss Red Cross and wanted to speak to the colonel in charge. This impressed him enough to let me enter. I went straight to the office and was told that the colonel was not expected until late morning. When I said that I would come back later, nobody asked me where I was going to wait in the interim. When I walked out of the office I pretended to just amble along without any set destination and wandered toward my father's barracks. When I got there my father was playing cards with some of the other inmates. We left the barracks and sat outside and I showed my father the documents. A few people had already been released from the camp. Apparently the French weren't too anxious to keep Jewish foreigners in the camp and Vichy had not issued any policy instructions to the contrary.

After about an hour, I returned to the office and the lieutenant took me into the colonel's office. I had the impression that he was friendlier than he had been at my first encounter with him and I was hoping that this observation was correct. After the usual courteous exchange, we came to the subject of my father's release. I presented the various letters and affidavits. Based on this submission, the colonel agreed to release my father forthwith. It was difficult for me to contain my joy and I realized I had to be careful not to press the colonel to issue the order immediately. Instead I told him that I was committed to another speaking engagement in Rodez the following day and would appreciate it if he could let me escort my father to Naucelle. He called in his lieutenant and told him to prepare things right away while I waited for his signature on the order for my father's release. It was one of the longest half-hours I've ever experienced and I could imagine my father's anxiety at not knowing the outcome of my meeting. When the lieutenant handed me the release order I thanked him and immediately went back to my father.

When I got to the barracks, my father could see from the expression on my face that we had been successful and said, "Alright let's go, I'm packed." We left like fugitives, avoiding the other inmates with families in Naucelle. At the gate the soldier hardly paid attention to the presentation of the release order and I began to wonder if the inmates couldn't just walk out. Nobody would really know where to look for them. It must have been the fear of the unknown that prevented people from doing it. My father had spent almost three months in the camp and while he didn't suffer any hardships during that time, it was nevertheless a deprivation of his freedom. I wondered what would have happened had he left with me during my first visit.

After sitting in the railway station restaurant for three hours, we caught a train to Naucelle. The trip was uneventful except that I felt happier than the last time I had made this journey. During the train ride we discussed our plans for the future. My father thought that it was time for us to plan our departure from France. I told him what I had learned about visas. I could probably finagle a trip to Marseille to get information about the requirements for obtaining visas, but I would also need to go back to Vichy to visit the ministry of the interior for an exit permit. Arranging a return visit to Vichy would be more difficult unless they invited me. It occurred to me that I might be able to convince my Rodez Boy Scout contact that it would be a worthwhile trip considering that it was the seat of government where the Jeunesse de Pétain had originated.

I didn't convey any of these thoughts to my father as he was more concerned with the bigger picture – he feared for our lives if we remained in France. I assumed that his stay in the camp had made him realize how vulnerable we were with the Germans controlling most of France and dictating terms to the Vichy government. The Germans had been clear that their intention was the murder of all the Jews and now they could extend this to the occupied countries, particularly Poland with its large Jewish population. I'm sure that my father was remembering our narrow escape from deportation to Poland in 1938 and our flight from Brussels one day ahead of the German occupation. All our feelings of persecution came to the fore when we learned that the Vichy French had arrested Leon Blum, the prime minister of France in 1936, and charged him with contributing to France's defeat by Germany. Being Jewish and a socialist added to the attraction of making him a scapegoat. At a time when French women had no political rights, Blum appointed three women as junior cabinet ministers. He also introduced the shorter work week, for which he was maligned by the French ruling classes.[15] The Blum arrest echoed the injustice done to Captain Alfred Dreyfus who had been prosecuted for espionage in 1894.

~

It was dark by the time we arrived in Naucelle and I was glad. It occurred to me that we might encounter problems from the other refu-

---

15 Léon Blum was the first Jew and the first socialist to serve as prime minister of France. Vilified by the Catholic and antisemitic right, he was one of the French members of government who refused to grant full powers to Pétain. He was charged with treason during the war, but his trial became such an embarrassment to Pétain and to the Vichy regime that the Germans ordered it called off. The Nazis deported Blum to Buchenwald in 1943 and then to Dachau in 1945. He was liberated by the Allies in May 1945.

gees when they found out that my father had been able to leave the camp while their husbands were still there. When we arrived at the mayor's house, my mother was overjoyed to be reunited with her husband and have her source of moral support back. It had been difficult for her to assume the duties of head of the household and make decisions that affected all of us. While she looked to me for concurrence, in her mind I was still a little boy.

I asked the mayor for advice in regard to the possible discord we might encounter within the camp. He said that he would speak to his friend, the mayor of Viaduc du Viaur, about granting us residence rights. Viaduc du Viaur was only about fifteen kilometres from Naucelle and was serviced by a bus route. I had no doubt that the Belgian police inspector would use this event to undermine my authority with the other residents. And so three days after my father's arrival, we moved to Viaduc du Viaur where we were housed with a local woman whose husband and two adult sons had been conscripted at the beginning of the war. We now each had a separate bedroom and my mother and aunt had the full use of the kitchen – we pretty well had the run of the house.

The owner was delighted to have company and the additional money paid by the government for our stay contributed to her meagre income. Most of the people in this area were farmers and the absence of the men caused the women tremendous hardship as they struggled to work the farms. Her neighbour was an old farmer – old to me at least – whom I befriended; he helped out our landlady as well as tending to his own farm. On one occasion, after I had returned from a trip to Vichy where I had once again tried to overcome the difficulties associated with obtaining an exit permit, I was feeling very low. Recognizing that something was wrong, the farmer asked me if I could help him; I jumped at the opportunity to do something to change my mood.

I was determined to move heaven and earth to assure our early departure from France. I had to somehow make a trip to Marseille to find what was required for a visa. As it happened, when I checked with my Scout contact in Rodez, he asked if I would be interested in going to Marseille and Perpignan for speaking engagements. He said that the only problem was that I would have to leave within a few days – little did he know how anxious I was to make the trip. After we had worked out the details, I received my travel documents by bus delivery two days later, along with my itinerary.

My parents, Aunt Rena and I had talked extensively over the last few days about what I should do in Marseille to find out about getting visas. We decided that I should take our passports with me just in case visas were readily available. We managed to locate Kurt Berliner, my aunt's fiancé, in an internment camp in Perpignan with the help of the Red Cross, and my aunt wanted me to visit him to see if I could get him out so he could join us when we were ready to leave France.

In mid-September I took the bus to Naucelle and then boarded the train for Marseille. I was aware that I was on a serious mission and that our lives depended on it. The train ride to Marseille was very long and I had to change trains in Toulouse. I really stood out because of my uniform – people hadn't seen one like it before. All of the other passengers in the compartment wanted to know what it represented. It was difficult to get across to them that it was the uniform of a Belgian unit of the Boy Scouts and that I was on a promotional trip for the organization. I had been warned not to mention the campaign against the Jeunesse de Pétain lest I encounter problems from Vichy officials. While the campaign wasn't exactly clandestine, it was nevertheless aimed at convincing French youth not to participate in the government's recruitment efforts. The organization was also afraid that the Vichy government would abolish the scouting movement at the request of the Germans and, as in Germany, allow only one youth organization to legally exist in France.

I arrived in Marseille in the early evening and went to the house where I would be staying for two nights. I was scheduled to speak at two different schools that were now in session. Both engagements were in the middle of the day, leaving me plenty of time to visit the various consulates and submit visa applications. My host was a fifteen-year-old Scout named Pierre and he and his mother occupied a large apartment close to La Canebière, Marseille's famous avenue.[16] His father was a medical doctor who had been conscripted in April 1940 and was now a prisoner of war in Germany. Because he was a doctor, they thought that he would probably be one of the last people released from the German internment camp – they would want to keep him so that he could attend to the remaining inmates.

After dinner Pierre took me for a walk and I admired the width of La Canebière. Never had I seen such a wide avenue so crowded with people and with so many shops, coffee houses and restaurants. Even the many lights illuminating the entrance to the movie theatre was a novelty for me. Pierre accompanied me to the Boy Scouts' meeting hall so that I could find it on my own next day; he had to leave for school at 7.30 A M. That would leave me time to visit one or two of the consulates before to my noon meeting. When we got back to the apartment, I looked up the addresses for the Siamese, Spanish and Portuguese consulates. Pierre's mother had told me that they were close to each other and that she could take me there. We chatted about the German occupation but, being so far away from Vichy, people in Marseille didn't seem to be too concerned. I spent the next day giving speeches and visiting the consulates to fetch the application forms. In the evening Pierre suggested that we go for another walk so that he could show me where I would be speaking the following day. When we returned I sat in my room and filled out the application forms that I intended to deliver the next day.

~

16 La Canebière, modelled on the Champs Elysées, is a vibrant commercial thoroughfare filled with smart shops and restaurants; it was the undisputed hub of Marseilles.

As morning approached, I had a dream that somebody was playing with my genitals. When I finally woke up from this pleasant sensation, I saw Pierre's mother sitting on my bed in her nightgown, holding my penis in her hand. She put her finger to her lips and then lifted the blanket off me. I was lying on my back and she loosened the cord on my pyjama trousers and fully opened the fly so that I was completely exposed. At first I didn't know what to do, but she was a very attractive woman and I began to look forward to this experience. She obviously didn't want me to do anything and I believe that she was aware that this was a new experience for me.

The stroking slowed and she bent over and placed my penis in her mouth. It wasn't too long before the pleasant sensation of an ejaculation came over me. This was the first time that somebody else had brought me to this feeling and I enjoyed it so much more than when it was self-induced. Afterward, she began stroking me again and I could feel the beginnings of another erection. Now she spoke for the first time – while continuing to caress me, she asked me if I liked it. I told her that I enjoyed it very much and I moved my hand toward her breast. She shook her head and said that we should go to her bedroom. She took me by the hand and we walked to her room where there was a huge bed. She took off her nightgown and made me take off my pyjama top. We stretched out on the bed and she took my hand and guided me inside her. I followed her instructions and after a while, she started to moan and arch her back. I asked if I was hurting her and she whispered that I should continue doing what I was doing. After a few minutes a soft scream emanated from her.

At this juncture I had no idea what I had done to bring about this reaction and just lay back quietly, waiting to see what would happen next. After a while she raised her head and bent over to kiss me on the lips. I had kissed my mother and aunt on the lips and was therefore surprised when her tongue forced my mouth open and found my tongue. The circular movement of her tongue in my mouth aroused me. Her hand continued to stroke me while her tongue continued its circular activity. After a while she removed her tongue and lifted herself up and started to straddle me. Soon she started to moan again and suddenly she uttered a short shriek. This didn't stop her from riding me and all of a sudden I felt the pleasant sensation that I was going to ejaculate. Somehow she must have felt it too, since she increased her movements, shrieked and then went limp.

After this she got off me and lay very still beside me. Then she grasped my hand and placed it on one of her breasts and with her hand took two of my fingers and made me pinch her nipple in a circular movement. When I was pressing too hard she whispered to ease off and do it gently. While I was massaging her nipple she asked me to kiss her and I reached over and placed my lips on her mouth and immediately her tongue found its mark. This was an exhilarating experience and I didn't want it to end. My thoughts wandered as to how I could get her to sigh or shriek some more because somehow I sensed that this was related to her pleasure. She seemed so hungry for more and I wondered if this was the first sexual encounter she had had since her husband left. It was still early in the morning and there was no danger of Pierre returning from school until lunchtime. Any thought of visiting the consulates had completely vanished. I was revelling in this new feeling of sexual satisfaction – and like her, I desired more. We were quietly lying there, I suppose each with our individual thoughts. Needless to say, I was too shy to make the first move for a repeat performance.

After what seemed like an unendurably long time, she got out of bed and disappeared into the hallway bathroom. When she returned, she had a washcloth in her hand. She sat down on my side of the bed and started to wash me. Almost immediately I had another erection, which brought a sweet smile to her face and the question if I was ready for more. Her nakedness revealed a beautiful body; I had never seen a naked woman before. She must have noticed my staring at her body, but there was no shyness in her parading around the room. After a while she came back to bed and we began again. Afterward, I moved up to lie beside her again but instead she pulled me on top of her. At this point, it was clear that the time had come when we were both satisfied and any prolongation would destroy the sweetness of this event and make it vulgar.

She initiated what became my first sexual experience. It was educational and taught by a woman who had her own needs but who also understood the situation of a young man who had no knowledge of the act or its refinements. The way she instructed me was without pressure or signs of recognition that I was a total novice. I shall always be grateful for that. It had awakened my sexuality.

After I had my bath and dressed, I served myself breakfast and called to her when I was leaving. I wouldn't be coming back because I had a train to catch in the late afternoon. When I moved to kiss her goodbye, she held out her cheek and it was now a kiss on the cheek, different from the one we had exchanged in the bedroom. She was telling me in a nice way that what happened was over and should be forgotten. In all likelihood I would never see her again and nobody would be any the wiser as to what had happened in that bedroom earlier in the morning.

~

While I had to go to my first speech at noon, my thoughts were focused on my visits to the consulates and finding out what was required to obtain the exit visas. My address to the kids would last about forty-five minutes and the three consulates that I wanted to contact were Siam, Spain and Portugal. I knew that without an end destination the Spanish or Portuguese consulates wouldn't give me any consideration. In the early afternoon of September 14, I presented myself to the Siamese consulate with our passports and applications and spoke to the consul general. I had to convince him that we required a permanent residence visa, not the transit one he was prepared to issue. After promising him that I would participate in the fledgling Boy Scout movement in Siam he agreed to issue a permanent residence permit. Now I had to obtain the transit visas for Portugal and Spain. I was shocked to have confirmed what my acquaintance in Toulouse had told me – that all applicants had to make a personal appearance to obtain their visas. This meant that my parents and my aunt would indeed have to come to Marseille. And I remembered that the man had also told me that the Spanish consulate might require proof that we weren't Jewish in order to grant a transit visa.

I had promised Aunt Rena that I would visit Kurt Berliner at the camp in Perpignan. Apparently people who had been summoned to the police station in Brussels and who weren't as resourceful as my father were deported to that camp. Late that afternoon I took the train to Perpignan and checked into the hotel. The next morning I presented myself at the camp gates and used the same ruse that I had used to gain admittance to my father's camp in Albi. These camps were also run in a very lax fashion and, as in Albi, as long as one was present for the roll call, nobody cared what anyone did the rest of the time. The inmates could get out to the city and most of them did so. After asking a few people, I was directed to Kurt's barracks.

Kurt was wearing a beret on his almost-bald head and had lost some weight; otherwise he didn't seem to be suffering from his detention. After we exchanged news, I suggested that he give me his German passport with the J imprinted on it so that I could try to get visas for him as well. I was hoping that I could sneak it through when we were all in Marseille with some excuse for his absence. I was shocked when he asked, "How can I be here in camp without my passport?" I asked him when he thought he would need it in the camp, but his resolve to hold on to it was unshakable. I knew this would upset my aunt so I tried to convince him, to no avail. I left a couple of hours later and told him that we would let him know when we would be coming through Perpignan on our way to Portugal.

When I returned to Viaduc du Viaur and I told Aunt Rena about my encounter with Kurt, she was very upset that he wouldn't trust me with his passport. She undoubtedly realized that this would mean a long separation when she left for Portugal with us.

During my absence my parents had become acquainted with a couple from Antwerp who had fled about the same time we did and were quartered in one of the adjoining villages. They had a very pretty daughter and when I met her my thoughts strayed to the possibility of exploring my newly discovered sexuality. Even though she was few years older than me, she appeared to like me and we went for lengthy walks along the banks of the river Viaur. I didn't quite know how to broach the subject of intimacy. After a while we started holding hands and kissing. The third time we went for a walk we sat down by the riverbank to rest for a while and kissed. This led to us taking things even further. For the next few days we went for walks every day and shortly thereafter I left for Vichy. Our respective parents had obviously discussed the purpose of my trip since the day before I left she mentioned that her family also wanted to leave France.

Despite my amorous encounters, I was pretty depressed and decided that manual labour was the answer to my problem. I had helped our landlord in the fields in the past and asked him if he could use some help now. His sons were still in the army and his daughter was pregnant. He was a very down-to-earth person with a lot of common sense that he had acquired over the years. He had been mayor of Viaduc du Viaur but resigned for a while when, as he put it, the "dirty Germans" took over the country. He refused to subscribe to the idea there was an "unoccupied France" governed from Vichy – he maintained that the government was sitting in Berlin. He told me stories of World War I when he was a soldier and lived through France's final triumph with the signing of the armistice in Versailles. He had felt deeply ashamed for France when the country signed over its own defeat in the same railway car that had been used for the signing of the German defeat in 1918.[17] As we bundled hay, he saw how down I was and asked me what was wrong. I told him about the problems I was having getting visas and exit permits and how these matters affected me. He said that worrying wasn't going to change anything and that I should always keep in mind that "La vie est belle seulement il faut la comprendre a vivre." (Life is pleasant but one must understand how to live it). When I thought about my circumstances this way, my life wasn't so bad. After all, we were clear – for the time being – of the German menace and unless we were refused the opportunity to leave France, we had every reason to hold onto hope. An optimistic attitude would strengthen my resolve to get us out of the country and would assist me in my future endeavours. My spirits were lifted and I was immensely grateful to this farmer for his insight and ability to reach my soul and alleviate my burden.

The grapevine reported the latest news about what was happening to the Jews in Belgium as the Nazis moved to eliminate them with a number of decrees and manipulations. Fortunately, we had no immediate family there and while we knew that my Uncle Dadek had left Brussels, no one had heard a word from him.

The transformation of the Breendonk Fort into a concentration camp for "Jews and certain dangerous internees" began on September 20, 1940. A month later, on October 28, 1940, the first ordinances on the status of Jews were decreed, followed by a whole series of successive orders set forth by the Nazi occupiers. Jews were transformed into social pariahs: they had to be registered; they were barred from certain socioeconomic and professional sectors; and they had to have their identity cards stamped with the word "Jew." Jews could no

---

17 When the French government signed the armistice with Germany on June 22, 1940, Hitler insisted that the official ceremony take place on the railway track in the clearing in Compiègne forest, about eighty-five kilometres northeast of Paris, where Germany had been forced to sign the armistice with the Allies in 1918 after the German defeat in World War I.

longer appear in most public places.[18] They had to set up a so-called "Association of Jews in Belgium," or AJB, which, cynically, created a body of Jewish spokespeople to serve as forced intermediaries in the efficient enforcement of anti-Jewish measures.[19] Jews were regrouped in certain major cities and had to observe a curfew created especially for them. Their assets were blocked and their businesses confiscated. This news from Belgium fortified our resolve to leave France as quickly as possible should the Vichy authorities commence a similar operation.

About ten days after my return from Marseille, we decided that it was time to go back there to see about getting the Spanish and Portuguese visas. We arrived on the evening of September 30 and presented ourselves to the Portuguese consulate the next day. We gave them the Siamese visa in our passports and received a transit visa with a notation that our end destination was Bangkok.

Before going to the Spanish consulate we stopped for something to eat on Marseille's famous thoroughfare, La Canebière. My father couldn't believe his eyes when he saw his friend Kuba Ader and his wife sitting there having lunch. This chance meeting turned out to be crucial for us. At first the two friends exchanged stories about what had transpired since they last saw each other in Leipzig. When my father told him the purpose of our visit to Marseille, Mr. Ader con-

---

18 In a series of increasingly restrictive measures enacted between 1940 and 1942, life for Jews in Belgium became more and more circumscribed. Jews were required to register with the local authorities; were no longer allowed to visit public places such as swimming pools, parks, theatres and cinemas; and were forbidden to travel on the public transportation system. Jewish children were no longer permitted to attend public school. After May 1942 wearing the yellow Star of David became compulsory.

19 The Association of Jews in Belgium (AJB) was established by the Nazis to consolidate all the Jews in Belgium under one administrative umbrella. For more information, see the glossary.

firmed once again that the Spanish consulate frequently refused to grant transit visas to Jews even though Portuguese visas had already been granted. He emphatically stated that the only way we could be sure to get Spanish transit visas would be to somehow prove that we weren't Jewish – if the Spanish consular officials refused us, they would never let us make a second application. While he had no personal knowledge about to how we might overcome this potential obstacle, he said that some people knew Catholic priests who were willing to help by giving letters of testimony. We surmised that this would no doubt cost a considerable amount of money. Mr. Ader was going to check with some people he knew to see if he could find a contact for us. We agreed to meet again the next day.

At the restaurant we enjoyed a delicious dinner of garlic bread with tapenade, a paste of capers, olive oil, and anchovies, and the famous Marseille bouillabaisse, a fish soup with many different ingredients. The French rave about this dish, although I still hadn't been able to eat fish ever since my grandfather's near-choking experience. My parents and Aunt Rena loved this delicacy. But after the Aders had left, we returned to our discussion of how to proceed with obtaining a Spanish visa. We could hardly take the chance of applying and being refused.

Throughout the evening the question of what to do kept creeping into our conversation until finally my father in his wisdom said, "Let us sleep on it." We all went for a walk after dinner and admired the activities on La Canebière and the crowds. After all, we had been sequestered in small towns and villages for the last four months and seeing people walking on a boulevard was a major event. There was not much sign of either the war losses or of the German occupation and we could almost forget the adversities facing us. When we returned to the hotel we went to our respective rooms for the night. As I undressed, however, I noticed my new belt buckle with the cross entwined in the *fleur-de-lys* that was the logo of the Catholic Scouts of France. I wondered if it could help in getting a certificate stating that my family was Catholic. I devised a plan and had to test it, but I didn't want to say anything to my parents in case it failed and their hopes were dashed. The next morning I told them that I was going to see somebody I had met during my previous trip and would return shortly. I asked at the front desk where the bishop of Marseille's residence was and was told that it was next to the cathedral. I had noticed the cathedral on my last visit and headed straight over there.

The Cathédrale de la Nouvelle Major was an imposing structure off the rue de l'Éveche, about a fifteen-minute walk from our hotel. The weather was beginning to cool, but I was perspiring. Realizing what was at stake, it took all my willpower to mount the few steps and enter the office part of the building. My uniform had always served me well and this time I made sure that my belt was visible. The priest sitting there wanted to know what my business was and I stated in as firm a voice as I could muster that I would like to see the bishop. I had found out his name before I arrived and, after waiting about an hour, I was ushered in to see the Most Reverend Jean Delay, bishop of Marseille.

My first impression was that he was a kindly man with empathy for the current situation faced by a segment of the population. Without ever actually saying that my family and I were Catholics, I simply stated the fact that Catholics got preferential treatment for transit visas through Spain. Sitting behind his desk, he glanced at my belt, which was clearly visible as I stood before him. After I left, it occurred to me that he never extended his hand to me so that I could kiss his ring, a custom typical when a Catholic meets with a senior cleric. Without asking any other questions, he declared that he would be glad to give me a document confirming that my family and I were Catholics. He called in his priest secretary and directed him to prepare it for him to sign. He had apparently issued such letters before. The priest asked me for the names of the people involved and said that he would return shortly. The bishop asked me how long we had been in France and where we had come from. He wanted to know if we were being treated fairly by the authorities and if there was something he could do to help. I assured him that giving me the letter was all I wished to ask of him and thanked him for his help and concern. He then directed me to wait outside, saying that his secretary would bring me the letter. Again, he didn't extend his hand to me but gave me a wave and wished me Godspeed. I waited for about half an hour and then the priest came out and handed me the letter signed by the bishop. I floated out of the rectory. I don't quite remember how I returned to the hotel. I will never forget the compassion of this man who was surely aware that this letter would save our lives.

When I returned to the hotel, I told my parents what I had done and showed them the letter signed by the bishop. We were all elated since we believed this was the last stumbling block to obtaining a Spanish transit visa. It was the evening of the beginning of Rosh Hashanah, the Jewish New Year, but we had no way of attending synagogue. For my father, this was probably the first time in his life that he didn't attend services for the High Holidays. I joked with him that after all a Catholic wouldn't observe the Jewish New Year, but he didn't appreciate my warped sense of humour.

The next morning, armed with the letter from the bishop and the completed application forms, we went to the Spanish consulate and presented them to the clerk. He checked everything and asked for thirty francs. I believe that this was the best thirty francs we had ever spent. The documents were accepted and we would be getting our transit visas. When I returned to the consulate that afternoon to pick up the passports I still had a nagging feeling that something could go wrong at the last minute, but when the clerk handed me the passports these misgivings quickly vanished.

That afternoon my parents met with the Aders and told them what had happened and that we would be leaving France within a few weeks. We stayed in Marseille another day because my father didn't want to travel on Rosh Hashanah. While the Holy Day had been good to us in obtaining the Spanish visas, I assume that my father didn't want to tempt fate any further. In some ways he was a very superstitious person. He believed, for example, that touching the hump of a hunchback would bring good luck and always had such a person meet him before he went on a difficult business trip. He wouldn't deal with redheaded men because he thought that it was bad luck and would bring failure. I never told him that the man in Vichy who issued our exit permits had flaming red hair and that I did feel a bit uneasy when I first saw him. So much for influencing the behaviour of your children; had I believed this superstition I would have walked away when I saw him.

On our return trip to Viaduc du Viaur we discussed our plans for a departure from France as soon as possible. Both the Portuguese and Spanish visas were only valid for thirty days, so we would have to leave before the end of the month. This gave us about three weeks to obtain an exit permit, get packed and cross over the French border into Spain.

The day after we returned from Marseille, the Vichy government announced its new racial laws, consisting of twenty-eight laws and nineteen decrees. In some respects, they were harsher than the ones published in Germany in 1935. Under these laws Vichy could incarcerate foreign Jews living in France. It clearly demonstrated that some of the French population was willingly collaborating with the Germans. That government had already demonstrated its bad faith when it had arrested former prime minister Leon Blum. At the same time, the newly formed Commissariat general aux question juives – CEQJ, or the Commissariat for Jewish Affairs – was created and accorded great powers over any issues that concerned Jews. Judging from the text of the laws it was quite obvious that the Vichy government was not only cooperating with the Germans but was outdoing them. The covert antisemitism of the Dreyfus days was now becoming overt. It also seemed that Joseph Barthelemy, the minister in charge, was out to make a name for himself at the expense of both French and foreign Jews.

About 60,000 foreign Jews were living in Paris at the time, including my Uncle Willy, and their lives were now in jeopardy. The rumours emanating from Paris seemed to indicate that Parisian lawyers were neither cooperating with the German authorities nor recognizing the Pétain government or its laws. This resistance, however, would only help in trials – not with everyday life. The realization that we could be arrested any day weighed heavily on our minds and strengthened our resolve to get out of France as soon as we could.

When I arrived in Vichy in the late afternoon of October 10, 1940, I searched for a hotel but all were full. At one of the small hotels, late in the evening, the clerk offered to let me sleep in the lobby until about 3 A M, at which time I would be able to a room when one of the other guests left at that early hour. I gladly accepted this offer because I was getting very tired and had very little hope of finding anything better. Without removing my riding boots, I went to sleep on a couch only to wake up when I felt something stinging my legs and feet. Just then, the room clerk came over to tell me I could go to my room and it couldn't have happened at a better time. The biting continued and I was anxious to remove my boots to see what was causing it. I discovered that three fleas had got into my boots and were having a marvellous time at my expense.

After I took a bath and thoroughly cleaned the inside of my boots I went to sleep in the bed that had been occupied by the previous guest without even a change of sheets. I was fast asleep until the sound of banging on my door woke me up. Apparently the room clerk had entered my name in the guest registry and the police had come to check his register since he hadn't filed a police form. He had probably intended to pocket the money I paid him for the room and the police were suspicious about an unreported occupant. When I produced my official travel papers, they accepted the fact that I wasn't a fugitive and that this had probably only been an oversight on the part of the room clerk. It was now 6 A M and I had hardly had any sleep, but the anxiety about my fateful task kept me from going back to sleep.

I went to the ministry of the interior at 8 A M – I wanted to be one of the first people there. I had made up my mind that it would be best to speak directly to the head of the division rather than to the civil servant at the front desk. When I reached the proper department there were about ten people standing in line. Without hesitation, I headed straight to the person behind the counter and loudly demanded to speak to the head of the department right away. The clerk wanted to know what it was about and I told him that I would only disclose my business to the head of the department. The clerk was so taken aback by my attitude that he left his post and disappeared into one of the offices. He came out with another man and pointed at me. The man nodded his head and the clerk came back and escorted me into the office.

After the introductions I produced my official travel documents and said that I was there on official business with a very tight schedule and had no time to queue up to request an exit permit. I produced the completed questionnaires and the passports and the residence permits for Siam. I asked whether, given my time constraints, he would consider issuing the letter of instruction to me as my family and I were leaving within the next two weeks. The regular procedure was for the ministry to issue a letter of instruction to the *préfet* of the department responsible for the chosen border crossing. This letter was the *préfet*'s authority to issue an exit permit. In my case, I was asking that Perpignan be our exit point since we intended to cross the Spanish border and travel through Barcelona and on to Portugal. The exit permit was usually only good for a very short duration so people had to have all their travel documents and visas before requesting the issuance. The man I saw was most accommodating and asked me for the details required for the letter. He told me that if I returned in an hour, he would have the letter prepared, signed and ready for me to pick up. I thanked him profusely and assured him that I would be back at the appointed time. As I walked out of his office, I noticed the line now contained about twenty to thirty people and seemed to be advancing very slowly. I was relieved by my foresight in coming early.

The Boy Scout headquarters was not far from the ministry so I decided to visit people I had met on my previous trip. They wanted to know how long I was staying and if they could arrange for me to speak to a group of youngsters on short notice. I told them that I intended to return home shortly, but if they were able to arrange something I would be happy to oblige. I was glad to have some diversion since the hour was a long one. One never knew in present-day France what new laws or regulations would be issued on a daily, if not hourly, basis. The Germans were pulling the strings even in unoccupied France and a curtain could descend at any moment to prevent Jews from escaping the country. An hour later I was back at the office in the ministry and picked up my letter. My sigh of relief could have been heard all over Vichy. To reward myself, I decided to go to one of the better restaurants for lunch before returning to the Boy Scout office.

After I sat down in the restaurant, the waiter came over to take my order. Lo and behold, it was the same waiter I had gotten to know in Toulouse. Apparently, his wife worked for the government and had been transferred from Toulouse to Vichy. He remembered my uncle and asked if he was with us. I sadly informed him that he was still in Paris. As I was finishing my meal, two German army officers entered the restaurant. My waiter tried to take their order but neither spoke French. I noticed the waiter making a sign that they should wait a minute and then, to my horror, he came straight over to my table and asked me if I would interpret. The two officers were watching him and this put me in a very perilous position should I refuse. With severe palpitations I approached their table and told them that the waiter had asked me to assist them in their order. They asked me to sit down and although I tried to decline their offer, they insisted that I finish the rest of my meal at their table.

After ordering their meal, they were very inquisitive about my uniform and where I had learned to speak German. Before I answered, I asked them the reason for their visit and was told it was of a private nature, to partake of the spa. One was a colonel and the other a major, and they were stationed in Holland. Answering their questions could have landed me in trouble unless I could concoct something quickly that would satisfy their curiosity. When I realized that they were tourists, I told them that the uniform was created for a unit to work as liaison between the Boy Scouts and the Jeunesse de Pétain. I told them that we travelled through unoccupied France to assure cooperation between the two organizations. Then I informed them that I learned German in Leipzig where my father had business interests and I had spent two school semesters. Every now and again I would search for a German word and also I adopted a slight accent that they could believe to be French. I grew more at ease once I realized that they had no connection to France nor were they likely to cause me any problems.

I was glad that they didn't bring up the subject of the attack in Dakar by the British and Free French forces that had just started. The French were talking about it and when I visited my friends earlier in the day they expressed the hope that Dakar would fall to the Free French forces. As soon as I started to take my leave the Germans insisted on offering me a lift to wherever I was going. As we left the restaurant a chauffeur-driven Mercedes limousine pulled up at the curb and I found myself seated between the two officers telling their chauffeur where to drop me off. I scooted down in my seat since I didn't wish to be seen by anybody who could identify me. I asked the chauffeur in French to stop one block before the Boy Scout office because I had to buy cigarettes. I certainly didn't want my peers to see me arriving in a German army staff car. After we said our goodbyes, I got out of the car and breathed an inaudible but deep sigh of relief as it pulled away from the curb and disappeared. I made a mental note to avoid that restaurant should I ever come back to Vichy.

My friends had not been able to find a speaking engagement for me on such short notice, but were kind enough to drive me to the railway station, where I caught the first train for home. I was relieved not to have to speak to a group because I was mentally exhausted after the incident with the German officers. I had not been this close to Germans since I left Leipzig and was certainly not prepared for such encounters. The nagging feeling of being drawn back into the net of Nazism was frightening and psychologically devastating, heightening my sense of survival and desire for flight. Nothing mattered as much as finding a way out as fast as possible. I was also confronted by the inevitable fact that many paths leading to escape are so dependent on people and events over which I had have no control.

These thoughts ran through my head all the way home and I wondered if my parents were experiencing the same misgivings. We hadn't heard from my brother in months and had no idea where he was. There were rumours that people of German origin had been interned in England, but we thought that this wouldn't apply to Jewish school children. In any case, we consoled ourselves with the thought that my Uncle Arno would be looking out for Heini. Telephone or mail communication between England and unoccupied France was scant after the French and Germans had signed an armistice.

After my return from Vichy, my parents' newfound friends came over with their daughter. We took off and visited our usual spot where we could find privacy. When we returned, the family left and my father took me aside to tell me that her father had approached him to convince me to go to Vichy for an exit permit for them. He had offered my father two thousand dollars. My father had told him that it would depend on whether I was willing. To this, the man said to my father, "After all, we are a bit of *mishpoche*," using the Yiddish word for family. Hearing this I wondered how much his daughter had told her parents for him to make such a remark. I also thought that she may have acceded to my advances solely for the purpose of getting me to go to Vichy for them and that this was a planned sexual surrender. It was clear that I would have problems seeing the same man in Vichy to request an exit permit for strangers. While I could lie about their relationship to us, I didn't wish to do so. They could easily go to Vichy themselves and apply for the permit. I resented the "family relationship" remark as a way to manipulate me, but I couldn't tell my father this. Instead, I pointed out that the man in Vichy might get upset if I appeared again and that it could have undesirable repercussions. I said that we should devote our time to preparing to leave and I would not accept any more speaking engagements.

The Third Exodus

When we boarded the train for Perpignan on October 21, 1940, we intended to spend a few days there so that Aunt Rena could say goodbye to her fiancé, Kurt Berliner. We regretted that he wouldn't be coming with us and feared for his fate. This caused my aunt great anguish. As soon as we arrived in Perpignan we checked into the hotel and I went to the camp to get Kurt. The next morning I went to the prefecture to present the authorization letter for our exit permit and discovered that the permit had already been issued, but that it would only be valid for eight days. Since we could hardly afford to wait for the last day, we decided on October 24 as our departure date.

It had been five months since Aunt Rena and Kurt had seen each other and their reunion was tearful but joyous. We left them together, giving them the time and space they so badly needed. When they later joined us for lunch at the hotel, they told us that my aunt had decided not to go with us, but would be staying in Perpignan with Kurt. This came as quite a blow to my mother – she felt responsible for her youngest sister and was well aware of the possible consequences if Rena remained in France. My father took Kurt aside and tried to convince him to persuade my aunt to go with us since her future in Perpignan was perilous at best. He told Kurt that letting Rena stay behind with him was selfish – they wouldn't even have much chance of staying together because Kurt had to remain in the internment camp.

My father argued that he knew from his own stay in the camp in Albi that Kurt would require the camp commandant's consent to marry my aunt, that permission was hardly ever granted and that Kurt had limited means to support Rena. But all my parents' efforts failed to dissuade either one of them. Kurt and Rena's willingness to take this risk was all the more astonishing to us because Kurt had just informed us that the internment camp was being readied to accommodate Jews from Alsace-Lorraine and the Saarland as the Germans were deporting all Jews from those areas to Vichy France.[1] In the end my parents accepted the fact that Kurt and Rena had made up their minds and my father gave my aunt as much money as he could, promising to send more when we got to Lisbon.

Before we had left Viaduc du Viaur my mother had covered the oversized buttons of one of her dresses with cloth and hidden American dollars underneath the cloth covering. It was highly illegal to take much money out of the country or to even possess US currency, but American money was the only currency we could reliably use to get us across Spain into Portugal. We had acquired the *lokschen,* as US dollars were referred to in Jewish circles, in exchange for French francs on the black market. We were legally allowed to take only one thousand French francs per person out of the country and wanted to be prepared for whatever we might encounter on our trip to Portugal.

The next day Aunt Rena announced that she had changed her mind – she would go with us if she could spend at least another two

---

1   On October 22, 1940, the Jews of Baden, the Saarland and the Palatinate (all German regions bordering on France) and from those areas of France that the Nazis had annexed as a part of "Greater Germany" – Alsace and the Moselle region of Lorraine – were forcibly transported to internment camps in Vichy France as part of the "Wagner-Bürckel-Aktion." This deportation, named after the Nazi *Gauleiter* of these areas, went beyond Hitler's immediate plans and extended the concept of "cleansing" territory of Jews to the Reich itself.

or three more days with Kurt. My mother convinced my father to agree, but because of time limitations we thought it best to obtain an extension on the Portuguese visa. I travelled to Marseille the next day and presented myself at the Portuguese consulate to request an extension. It was granted, but only after much discussion. It turned out that Portugal had issued new regulations that required applicants for transit visas to already have valid residency visas for Canada or the United States prior to requesting Portuguese transit visas.[2] The vice consul didn't want to grant us the extension, but the consul argued on our behalf – saying that we didn't fall under the new guidelines because the original visas had been issued before the changes came into effect. After much discussion – which I couldn't understand except for the angry tone – the consul instructed his second-in-command to issue the extended visas and I returned to Perpignan. It was Simchat Torah, the day Jews celebrate the Torah, a day made all the more joyous knowing we could safely stay a little longer.

The next day Aunt Rena and Kurt announced that they had changed their plans once again – they were getting married and Rena would be staying in Perpignan. A rabbi in the camp had agreed to perform a Jewish wedding ceremony without the benefit of a civil one and, since there was no civil wedding, Kurt didn't need the consent of the camp commandant. The problem, however, was that the rabbi could not get out of camp for the next few days because of religious

---

2 The Portuguese government was concerned that Jewish refugees who fled to Lisbon from Nazi-occupied territories might try to stay in Portugal indefinitely. On October 28, 1938 – just before the Manns left France – the government passed a new regulation stipulating that Jews were forbidden to settle in Portugal permanently, although they were allowed entry as tourists for thirty days as long as they had a valid visa for another country (it was not limited to Canada or the US). It usually took considerably longer than thirty days for Jewish refugees to arrange passage to their final destination and although the Portuguese government did not actually expel them, the refugees constantly felt vulnerable and under pressure to move on.

commitments, so the wedding couldn't take place in the hotel until October 30. This meant that we wouldn't be able to leave for Cerbère, the border-crossing town at the Franco-Spanish border, until the following day, but our exit permit expired on the day of the wedding. On the morning of October 30, I had to visit the prefecture to requested an extension from them. Amazingly, the French officials agreed to grant us a five-day extension.

The wedding ceremony was very simple, without many of the customs that are traditional at Jewish weddings, although Kurt did step on and break a glass. The symbolism of this ritual has several interpretations. One is that the shattering of the glass simply sounds the beginning of the celebration and the guests usually respond with cries of "Mazel Tov!" meaning "Good luck!" Another interpretation is that the breaking of the glass brings to mind the destruction of the Temple in Jerusalem and the fact that, even at moments of personal joy, we must remember our collective sadness. Breaking the glass also reminds us of the fragility of personal relationships. There was certainly not very much merriment at my aunt's wedding. Her favourite brother, Uncle Dadek, whom she had always thought would give her away at a wedding, was absent – he had left Brussels two days ahead of us and was never heard from again. My mother, while happy for her sister, was upset that she had decided to stay in Perpignan, that she had chosen a very uncertain future with a man whose internment meant that he could barely look after her.

~

We arrived in Cerbère in the early evening of Thursday, October 31, and checked into a hotel. We had dinner in the hotel dining room, where we were the only guests. Cerbère is a small town of about three thousand inhabitants and its proximity to the Spanish border gave meaning to its existence as a border crossing. After dinner, when we went for a walk, my mother's anguish about her sister came to the surface and she suddenly declared that she couldn't go on. She suggested that my father and I continue on our journey and that she return to Perpignan. Fortunately, she regained her composure after a good night's sleep and the thought of staying behind was never mentioned again.

The next morning we took a taxi to the border and presented our passports to the officer in charge. He stamped them and then told me that we might have a problem with the Spanish authorities. The Spanish government had apparently announced the day before that they would only admit people who had US visas and that a number of people had been refused entry at this border station and had their transit visas cancelled. He also told us, however, that people had been allowed to enter Spain through the border-crossing at Fos, about fifty kilometres west of Perpignan.[3] From Les, on the Spanish side of the border, we could take a bus to Zaragoza. The French officer suggested that we cross on a Sunday, when fewer officers were on duty at the border. Having learned that one must listen to those with experience, my father was quick to accept his suggestions. He decided that we should go to Fos rather than take our chances in Cerbère, even though it meant another delay and our Spanish visas were due to expire within a few days. The customs officers cancelled our exit stamps without invalidating the permits and we left Cerbère.

In order to cross the border on Sunday, we had to remain in Perpignan for another two days – two more days that my mother got to spend with her sister. Early on Sunday morning, November 3, 1940, we boarded the bus for Fos, where we arrived at noon. There were a few other passengers on the bus but none of them seemed intent on

---

3 Spain – and other countries – kept changing regulations for border crossings on a daily or even hourly basis. In this atmosphere of confusion, whichever regulations were in place at any given time were enforced more or less stringently by the border officials, who could be more or less sympathetic to the plight of refugees fleeing the Nazis.

crossing the border. We took this as a good sign because it meant that there wasn't much border traffic at that location. The bus was an ancient Renault that didn't have any proper heating. We huddled in our coats and gloves to keep warm and were glad that the roads weren't icy. From the windows we could see the Pyrenees mountains that we would soon cross. The bus deposited us two blocks from the border and we walked to the small customs building, where the customs official greeted us with a cordial "Bonjour" and asked us about our end destination and what money we had with us. After we made a declaration that we each had one thousand French francs in cash, he stamped our passport and we were on our way.

The Spanish border was just next to the French customs building. As we crossed over to the Spanish side, our feelings of unease dissipated when the Spanish customs officer greeted us with a cordial "Buenos dias." He spoke fluent French and asked us where we were coming from. I told him that we had travelled from Marseille because saying that we had come from Perpignan might raise the question of why we hadn't crossed at Cerbère. Without giving him a chance to ask us anything else, I asked him if he could tell us the best way to get to Madrid. He immediately became a tourist guide and told us about the beauty of the region and that we should spent a few days there before going on to Madrid. The conversation sounded like music to our ears because it indicated that we wouldn't experience any trouble in Spain. He also asked us how much money we had with us and entered the information into our passports, stamped them and handed them back to us. He told us that a bus would be leaving for Zaragoza within an hour and the trip across the Pyrenees would take about four hours. The road we took crosses the mountains at various passes and on the incredibly beautiful drive we could see snow up toward the peak. The fact that we had safely made it into Spain lifted our spirits and we were able to enjoy the scenery.

When we arrived in Zaragoza in the early afternoon, we registered at a hotel recommended by the bus driver. We had intended to take the evening train but decided to spend at least a day in Zaragoza before continuing our journey. We had two rooms and my parents' room had see-through glass doors, so in order to get some privacy, they had to hang their overcoats on the doors to cover the top two-thirds of the glass. This was the first time in a long while that we would able to sleep without fear, so we went to bed early. The emotional burden of constantly facing death had weighed heavily on us – the whole time that we were in France we knew that we could be killed at any moment. The meeting between Hitler and Pétain on October 24, 1940, at Montoire-sur-le-Loire had reinforced the laws passed earlier that month that called for the persecution and eventual mass murder of Jews in France.[4] We hoped that we had escaped this horrible fate, though much still depended on an Allied victory. Mussolini's invasion of Greece at the end of October was bad news, but we heard in a BBC radio broadcast that the Germans had put off their attempt to invade Britain and that the Battle of Britain had come to an end. This kind of emotional rollercoaster had become part of our lives and we lived for the news of any German defeat.

After a pleasant but uneventful day in Zaragoza we boarded the evening train for Madrid on Monday, November 4. The trip to Madrid was about 250 kilometres and the train made a number of stops. At around 6 AM the police came through the cars requesting travel documents. Even though the civil war had been over for more than a year, Spain under the Franco regime was tightly controlled. My mother carried all our vital documents in the outside pocket of a big travel handbag secured by a zipper. She took out our passports and handed them to the policeman, who carefully checked the visas

---

4 Maréchal Pétain's meeting with Hitler in the small train station at Montoire-sur-le-Loire, while largely symbolic – complete with the photographic record of the two men shaking hands – nevertheless formalized the collaborationist nature of Pétain's administration. On October 3, 1940, Vichy had enacted its own anti-Jewish legislation, the *Statut des Juifs*, modelled on the Nazis' Nuremberg Laws.

and entry stamps and decided that we were legal travellers. In good Spanish fashion, he handed the passports back to my father, recognizing the man as the head of the household. My father placed the passports in his inside jacket pocket.

We arrived in Madrid at around 8 AM on Tuesday, November 5, intending to connect to the evening train for Lisbon. To do this we would have to change railway stations since the trains for Lisbon left from the Atocha Station, just south of the centre of Madrid, and we had arrived at Chamartin Station in the northern part of the city. We had three suitcases and an overnight travel bag and my father and I shared carrying the bags between us. When we left the building to take a taxi to a Wagons-Lit Cook office to exchange money, we were surrounded by a flock of beggars asking for money and had to fight our way through them in order to reach the taxi stand.[5] After we settled into the taxi and gave the driver instructions, my mother noticed that the zipper on her handbag was open. When she looked inside, she found that the leather pouch containing all our documents was missing.

We went into shock – we didn't remember at first that my father had put the passports in his jacket pocket. We had lost some other important documents – including our birth certificates and my parent's marriage license – but no money. Most of our cash was still hidden under the buttons on my mother's dress; she hadn't changed her dress in Zaragoza because she didn't want to risk putting the dress into a suitcase that might get lost. We went into the currency exchange shop to consider our next move, which was when my father realized that he had the passports in his pocket. What a relief! We considered re-

---

5 The travel agency Wagons-lit Cook was created when British agency Thomas Cook and Son was acquired in 1928 by Belgian hotel and railway travel company La Compagnie Internationale des Wagons-Lits et des Grands Express Européens – the firm that owned almost all the sleeping cars in Europe and ran the Orient Express from Paris to Istanbul.

porting the theft to the police but decided that it would serve no purpose since we were in transit. We also didn't want to do anything to draw attention to ourselves. It's never wise to take unnecessary risks involving the police in a totalitarian state. We considered ourselves lucky that my father had the passports in his pocket – the documents that had been stolen could be replaced. My father exchanged some French francs into Spanish pesetas and purchased our railway tickets to Lisbon.

We went to the station, checked our bags and went for lunch – our first encounter with Spanish eating customs. We discovered that restaurants in Madrid didn't open for lunch until after 2 P M, so we headed back in the direction of Wagon-Lit Cook and waited. At 2 P M we found a small restaurant that was open, but to our dismay nobody there spoke anything other than Spanish. We ordered some food from the waiter by pointing to a nearby table where people were eating a dish that looked appetizing. When it arrived at our table and we tasted it, however, we found it too pungent and stringy. We couldn't figure out what kind of meat it was so when the waiter came back I tried to ask. He kept saying that it was *conejo*, which meant nothing to me. A gentleman at another table observed our attempts to communicate and leaned over to tell me that we were eating rabbit. We asked the gentleman to please tell the waiter to charge us for the rabbit but that we would prefer to eat a beef dish. Soon after, the waiter brought us a delicious beef stew. Fortunately, the word coffee is universal and we ended our meal with something we could order ourselves.

After we had finished our lunch, we had still about five hours before we could board the train. The Palace Hotel was nearby so we decided to drop in there and sit in the lobby for a while. We thought that they would probably be serving tea and that there might be somebody who spoke French to help us order. We would be having dinner on the train since most people in Madrid didn't eat dinner before 9.30 P M. The Palace Hotel is one of Madrid's best hotels and we heard quite a bit of German spoken. This didn't surprise us because we were aware that Franco favoured the Germans and there was a distinct possibility that he might join them in the war. Hitler had supported Franco during the Spanish civil war and given his Fascist Falangist movement weapons, ammunition, planes and other war *matériel* from Germany.[6] The Germans were putting pressure on Spain to refuse transit to Jews, but so far Franco had not obliged. He did accede to the Germans' request that the Spanish intern military-age refugees passing through the country, but he didn't turn them over to the Nazis. None of this made us very comfortable as we travelled through Spain.

At around 8 PM that evening we headed back to the Atocha Station, retrieved our luggage and made our way to the platform. We could board the train early even though it wouldn't be leaving until 11 PM, so we found our compartment and made ourselves comfortable until the dining car opened 9 PM. There weren't very many passengers on the train and we were the first guests in the dining car. Ordering was easier because the steward spoke French. We spent a couple of hours in the dining car, which was full by the time we left. The distance between Madrid and Lisbon is about 525 kilometres and we expected to arrive in the Portuguese capital at around 9 AM. We had reserved rooms at Lisbon's Hotel Tivoli from Madrid.

We arrived at Valencia de Alcantara on the Spanish-Portuguese border at 5 AM, where the train stopped for visa inspection. The Spanish border-control officer opened our compartment door and asked us for our passports. My father handed him our documents and he verified them. Then he said that he would be back in about half an hour. A little later a customs officer came in and asked us to open one of our suitcases. He also wanted to know if we had any Spanish

---

6 In the civil war that followed General Francisco Franco's right-wing rebellion against the democratically elected government of the Second Spanish Republic in 1936, Hitler supplied Franco with tanks, troops, planes, large guns and other war *materièl*.

pesetas left because we would have to change them for Portuguese escudos. My father told me to ask the officer if he could also exchange US dollars into escudos and he said that he could. About forty-five minutes later our passports still hadn't been returned and we became alarmed. I got off the train to ask what was happening at the visa office. We knew that we would be stopped for about an hour so it was safe for me to disembark. I found the visa office and asked about our passports. The customs officer told me that all the passports had been returned about fifteen minutes before and didn't believe that we hadn't received ours. At that moment I just happened to look down on the floor and saw three passports lying under his desk. I pointed them out to him and he reached down to pick them up. Sure enough, they were our passports. They hadn't been stamped yet, which he promptly corrected and handed them back to me. It's hard to describe how I felt. To the officer this was possibly just an everyday occurrence – a simple oversight – while to us it meant life or death. Little did he understand how deeply this incident affected us. It struck a deep fear in our hearts and my parents were badly shaken. Once the train started moving, we were in Portugal within minutes and finally felt safe from Hitler.

~

When we arrived in Lisbon at around 8 AM on November 6, 1940, we left the train and took a taxi to the Hotel Tivoli. The taxi drove along a magnificent avenue that we later discovered was Avenida da Liberdad. The hotel was located on the Avenida and our rooms overlooked it. We were a bit tired having spent two nights in trains, nevertheless, we were too excited to sleep so we decided to freshen up and go for a walk. It was a beautiful sunny day. The Avenida, with its tree-lined medians, looked more impressive than the Canebière in Marseille. An array of flowers decorated the centre walks as the traffic flowed in between. The width of the Avenida was considerable and the buildings on either side had a great number of shops. As we walked along, we passed the railway station and Rossio Square.

We began to get hungry and decided to go into one of the coffee houses. Café Suica was one of those typical European cafés that served both light meals and some of the best pastries in the world. I'd had a love affair with whipped cream my whole life and hadn't been able to get any since we left Brussels. My father, knowing of my weakness, ordered a plate of twelve pastries, each one of them filled with cream and topped with whipped cream. My parents ate one each and I devoured the rest. My parents were happy to see me eat them, but feared the consequences of this overindulgence.

On our way past Rossio Square, my father had noticed Café Palladium, a coffee house that appeared to be filled with refugees – he had really developed an instinct for finding kindred spirits. On our way back to the hotel we stopped into the café but didn't see any familiar faces. By now the lack of sleep began to take its toll on us, so we returned to the hotel and took a nap. It was easy to sleep when our minds weren't clouded with fear. For the last six months we had lived with the dread of facing the Nazis at any moment. The Allies hadn't been doing particularly well during that period of the war, but rumours abounded and it was hard to discern truth from fiction. We had heard that all the refugees in Toulouse had been rounded up and sent to a camp.[7]

The next day we went to the post office and sent telegrams to my uncles in London and Paris, to my aunt in Perpignan, and to my grandfather in Leipzig. While we were in France we had received one letter from the manager of the old folks' home where my grandfather was living, telling us my grandfather had been operated on and that three of his toes on his right foot had been removed. Then we went

---

7 The Jews rounded up in Toulouse would still be in French internment camps – no deportations to Auschwitz or other death camps in the East took place before 1942.

to Café Palladium and my father saw some people he knew. He went over to talk to them and returned full of information. Apparently, all refugees were supposed to register at the Comissao Portuguesa de Assistencia aos Judeus Refugiados, the Portuguese Commission for Assistance to Jewish Refugees, run by the Portuguese Jewish community and subsidized by the American Jewish Joint Distribution Committee (JDC).⁸ The JDC, which had its head office in New York, assisted Jewish refugees with financial matters and with procuring visas for other countries. It was important that all Jewish refugees be registered – the amount of the JDC's subsidy to the Jewish Refugee Committee depended on the number of refugees registered.

My father also learned that the American embassy was issuing visas to people who could prove independent financial means. These entry permits were categorized as "capitalist visas" and were subject to a quota based on the country of birth. The Americans had managed to devise a means of restricting Jewish immigration without seeming to be antisemitic. The quota was related to population size and since the Germans had already occupied the European countries with the largest populations, there was little danger of those countries producing too many applicants to the US. We later heard the story of a Romanian Jew who applied for a visa and, after he had produced all the required documents, the US vice consul confirmed his eligibility. However, the vice consul told the applicant that the Romanian quota had already been filled – Romania had a very small quota – and that he should return to the consulate in three years to have his passport validated for entry into the United States. The man accepted this news without argument and as he left turned to the vice consul and asked, "In three years from today, Mr. Vice Consul, should I come in the morning or the afternoon?"

---

8 The American Jewish Joint Distribution Committee was established during World War I and charged with distributing funds raised by the American Jewish charities for the relief of Jews in Europe and Palestine. For more information, see the entry JDC in the glossary.

The next Monday we went to register at the offices of the Refugee Committee at Rua Rosa Araujo 12. My father had also been told that the people at the committee office had a list of addresses of apartments for rent. This was important because it was expensive to stay at the hotel. Unfortunately, as we soon found out, the committee wasn't very organized yet – they hadn't been operating very long. The registration process mainly focused on confirming that the applicant was Jewish. There was no thought given to my need for schooling. I did look older than my age, but the person taking down my personal information was well aware of my birth date. There were very few people working in the office and there were definite language problems. The Portuguese man interviewing us could only speak a little English – which we didn't know – and almost no French or German. He somehow managed to communicate because we had a common interest. During the interview a gentleman came in who spoke German with a Hungarian accent. We found out later that his name was Tibor Braun and that he was the committee treasurer. After looking at our file he offered us a weekly stipend to assist us financially and supplied us with three rental addresses. He told us that if none of the places was suitable, we could come back for others. We thanked him for his help and he said that we should come to the office once a week to pick up our regular stipend. Tibor Braun also informed us that we had to register with the police to obtain permission to stay in Portugal.

We went to see a furnished apartment at Largo de Sao Mamede 3, on the third floor of a four-storey house. The apartment had two bedrooms, a living room, kitchen and bathroom, and the furniture was adequate. The owner of the house, Professor Dr. Luis Betancourt, spoke fluent French because he had studied in Brussels. He ran a private school on the ground floor of the house that turned out to be very beneficial to me later on. We immediately rented the apartment on a monthly basis and agreed to move in the following day. The house faced a small square and was a ten-minute walk from the Avenida, located conveniently close to the areas we were to frequent most.

We returned to the Hotel Tivoli by walking down Rua do Salitre to the Avenida and we were to become very familiar with the street's steep ascent. We discovered later that we could take the funicular – the cable railway – from the Avenida to the Bairro Alto – the Upper District – a short walk from the apartment. We could also take the Elevator de Santa Justa – the Santa Justa Lift – from the Rua d'Ouro and while this required a longer walk, it was a suitable way to get home from downtown. These two methods of transportation required buying tickets, however, whereas walking uphill was free. From downtown we could also walk through the Chiado district with its many shops, restaurants and clubs where Fado singers performed. Traditional Portuguese Fado tends to be full of pathos and is a particularly melancholy kind of music. The Portuguese take this music very seriously and expect total silence when a performer sings it. As refugees, we hardly needed this type of music because our own circumstances created enough natural sadness. While the coffee houses were packed every day, there was little refugee traffic in the Fado clubs.

Lisbon was built on seven hills, each with a charm of its own, and our apartment was on a hill in a district known as Rato. It was in the general area of the Bairro Alto that contained some of the most elaborate old homes in Lisbon and a ten-minute walk to the Refugee Committee offices.

The very centre of Lisbon was destroyed by a terrible earthquake in 1755 and the city had to be almost completely rebuilt, which gave the Marques de Pombal – prime minister to King Joseph I – the opportunity to create wide avenues and streets. The Baixa, as that district was known, is the very heart of the city and Pombal named the streets in accordance with the dominant trade in the surrounding areas. Rua do Ouro – Gold Street, for the banking; Rua da Prata – Silver Street, for the silversmiths; Rua dos Sapeteiros – Shoemakers' Street, for those tradesmen; and Praça do Comércio – Commerce Square, for the traders selling their wares in the square. The fish market at Cais de Sodre was where panhandlers bought their goods and put them in a basket skilfully balanced on their heads. Lisbon's Alfama district is the oldest surviving area of the city. A muddle of very narrow streets and small squares create a glimpse of a forgotten age. On Tuesday and Saturday mornings there is the flea market on the outskirts of Alfama where one can buy almost anything. The Bairro Alto district, where we lived, is on the opposite hill from Alfama and is linked to Baixa by a well-known shopping area named Chiado.

That evening my father offered to treat us to dinner on the hotel's roof-top restaurant with a stunning panoramic view of the city. As we were having dinner, we saw Mr. Braun enter the restaurant. After he was seated my father went over to his table to thank him for his assistance in finding our apartment and invited him to joined us for dinner. Mr. Braun seemed to be a very lonely person and was pleased to have some company.

He told us the story of his arrival in Lisbon in September 1939. He left Budapest shortly after war was declared because he had tragically lost his wife and was looking for new roots. He was a professional accountant in Hungary and thought that he could practice his profession anywhere in Europe. He spoke some Spanish, but when he couldn't get a permit to live in Spain, he decided to come to Portugal. He had become the treasurer of the Jewish Refugee Committee when it was established about six months ago. The operating head of the Jewish Refugee Committee was Mimi Sequeira, a slightly obese Portuguese Jew who was more interested in promoting her engagement to the president, Dr. Esaguy, than attending to the business at hand. Nonetheless, she was a kind woman who had been catapulted into a job for which she wasn't really qualified. Consequently, Tibor Braun was very powerful in the committee.

He mentioned that before the war there had only been about 250 Jewish families in Lisbon and that the Jewish population had greatly increased with the influx of the refugees. The reason for such a small Jewish population was that the Jews had been expelled from Portugal in October 1497, as an extension of the Spanish Inquisition, and had never returned in any numbers. Like so many other cities in Europe, Lisbon has its Jewish street, Rua Judiaria. The Jews living in Portugal now can trace their lineage to those known as crypto-Jews, Jews who hid their religious observances at home but appeared as Christians in public. One can still find examples of Jewish practices by these *conversos*, converts to Christianity, or *marranos*, the derogatory antisemitic term for them. Of course, during the turbulent times when Hitler was persecuting Jews, there was hardly a "crypto" who would wish to own up to his Jewish faith.[9]

Tibor Braun appeared to enjoy his time with my parents and after a couple of hours chatting they decided to have dinner together again soon.

The next morning, we received a telegram from Uncle Arno in London, expressing his delight that we had escaped from France and telling us that my brother had been sent to Canada. He added that a letter of explanation would follow. We sent him a return telegram with our new address. We also sent telegrams to Aunt Rena in Perpignan and Uncle Willy in Paris. Fortunately there were no restrictions placed on sending telegrams from Portugal. However, the Portuguese post office could not guarantee delivery in France. When we returned to the hotel, we packed our three suitcases, checked out and took a taxi to our new apartment.

Professor Betancourt and his wife, Mimi, received us cordially and escorted us to the apartment. They invited us to join them for dinner that evening and we gladly accepted. We expected it to be a little awkward because of the language barrier, but it turned out the

---

9 The Portuguese Inquisition was formally established in 1536, although the targeting of Portuguese Jews began immediately following the expulsion of Jews from Spain in 1492. As the author describes, many of the Portuguese and Spanish Jews who participated in these forced conversions maintained their adherence to Judaism in secret. See also "conversos" in the glossary.

Betancourts spoke French and I acted as interpreter. The Portuguese eat dinner at about the same time as the Spanish, which meant that dinner was around 9 PM. The Betancourts lived on the first floor of the house and their apartment was beautifully furnished. My father had sent me out to buy a dozen pink roses and a bottle of French wine for Mrs. Betancourt. At dinner we met their eleven-year-old daughter, who also spoke French.

In the course of the evening Professor Betancourt told us that he had been dismissed from the University of Lisbon because of his political leanings. We learned from him about the dictatorship of António de Oliveira Salazar, the undisputed leader of Portugal. Mr. Salazar was not only the prime minister, but also the minister of foreign affairs and minister of war. Under his dictatorship, Portugal had become a one-party state and no opposition was tolerated. He came to power in 1932 and in 1933 declared the Estado Nova, or New State. Salazar was a sympathizer of Spain's General Franco and had supported him during that country's civil war. Professor Betancourt, on the other hand, had openly supported the legally elected government of Spain and when he declared this at the university, he was summarily dismissed. This precluded him from getting another teaching job and, as an alternative, he opened a private school on the ground floor of the building. The school had four other teachers, about twenty students ranging in age from fourteen to eighteen and five classrooms. The Betancourts had originally occupied the whole house as a residence, but when Professor Betancourt was dismissed from the university, they began renting out part of the house for additional income. An Argentinean couple who were both professional dancers occupied the fourth floor.

During our first week in Lisbon we explored the city and found some interesting sites to visit. One of them was the Hotel Aviz, Lisbon's most exclusive hotel. The hotel's most famous resident guest was Mr. Calouste Gulbenkian, also known as Mr. 5 Per Cent, an oil

and financial magnate who introduced the international oil compa-
nies to the Middle East and was paid for his services with 5 per cent
royalties. It was at the Hotel Aviz that we were first introduced to the
British tradition of five o'clock tea. After about a week of relaxing and
going for walks, exploring the seven hills and the culture, it was time
to think about the future.

We registered with the police and received a fifteen-day extension of our visitor's visa. The following week, my father presented
himself at the American embassy to apply for a capitalist visa to the
United States. Under the regulations, as long as the applicant could
prove ownership of sufficient funds, a sponsoring affidavit from an
American citizen was not required. My father had arranged for my
uncle in London to submit the necessary financial documentation,
but when my father met with one of the vice consuls who spoke
German, he was asked to show our birth certificates and passports,
and my parents' marriage license. My father produced the passports
and explained that our other documents had been stolen in Madrid.
Nonetheless, he said, the passports provided all the same information.
The vice consul asked if we had reported the theft to the Madrid police and was sceptical when my father told him that we hadn't. He was
clearly oblivious to how terrifying it would have been for people like
us to call on the police in a fascist country. The vice consul informed
my father that the regulations required presentation of all the documents before they could issue a visa. When my father explained that it
could take months for us to replace documents from Vienna, Leipzig,
and Poland, the vice consul merely assured him that once we had everything, there wouldn't be any obstacle in granting us our visa.

∼

Toward the end of November 1940, news began circulating among the
refugees that the Germans had created a ghetto in Warsaw that was
comprised of hundreds of thousands of Jews and completely sealed

off. Rooms were occupied by more people than there was space and a great many of the Jews had to sleep outdoors in the cold winter. The Germans obviously thought that this would be a good way of decimating Warsaw's Jewish population, almost a third of the city's total number of residents.

We had to present a valid passport to the Portuguese police for the visa extension for our stay in Lisbon, but the Polish consulate in Lisbon had run out of passports, so the consul put my mother and me onto my father's passport. The Polish consulate was acting under the authority of the Polish government-in-exile in London under President Władysław Raczkiewicz and Prime Minister Władysław Sikorski.

We spent New Year's Eve 1940 as guests of the Betancourts. Mimi Betancourt's mother and brother were there too, as well as the Argentinean couple from upstairs and some other friends of the Betancourts. A Portuguese specialty of pork and mussels deliciously prepared by Mimi's mother was served as the main course. It was during that dinner that the Argentinean woman made a pass at me that led to an affair that lasted several months. By the age of seventeen I had had two excellent teachers in sex – the first in Marseille and the second my Argentinean neighbour.

On January 31, 1941, my parents and I applied for visas to the United Kingdom. My uncle had made representations to the foreign office in London to get us admitted, but our application was denied in March 1941. The question of documentation did not come up because the British consulate accepted our passports as sufficient identification. Now that we had spent a little more than two months in Portugal, going to London was not that appealing because of the hardships the British people were suffering at the hands of the Germans. The threat of a German invasion was constant and we had no desire to go from the frying pan into the fire. My parents also weren't too upset about the visa rejection because my brother was now in Canada and wanting to join him had been their main reason for applying to go to England. We had received a letter from Uncle Arno telling us that about two thousand German-born refugees had been deported to Canada. He had heard from my brother who was now in an internment camp in New Brunswick. We thought that it sounded strange that the British had forced Jews into an internment camp in Canada until we learned that Winston Churchill was afraid that there might be spies among the German-born refugees and he wanted them at a safe distance from Britain.[10]

It had now been six months since I had been in school and Professor Betancourt offered to give me private lessons to further my education. My timetable varied because it depended on Professor Betancourt's free time. So one day he would teach me between 8 and 10 AM and on another day my lessons would be from 4 to 6 PM. These flexible hours left me with considerable free time. Professor Betancourt was an excellent teacher and could pack more knowledge into a single hour than I could acquire in a whole day elsewhere. The curriculum he suggested included mathematics, physics and, using French educational materials from his own library, subjects such as history and geography. While he didn't teach me history, he made sure that I read up on it and assigned me plenty of homework, which usually took two hours to complete. Sometimes, he would make me write essays on the books he had supplied. He would take the trouble to mark these essays and discuss the contents with me. In other words, I had the benefit of a university professor teaching me high-school curriculum.

The courses that Professor Betancourt laid out for me were comparable to the matriculation preparation taught in his school. While I

---

10 Fearing a German invasion and unsure of the loyalties of many who had emigrated to Britain from Germany and Austria, the British government summarily interned many German men in camps as enemy aliens in 1940. As the threat of a German invasion became more urgent, many were shipped overseas to Canada so that they might not be able to aid a possible German invasion.

was chronologically two years behind his study group, he determined that I could handle it. My only problem was being able to matriculate in Portuguese. By the summer of 1941, nonetheless, I had reached the matriculation level for all the subjects he had taught me. He tested me and I passed with flying colours, even though it wasn't officially recognized and he couldn't award me the diploma. In any case, by that time I was working for the Jewish Refugee Committee.

Whenever I was finished with my lessons and homework, I joined my parents at one of the two coffee houses – Café Palladium or Café Lisboa – frequented by the refugee crowd. Both were on the Avenida, a few blocks apart, and they each had an outdoor terrace. Even in the winter months Lisbon's daytime climate was never below 10 degrees Celsius and one only occasionally required a topcoat in the evening. We had met a couple from Leipzig named Ruth and Simon Prisel and become very friendly with them. Even though there was a fourteen-year age difference between us, Simon and I became friends. Simon introduced my father to a circle of poker players who held weekly games at the apartment of a German Jew, Mr. Neustadt, a permanent resident in Portugal and the owner of a thriving import business. Since Mr. Neustadt was a bachelor, Ruth frequently acted as his hostess during these games. My father was a pretty good poker player and won most of the time, which made him a desirable member as they all wanted to get even with him. Neustadt liked the Prisels very much and helped them financially. In 1941 Ruth became pregnant and gave birth to a baby girl. The little girl was born in the Jewish hospital next door to the "restaurant" run by the Refugee Committee that fed lunch to about five hundred people every day.

During one of our dinners with Mr. Braun, he asked my parents if they would let me work for the Refugee Committee. My main duties would be to meet the incoming train from Germany every Tuesday evening and make housing arrangements for the arrivals for their brief stay over in Lisbon before boarding a ship to the United States. I would also check out their credentials to make sure that they were really Jewish. My father agreed, as long as it didn't interfere with my schoolwork. After I told Mr. Braun my school schedule, he felt that there wouldn't be any conflicts. So in March 1941 I started working at the Refugee Committee. Since the office was a ten-minute walk from our apartment, I was able to keep up with both my new job and my schoolwork without spending a lot time in transit.

I was teamed up with Hans Leinung at the Refugee Committee. Hans was about ten years older than me and tried, at first, to play the part. His family had immigrated to Portugal in the mid-1930s and had full residency status, so Hans spoke Portuguese fluently, which was an asset in communicating with the people at the railway station.

Hans and I would go to the railway station off the Avenida every Tuesday night to meet the 10 P M train from Madrid. The train would arrive with one special railway car attached, a car that origi-nated in Germany and carried German Jewish refugees. These were people who had obtained American visas in Germany and had been sponsored by their American relatives. I was told that this process had started in December 1940 and was quite a surprise to the Jewish community in Lisbon. Even though German policy still officially en-couraged Jewish emigration, it was hard to believe the Nazis would be so benevolent as to allow Jews to leave Germany.[11]

Early in January 1941, the Refugee Committee had discovered the Nazis' real reason for promoting this program was to infiltrate the Jewish refugee community in Lisbon. When the second or third transport arrived, one of the families fell under suspicion after the other passengers reported that they had kept themselves secluded from everybody else. Their documents were checked and their pass-ports had the customary J imprint along with the addition of the middle names "Israel" and "Sara," but as soon as Refugee Committee officials questioned them about their background, it became obvi-

11 Until October 1941, German policy officially encouraged Jewish emigration, but in fact the Nazis made it increasingly difficult for German Jews to leave the country.

ous that their knowledge of Judaism was limited. Even though they claimed that they hadn't practiced their religion before Hitler came to power, it raised suspicions that they were Nazi spies.

In another case, when I was already working at the Refugee Committee, one of the arrivals was reported to have been seen entering the German embassy in Lisbon a number of times. It became my task to investigate this family of husband and wife and two children. I called the husband in and asked him for an explanation. At first he refused to answer my questions but when I mentioned some of the consequences of refusing, he opened up. This was indeed a bizarre story that was so strange it actually seemed plausible. He told me that his family was related to German Air Force Field Marshal Milch through their grandmother. We had heard rumours that General Milch was of Jewish ancestry and that when this was brought to Field Marshal Hermann Goering's attention, he said, "I decide who is Jewish."[12] When the family was leaving General Milch told them to go to the German embassy in Lisbon where one thousand dollars would be waiting for them. They believed that the money had been transferred from General Milch's Swiss account. He did produce the one thousand dollars and a copy of a receipt that he had signed at the German embassy.

We had to be very careful with the people who were suspected of being German fifth columnists since we didn't want to endanger the program of German Jews arriving in Lisbon. Each transport brought in between forty and fifty people and while the numbers were small, it did mean that lives were being saved. We realized that these trans-

---

12 Field Marshall Erhard Milch, who oversaw the development of the Luftwaffe (the German air force), was born to a Jewish father and a Christian mother, although evidence indicates that his mother was also of Jewish ancestry. When Milch's ethnicity came into question before World War II, Hermann Goering quashed the Gestapo investigation by producing an affidavit signed by Milch's mother stating that Anton Milch was not his real father.

ports could only continue as long as the Germans believed that they could get spies through to the US by posing as Jews and as long as we appeared ignorant.

We took certain precautions by requesting that all arrivals undergo a medical examination. The reason we gave them was that the American authorities had requested that this be done before the refugees boarded the ships. The real purpose, of course, was to verify that the men were circumcised. The Nazis, however, were equally aware that this may be checked, so we found that even the suspicious people had been circumcised. Consequently we had to design other verification tests. We devised a questionnaire that asked for the respondent's parents' Hebrew names, their Hebrew teacher's name and which schools they, or their children, had attended since 1933. They were also asked the year and place of their bar mitzvah and the name of the attending rabbi. This helped us to evaluate whether they actually were Jewish. We knew that we had a moral obligation to the Americans to ferret out the spies on this side of the Atlantic and let them know our findings. Whenever we notified the American officials in Lisbon of any dubious families, they would in turn notify the authorities in the United States and the people in question would be placed under surveillance. We regretted that we had to allow the suspicious individuals to board the ships. Interestingly, the American authorities gave greater credence to our information than the JDC did.

Among the male refugees were a number who had been inmates at Dachau, Sachsenhausen or Buchenwald – three concentration camps inside Germany that were governed by the SS. The former inmates who arrived in Lisbon told us of the cruelty and abuse inflicted on Jews in the camps. We learned, for the first time, about the wanton killing by the SS guards through the most cruel methods. Victims were forced to line up in kneeling positions in front of a ditch and then they were shot in the neck. Others were taken to open pits and machine-gunned on site. Inmates were intentionally underfed and many died of starvation. The disease rate was extremely high and there was scant medical treatment. We were told there were between fifty and a hundred deaths per day.

Some of the wives of camp inmates told us that SS men showed up at their homes and told them that they would arrange special treatment for their husbands in the camps in turn for sexual favours. Some women were forced to have sex with two to three SS men per night. Yet they never knew if their husbands benefited from this sacrifice because no correspondence was allowed. Some of the wives were deeply ashamed of what they had done and made us promise not to tell their husbands.

Wives who had managed to obtain American visas had to present themselves at the Gestapo headquarters to file an application for their husbands' release from camp. The Gestapo would insist that they sign over all their belongings to the German government and leave Germany with only ten Reichmarks each.[13] We thought that when this information was passed on to the JDC it would be publicized, but that never happened. It's a mystery why the JDC never informed the public – and the American government, in particular – to help save Jews. Thousands could have left Germany before October 1941, but Hitler was well aware that nobody wanted them and killing them wouldn't generate any reaction in the rest of the world.

On October 23, 1941, the German government prohibited any further emigration of Jews from Germany but, oddly enough, the

---

13 The Germans viewed the Jews' belongings and their financial capital as German property, and they had no intention of allowing refugees to take anything of material value with them. Most of those who fled had to relinquish their titles to homes and businesses, and were subject to increasingly heavy emigration taxes that reduced their assets. Furthermore, the German authorities restricted how much money could be transferred abroad from German banks, and allowed each passenger to take only ten Reichsmarks out of the country. Most of the German Jews who managed to emigrate were completely impoverished by the time they were able to leave.

transports to Lisbon continued until December 1941, when Germany declared war on the United States.[14] These arrivals were vital because they were able to tell us what was happening to Jews in Germany and elsewhere in Nazi-occupied Europe. We learned that the deportation of German Jews to the various concentration camps had started in October 1941 and that they were killing Jews all over German-occupied southern Russia.[15]

During those transport days, Hans Leinung and I had very active love lives. When the families came off the train we gathered them at the platform and took down their names and the number of people in each family. We then assigned them to their lodgings, which were mainly in small bed and breakfast places. Housing them in hotels was too expensive as the funds allotted to the program were limited. We also arranged for taxi drivers to stand by to help with the luggage and take people to their destinations. Sometimes, when a family arrived with a pretty daughter, we would tell them that we had only enough beds in a given bed and breakfast to accommodate the parents. We then offered to escort the young woman to other accommodations. Since each family usually stayed in Lisbon for two to three weeks before leaving for the United States, this gave us enough time to get to know the young women.

It was during this time that I discovered that it pays to have a double. I had met another boy about my age, Leo Schmalz, and in profile we looked very similar. One day Leo told me that a girl he had never met before had walked up to him, berated him for standing her

---

14 Four days after the Japanese bombing on Pearl Harbor in Hawaii on December 7, 1941, Germany declared war on the United States.

15 Tens of thousands of German Jews began to be deported to ghettos and camps the Lublin district in the *Generalgouvernement* at the end of 1939 and beginning of 1940. German troops moving into the occupied territories in Eastern Europe were followed by mobile killing units that murdered local Jewish populations in mass open-air shootings, sometimes with the assistance of local pro-Nazi collaborators.

up the night before and slapped him hard on the cheek. Leo figured that the slap must have been intended for me. He tried to tell her that he wasn't me but to no avail. From Leo's description I gathered that she was one of the girls I had met when she arrived from Germany.

It was well known that some of the Portuguese "crypto-Jews" still performed certain rituals related to Judaism. My curiosity about them was aroused when I noticed that a private home not too far from our apartment only had the living room curtains drawn on Friday nights. One Friday evening, when I passed the house, there was a crack open between the curtains. I peeked inside and saw two silver candelabras lit with candles. The reason I was so curious was that the girl who lived there was extremely attractive. She was a pupil at Professor Betancourt's school and I had been trying to date her. I was elated when she finally consented to go out for a cup of coffee, but when I went to pick her up for our date, her parents, uncle and aunt suddenly joined us. This was my first exposure to Portuguese dating culture. By now I had learned some Portuguese and we managed to converse a little. However, the conversation I could have with her parents, and uncle and aunt was more limited.

It very quickly became clear to me that any one-to-one contact was not customary in Portugal and I understood why I had seen so many young couples in the company of older people. I also realized that the many young men I had seen standing on the street craning their necks to talk to girls looking down from balconies was part of that custom. This "Romeo and Juliet" way of communicating without touching was not the way I intended to court a girl. Never again did I give in to my desire to take out local girls. But I did discover that that girl's ancestry was indeed Jewish and her family background was unmistakably *converso*. She was the first girl I was infatuated with and I regretted not being able to be alone with her.

After we had assigned housing and arranged transport for the new arrivals, we would usually head out to a restaurant for a late supper. We always had a few of our friends join us because the bill was covered by our expense account. About four or five of us had become friends and would meet in one of the coffee houses. There was a billiard room in the back of the Café Palladium where we played English billiards – a game using three balls in which the white ball had to touch the other two in order to score. It was difficult to attend the cinemas because most films were either in English with Portuguese subtitles or in Portuguese. Only toward the end of our stay in Lisbon did we speak the language well enough to follow the dialogue.

In general life was very pleasant in Lisbon and we encountered no life-threatening insecurity. There was no food shortage, no gasoline shortage, no blackouts – in other words, no signs of war. If we didn't have to get an extension for our visitor permit every two weeks, we could have easily lulled ourselves into believing that this was a holiday. The city was inundated with refugees and very few had somewhere else to go. In the coffee houses along the Avenida, one heard more German and French spoken than Portuguese. Around the middle of 1941, the Portuguese authorities informed the Jewish Refugee Committee that if the refugee population was not reduced they would have to introduce forced residence in the countryside. This actually came as a relief to us since we were afraid the authorities would prohibit the entry of refugees into Portugal entirely. The Refugee Committee organized a team charged with researching residence possibilities outside Lisbon. The JDC in New York was notified and a budget for such an eventuality was submitted. Jacob Sequeira, the Refugee Committee secretary's nephew, was dispatched to New York to plead our case.

It was obvious that while the JDC was prepared to assist financially, the organization wasn't making any effort to procure entry visas into the United States for Jews stranded in Portugal. At that particular time the only countries willing to accept Jewish refugees without obstacles were Costa Rica, the Dominican Republic, Cuba, Siam and

Shanghai. The Canadians would issue immigration visas only with proof of Protestant religion. The Australians' immigration affairs, like those of the Canadians, were handled by the British and that precluded entry. Many other countries had no diplomatic representation in Portugal, which further hindered visa application. The local Jewish community had a weak relationship to the government, so we couldn't expect any intervention from those quarters.

While those of us who were already here didn't fear expulsion from the country, we did have to put up with the game the Portuguese authorities were playing with us. Because we had to renew our visitor's permit every two weeks, we could always tell the progress of the war by their actions. For instance, in February 1941, we received an expulsion notice at the beginning of the month and a cancellation of the order the second week of February. The reason was that on February 7, 1941, the Italian army had surrendered to the British at Bedafomm in Libya, which gave the advantage to the British. At the end of March 1941, we received another expulsion notice when the Axis forces, under Field Marshal Rommel, launched the North African offensive. While these notices were issued, we knew that they would never be enforced. This was the political game the Salazar government played to maintain its relations with Germany in case the Nazis won the war. Of course we watched these events very closely and every time there was a German success our spirits sank a little lower. There were a lot of ups and downs for us throughout 1941.

Our greatest relief came when Germany invaded Russia on June 22, 1941. We now knew that Hitler would not continue with his plans to invade Britain, and that had a direct impact on our safety in Portugal. We had been anxious to find out what Hitler's plans would be after he broke off the Battle of Britain in October 1940. We instinctively knew that if Britain were occupied then Portugal would quickly enter into an agreement with Germany to preserve its national identity. This was probably the underlying strategy of Hungary and Romania when they joined the Axis powers in November 1940.[16] Had Portugal adopted the same attitude, we would have been rounded up and shipped back to the Germans. It only took two months after Romania joined the Nazis for there to be a massacre of local Jews.[17] There was no escape from Portugal. As long as we remained in Europe we were at the end of the line. But now the Germans were beginning to have setbacks; before the Russian invasion, the Germans had seemed to be unstoppable. In April 1941 the Axis forces invaded Yugoslavia and Greece, even occupying Crete. They also made moderate advances in North Africa and exercised ruthless control in the countries they occupied.

The Jewish Refugee Committee had established a canteen to feed people a hot lunch because many of the refugees stayed in rooms where they couldn't cook and for many of us, lunch was the biggest meal of the day. While food wasn't overly expensive – Portugal had a thriving agricultural industry – the lack of cooking facilities forced people to eat in restaurants. Breakfast and dinner didn't present much of a problem since they weren't hot meals and sandwiches could be easily prepared in the rooms.

Occasionally, when my mother didn't feel like cooking, we would go to the canteen, where the food was always wholesome and appetizing. The canteen had at one time been an extension of the Jewish hospital and was only about five minutes from our apartment. It operated daily and usually fed about five hundred people a day in a main din-

---

16 In November 1940 Hungary and Romania became signatories to the Tripartite Pact that the main Axis powers – Germany, Italy and Japan – had signed in Berlin on September 27, 1940.

17 On January 20, 1941 the ultra-nationalist, antisemitic and fascist Romanian Iron Guard staged an unsuccessful coup against Prime Minister Ion Antonescu that was combined with a pogrom against the Jews of Bucharest.

ing hall that could accommodate approximately two hundred people per sitting. Every lunch, served from noon to 2:30 PM, consisted of three courses and there were no restrictions on second helpings, assuring that no refugee would go hungry while living in Lisbon. With the money paid to the refugees by the Refugee Committee, people could easily get by. The Refugee Committee's employees came from the refugee population and the work provided additional income to about thirty people. Food supplies were delivered daily and leftovers were turned over to the hospital.

In March 1941 Mr. Braun asked my mother to take over the job of assistant manager because the manager had left the country and the assistant manager had been promoted. My mother accepted, not knowing that the new manager was scheduled to leave in May 1941. So my mother became the manager of the canteen and held this position until we left for Jamaica in February 1942. She introduced a take-out service, reasoning that the food wouldn't spoil and people could eat it in the evening without having to spend money for supper. She also came up with the idea of serving Portuguese dishes once a week to encourage the Portuguese Jewish community to attend. After a six-week trial period, however, she had to abandon this plan because the members of the Portuguese Jewish community wouldn't attend and the refugees didn't like the food. Attendance on those days dropped by one-third. The hospital was happy, though, because they received more leftovers than usual.

About a month after my mother started her new job she became friendly with an elderly lady and her daughter, Trudy Mueller, who visited the canteen intermittently. They met for coffee in the late afternoon and my mother began to think that Trudy, in her late thirties, would be a good match for Mr. Braun. But there was a catch – it turned out that Trudy was the occasional girlfriend of a married Portuguese count.

Maintaining a mistress was an accepted way of life for Portuguese men from the upper classes. Their wives were considered the ones they had children with and their mistresses the ones they played with. It was a sort of compromise in a Catholic country where divorces were difficult to obtain. In other countries, couples may have separated but this wasn't an option for Portuguese men and certainly out of the question for the women. So the upper classes had their mistresses and the middle and lower classes their brothels. Lisbon had a great number of these establishments in all price ranges. Some were exquisitely furnished with bedrooms decorated in baroque style. There were also brothels where the men would sit in one big room while the girls obligingly performed their services by moving from chair to chair. It was therefore not surprising that the rates of syphilis and gonorrhea were extremely high. There were many men and women with visible signs of advanced syphilis, although they were frequently confused with sufferers of leprosy.

My mother persisted in her matchmaking plans and arranged a dinner for Trudy, her mother, Mr. Braun and my parents. Mr. Braun was smitten by the young lady right away and pursued a courtship with her, but Trudy wasn't exactly enamoured of this dishevelled middle-aged Hungarian. One afternoon we met the Portuguese count, who turned out to be a well-dressed, wealthy, cultured and well-educated man, so I could certainly understand why he impressed Trudy. Her mother, however, was looking for security for her daughter, something she could never expect from this married man. Trudy was a very obedient daughter, taught by her old-style European upbringing to respect her elders. Consequently, at her mother's insistence, Trudy married Tibor Braun four months later and over the next few months began to reshape her new husband. He became a well-groomed gentleman with manicured fingernails and polished shoes. He showered Trudy with gifts and was deeply in love. We could see a change in Trudy's attitude and believe that she fell in love with him after their marriage. Her mother lived with them and was in full control of that household.

～

A thirty-minute taxi drive from Lisbon, the playground of the rich and famous, was a place called Estoril. It was home to a number of deposed kings and royal aspirants, including Zog of Albania, King Carol II of Romania with his mistress Magda Lupescu, the Duc de Paris, and the usual retinue of dukes, counts and barons. The ones who didn't stay at the posh Palace Hotel occupied luxurious residences. King Carol was a frequent visitor to the casino, where he sat in the secluded Chemin de Fer salon with Magda Lupescu behind him. This was the man whom his father, King Ferdinand, had described as "like a Swiss cheese, excellent for what it is, but so full of holes."

To get to Estoril from Lisbon, three or four of us would get together and share the expense of a taxi. The arrangement was that the taxi driver would wait for us until we were ready to return to Lisbon, a cheaper and more convenient arrangement than taking the train from the Lisbon railway station. The casino had four restaurants, three bars, a movie theatre and all the gaming facilities such as roulette, baccarat – including chemin de fer and banque – and blackjack. One of our friends, Egon Reiss, was an accomplished pianist who had been hired by the casino to play in the piano bar. This was very opportune since his food and drinks were free and, as we had taken him for dinner with us many times, he ensured that all our meals and drinks at the casino were covered, as well as admission to the cinema. On some days when we went to the casino, we were handed a flyer at the entrance that said, "When playing roulette do not bet on a number more than three times." Egon told us that the reason for these instructions was that various spies were using the repeated-number-play system for identification – they were instructed to repeatedly play a certain number and place the same number of chips on that number; their accomplice was told which number to look out for. It was not unusual to see somebody with a swastika in his lapel who spoke perfect English. Lisbon was, after all, the hub for international spies. We would often go to Estoril on Saturday afternoons and not return before Sunday night. The facilities were open twenty-four hours a day.

There was also a fabulous beach in Estoril. Because Portugal was a very Catholic country, men's bathing suits had to have skirts and women's bathing suits required leggings to the knees.

~

During the war Britain used Portugal as a trade centre to acquire food, chemicals and other supplies, and as a jumping-off point to the United States. The Pan American World Airways Yankee Clipper made regular transatlantic flights from New York to Lisbon, a flight that took nineteen hours in a plane that carried seventy-seven passengers.[18] Many of us watched it with a heartfelt longing when we saw it fly off toward New York. The dream and fervent wish of almost every refugee in Lisbon was to emigrate to the United States, the country where, we were told, the streets were paved with gold.

As the Germans grew more and more successful in their military advances, we were conscious of our precarious position in Europe. The conquest of so many European countries, including Greece, Yugoslavia and now the invasion of the Soviet Union in June 1941, didn't suggest to us that Hitler could be stopped soon. In September 1941 we learned from arriving German Jews that all Jews in Germany were required to wear a yellow Star of David on their outer garments. The noose was tightening around Europe's Jews and the general belief was that if we could only get to the United States, we would be safe from Hitler's "Final Solution," only then would we be beyond his reach.

This belief, however, came to a screeching halt when the Japanese attacked Pearl Harbor on December 7, 1941, and the Germans and Italians declared war against the United States on December 11, 1941.

---

18 The Boeing 314a Yankee Clipper was a "flying boat" that flew a regular route, even during the war, from Lisbon to New York with a stop in the Azores islands.

Our immediate concern centred on how hard it would be to arrange transportation across the Atlantic now that American ships were no longer protected by neutrality. Portuguese ships would only be able to safely transport people across the ocean if the Germans respected their neutrality. While there was jubilation that the powerful United States was now actively involved in the war, there was an underlying fear that should Hitler succeed, there would be nowhere left to flee.

Around November 1941 the Portuguese government heightened its pressure on the Refugee Committee to find an immediate solution to the ever-increasing number of refugees entering Portugal. It threatened to not only institute an enforced residence area – such as a ghetto or a camp – refuse new arrivals and refuse to renew residence permits, but to permit German screening of the police registration lists. This was an implicit threat that they would turn Jews over to the Germans that we took quite seriously. Our intelligence information confirmed that the German embassy had made representations to the Portuguese government to stop or at least slow the influx of Jews into Portugal.

Jacob Sequeira had been in New York since the middle of the year but had not had much success in obtaining additional funding for the refugees. We began to realize that he had no intention of returning to Portugal, which proved to be correct when he obtained immigration status and began working in the US. It also raised doubts as to how effective he would be in speaking on behalf of the Refugee Committee. Various approaches were made to the representatives of foreign countries to accept the refugees. Cuba and the Dominican Republic were two countries that had agreed to issue visas. In December 1941 the Cuban consulate in Bilbao, Spain was instructed by its ministry to issue tourist visas to all applicants and my father decided that it was better to go there than to stay in Europe. On December 26, 1941, for the fee of about thirty pesetas, we obtained Cuban tourist visas.

About 450 passports had been sent to Bilbao through the auspices of the Jewish Refugee Committee and we informed the Portuguese government that this would reduce the registered refugee population by about 12 per cent. The real number of refugees was actually much higher, as about 1,500 to 2,000 people had crossed the border without registering. The number of visas granted created logistical and financial problems for the Refugee Committee as we looked for ocean vessels for those eligible to go to Cuba. We sent another message to New York asking Jacob Sequeira to make new representations for transportation funds. Most of the recipients of the Cuban visas didn't have the means to pay the fare, but there was the additional problem of financial aid once they arrived in Cuba. While the Cuban government had made no stipulation as to fiscal responsibilities of the "tourists," we were afraid that they might make certain demands that could negate the validity of the visas. President Fulgencio Batista could not be trusted. We all remembered only too well the *St. Louis* affair.

The *St. Louis* was a German ship that had set sail from Hamburg on May 13, 1939, carrying Jewish refugees. All 938 passengers had landing certificates for Havana, but only twenty-two were allowed to land in Cuba. After the United States, Canada and South American countries barred their entry, the remainder were forced to return to Europe in June. On the return trip, some of the refugees were accepted by other countries such as Great Britain, Belgium, France and the Netherlands. Most, however, perished in countries occupied by the Nazis.

∼

We spent New Year's Eve 1941 with Tibor Braun, his wife, Trudy, her mother and her former boyfriend, the Portuguese count. The count and I had become friends and we frequently met for coffee. One day he even took me to his home, a large apartment in a beautiful building that had only two apartments per floor. We went into his study and it was not long before a woman appeared with a washbasin. She sat down in front of him, took off his shoes and socks and proceeded to wash and dry his feet. She then produced a change of socks and shoes and put them on. When this ritual had been completed, she got up and, with a nod to me, left the room. A little boy and girl came in and kissed him and he introduced them as his two children. When I asked him about their mother, he told me she had just left. I realized that the woman who had washed his feet was not a servant but his wife. When I told this story to my parents, they couldn't believe it, but when I asked Dr. Betancourt, he informed me that this wasn't uncommon among the Portuguese upper classes.

Just before Christmas the count took me to a diplomatic tea-dance organized by the ministry of foreign affairs. All the various diplomats stationed in Portugal were there and the count drew my attention to the dancing partners, some of whom came from countries that were at war. This was my first introduction to the world of diplomacy and its peculiarities. Your country may be at war with that of your dancing partner, but when on neutral territory, enmities are overlooked. Lisbon was always full of surprises.

All kinds of people passed through Lisbon, some of them pretending to be what they were not, and others hiding their dubious connections. One of the funniest was an Abyssinian man who claimed to be a prince related to the emperor. We all kept an eye out for his appearance because whenever he spotted people he knew he would unceremoniously plunk himself down at their table, proceed to order, consume whatever he had ordered and then get up, wave goodbye and disappear. Sometimes he would pretend that he was going to the men's room and never come back. Nobody ever saw him pay for anything. He wouldn't have been welcome in Portuguese homes where, if you arrived while they were eating, you would be asked, "Are you served?" The expected reply would be yes, since saying no would be considered rude because it meant that they would have to feed you.

Another one of the refugees was a Mr. Rosenblatt whose family used to own a large construction business in Germany. Throughout his adult life, Mr. Rosenblatt loved to visit various casinos in Europe and gamble. When he arrived in Lisbon with only a few thousand dollars, he nonetheless continued this habit, oblivious to the fact that he no longer had an income. I frequently observed him at the roulette table in the casino at Estoril. After a few months I learned that he had obtained a US immigration visa. During a lull in his gambling we had a coffee and I asked him what he planned to do in there. He told me that he had heard of a bar in the Waldorf-Astoria Hotel in New York that was frequented by wealthy Americans. He intended to sit in the bar every day until he met somebody who would give him the money to start a construction business. I ran into him by accident in a restaurant in New York about fourteen years later and he confirmed that this was exactly what had happened. He was now a successful builder of family homes in New York State.

A number of people in Lisbon were trying to do some business through trading. One had to be careful, though, because the Germans were actively seeking raw materials – in particular, they were looking for tungsten required for their war machinery. Many Swiss were in Portugal arranging deals for the Germans while pretending that the goods were for Switzerland – they offered food items to the British, hoping to acquire merchandise needed by the Germans. The Portuguese also engaged in this trade and offered mostly fish products such as canned sardines to the British.

One day I was at Café Nicola with one of my friends and we were both smoking when suddenly I noticed my father standing in the entrance looking straight at me while I was holding a cigarette in my hand. He walked over to me, slapped my face and said, "I shall talk to you about this at home." My father had told me many times that even though he was a smoker, I was not to smoke until I was eighteen. Of course, I'd been smoking since we were in France, where I took up the habit to appear older. I always made sure that I hid my cigarettes when I came home and even though my father frequently ran out, I didn't dare offer him mine. Later that evening, he took me aside and told me that he had been told that smoking at an early age could stunt my physical growth and development and that that was the reason he forbade me to smoke. Fortunately, he didn't make me promise that I would abide by his instructions. The slap drove home the seriousness of his point – my father had only slapped me once before. I'd been pillow fighting with my brother one Sunday morning when my father came into our bedroom to ask us to be less noisy so that he and my mother could sleep a bit longer. Shortly after he left my brother and I resumed our pillow fight. My father returned, very much annoyed and, since I was closest to the door, he reached over, slapped me and said to both of us, "Do not make me come back again."

During the latter half of 1941 some of us knew enough Portuguese to go to the movie houses and theatres. I remember one movie that left a lasting impression on me was *Blood and Sand* starring Tyrone Power, Linda Darnell and Rita Hayworth. It was playing at the Tivoli theatre on the Avenida and an outdoor sign showing Tyrone Power covered almost the whole front of the building. The film was based on a novel by Spanish writer Vicente Blanco Ibanez and when I mentioned it to Professor Betancourt, he took the time to discuss the writer's background. Ibanez lived from 1867 to 1928 and was described as an early socialist. Movie houses in Lisbon had very interesting seating arrangements. They all had boxes with curtains you could draw so that you were entirely secluded from the other viewers. Most of the boxes had a couch and anywhere from two to four chairs. One would frequently see the curtains drawn during the performance – presumably because another performance was taking place inside the box.

My mother's chief cook was a young lady named Gisela who was about ten years older than me. Gisela took a great liking to me and told my mother that she couldn't understand why I didn't reciprocate. This put my mother in an awkward position because she didn't wish to offend Gisela by telling her that her son just wasn't interested. Whenever I was at the canteen, Gisela would find some way to manoeuvre me into a secluded spot. Unfortunately, I found Gisela totally unattractive and it was a pity I felt this way when she was so desperate to get my attention. I believe finally I managed to convince Gisela that there was no future for us and after that she no longer got me into any compromising positions. I really felt bad about it; she was a very nice and kind person.

~

In July 1941 we heard that there had been a mass killing of Jews near Vilna, Lithuania instigated by the Germans.[19] Not that the Lithuanians or Russians or Ukrainians needed much prodding to persecute Jews. They had been doing this voluntarily long before they had the assistance of the Germans. In October 1941 we learned of the deportation of German Jews to Auschwitz.[20] This hit close to home because my grandfather was still alive and in the old folks' home in Leipzig. The last news we had had was that his toes had been amputated but otherwise he was all right. He was now eighty-nine years old and it was a great relief when we were notified in November 1941 that he had died in his sleep at the home. At least he was spared the terrible experience of being transported to one of those death camps.

Dr. Esaguy had made representations to the British embassy in November 1941 to assist in the movement of refugees. On January 8, 1942, he received word by telegram that the British foreign office

---

19 In July 1941 *Einsatzgruppen* (mobile killing squads) aided by Lithuanian auxiliaries killed five thousand Jewish men at Ponary forest, eight miles outside Vilna. At the end of the month, the Nazis killed another 3,500 Jews at Ponary. A month after two ghettos were established in September 1941, the entire population of ghetto No. 2 – Jews considered unfit for work – was shot in the forest. By the end of 1941 the *Einsatzgruppen* had killed over 40,000 Jews, the majority of them from Vilnius. By the end of 1944 the number of murdered Jews in Lithuania would reach 70,000 –100,000.

20 Auschwitz (Oświęcim in Polish) was the site of a complex of concentration camps that included the Birkenau death camp. For more information, see the glossary.

would allow up to five hundred refugees to proceed to their colonial possession of Jamaica in the British West Indies.²¹ Those of financial means could live and work on the island and the JDC would have to make arrangements for the others. My father immediately decided that we should go to Jamaica where, he felt, British law and order prevailed, rather than to Cuba where the future was uncertain.

Then we heard about the mass killing of Jews in Kiev and Odessa in Ukraine and Kaunus in Lithuania.²² The news hit my mother very hard when we were told that a death camp had been opened near Lodz where my mother's sister resided.²³ That year ended with the massacres in Riga, Latvia and Simferopol in the Crimea.²⁴ The good news in early January 1942 was that Field Marshal Rommel was with-

---

21 In December 1941 the British government, the Polish government-in-exile and the American JDC agreed to send Polish Jewish refugees from Lisbon, which had become the refugee capital of Europe, to Jamaica. The year before, Jamaica had built a camp to house anticipated British refugees from Gibraltar. The first group of 152 Polish Jewish refugees arrived in January 1942, the JDC having guaranteed to pay for their maintenance. The Jamaican legislature was promised that none of the new arrivals would seek employment or citizenship.

22 In Babi Yar, a ravine in Kiev, the capital of Ukraine, more than 30,000 Jewish civilians were murdered by *Einsatzgruppen* units and local collaborators over two days, September 29–30, 1941. The Babi Yar massacre, as it came to be known, was the largest single Nazi mass killing of the history of the Holocaust. Between October 22 and 24, 1941, 25,000 Jews in Odessa in Ukraine were either shot or burned to death and more than 35,000 were deported. On October 29, 1941, the *Einsatzgruppen* and Lithuanian collaborators murdered 9,200 Jews from the Kaunas ghetto.

23 The Chełmno (Kulmhof) death camp was established on German territory approximately seventy kilometres from the Polish town of Lodz in December 1941. Before it was abandoned and evidence of its existence obliterated by the Germans in 1944, more than 300,000 Jews, mainly from the Lodz ghetto, were killed in the mobile gas vans at Chełmno.

24 In November and December 1941 approximately 20,000–30,000 Jews from Riga were murdered by the *Einsatzgruppen* especially sent from Germany for this

drawing his troops in Africa, but that was soon offset by the information that Rommel had launched a major counter-offensive toward the end of the month.²⁵ Germany's Japanese allies were gaining ground in the Far East, having occupied Manila in January and forced the American military to surrender; the Japanese took Singapore in February.²⁶ The fact that the Americans had lost in the Philippines was a moral blow, as we believed them to be invincible. We started to wonder how safe Jamaica would be. If we were to be caught on an island, where would we be able to run?

The number of European Jews under the Nazi heel and the fate confronting them was frightening. It appeared that Hitler was going to be true to his creed of destroying all European Jewry. We had expected that some of the Jews under Nazi control would meet a dire fate, but we never anticipated the mass killing we learned about later. At the Refugee Committee we were concerned that the Germans would begin demanding that the Portuguese deport Jewish refugees living in Portugal. We weren't sure how the Portuguese government would react to such a request. We received information from Poland that Jews with money could buy military hardware to defend themselves and that they were ready to resist the Germans if they had the

----

purpose. The murder squads also followed the Wehrmacht (German army) as it spread into the USSR, conducting mass killings in Simferopol and other cities in the Crimea.

25 Field Marshal Erwin Rommel, commander of the Wehrmacht's *Afrikakorps* who was popularly known as the "Desert Fox," was forced to fall back to El Agheila on the Libyan coast in December of 1941, but launched a successful counteroffensive in January 1942 that caused serious damage to the Allied Forces in North Africa.

26 In January 1942 the Japanese captured the Philippine city of Manila, including the Cavite Naval Base that was home to the US Asiatic Fleet. On February 14 the Japanese overran British forces at Singapore, massacring all the wounded prisoners in the barracks hospital. The British surrendered the next day. Winston Churchill called the ignominious fall of Singapore to the Japanese the "worst disaster" and "largest capitulation" in British history.

means to do so.[27] This information was passed on to the JDC in New York, but we never heard of any follow-up or received requests for further information.

On January 15, 1942, the British Passport Control issued us entry visas for Jamaica that were "good for a single journey" and "port of entry: optional." Arrangements were made to charter the SS *Serpa Pinto*, a Portuguese passenger ship set to sail to Jamaica and then on to Cuba. It would also be making a stop in Casablanca to take on about fifty refugees stranded there and in danger of being handed to the Germans by the Vichy government. A few days before our departure, Mr. Jacobson, the American representative of the JDC, arrived by Yankee Clipper to facilitate our entry into Jamaica. We couldn't understand why he couldn't have met us in Jamaica, but the reason became clear two days before we arrived there.

---

27 Jews inside the Warsaw ghetto received few arms from the Polish resistance who were hard-pressed for arms and sometimes disinclined to assist Jews. Polish organizations such as the Armia Krajowa (Polish Home Army), the National Security Corps (PKB), the Polish People's Independence Action (PLAN) and the communist People's Guard (GL) did share some of their scarce armaments with the Jews who were readying themselves for combat inside the Warsaw ghetto.

The Fourth Exodus

On January 24, 1942, my parents and I boarded the SS *Serpa Pinto* for our journey to Jamaica. A passenger ship belonging to one of the Portuguese shipping lines, the *Serpa Pinto* had huge Portuguese flags painted on the port and starboard sides, covering about two-thirds of the length of the ship, that were lit up at night to ensure visibility. Despite this, however, we were stopped by a German submarine and boarded the second night out. We later learned that Nazi agents had copied the passenger list and ordered the captain to wait for their instructions. We all assumed that the Germans on board the submarine had forwarded the list to Germany to make sure that there were no "undesirables" on the ship. After about four hours, we were allowed to continue our journey to Casablanca.

When we docked in Casablanca early the next morning, Vichy French officers came aboard and also checked the passenger list. We were told that we would stay in Casablanca for about eight hours to await more passengers. I approached one of the French officers and asked if we could disembark to look around the city. At first he refused, saying that we didn't have visas for Casablanca. I assured him we had absolutely no desire to stay and that all our belongings were stored in the hold of the ship and therefore inaccessible. I believe that was the argument that convinced him; he allowed us to disembark and to bring the Prisel family along with us. Despite our age difference, Simon Prisel and I had become good friends. There was a foreign exchange booth on the dock so my father converted some American dollars into French francs. We hired a taxi and drove around Casablanca and then stopped at a café for a snack. The city was filthy and reminded me of the Arab quarter in Marseille, although one of the residential parts we drove through had some of the largest villas I had ever seen. I remember that throughout our drive the Prisels' baby girl cried incessantly.

When we got back to the ship, a number of people wanted to know how we had managed to get permission to go ashore – we told them that we had simply asked. Shortly after our return, a bus arrived with the new group of refugees and their luggage. There were some Orthodox Jews among the new arrivals – not that we'd been short of a *minyan,* the quorum of ten adult male Jews required for daily prayers. We were all advised that we would arrive in Jamaica in about fourteen days, weather permitting.

My father and I shared a small cabin on the ship while my mother shared a cabin with two other women. Meals were served in two shifts since the dining room couldn't accommodate all the passengers at the same time. There wasn't really much to do on board; people played cards or just sat on deck when the climate began to warm up. There was also shuffleboard, although we had to book a time if we wanted to play. Opening the porthole at night allowed some fresh air in but it was still very warm in the cabins. On our first night out of Casablanca we were stopped and boarded a third time, but this time it was by a British submarine. After visiting the captain and checking the ship's manifest to confirm that we were heading for Jamaica, the crew allowed us to proceed without further incident.

The first few evenings as sea were cool and we wore light topcoats whenever we went on deck, but about a week later the weather turned warmer and my father decided to pack our topcoats in one of the suitcases. We were now travelling with about eight suitcases between us – a slightly improved situation over our arrival in Lisbon sixteen months earlier. When my father checked the pockets of my topcoat before putting it into a suitcase, he discovered a pack of cigarettes. As soon as I came into the cabin, he confronted me and asked me if I had disobeyed his instructions about not smoking. Thinking quickly, I said that Simon Prisel and I had been walking on the deck and Simon asked me hold his pack while he was trying to light his cigarette and that I must have inadvertently put them in my pocket. I figured that my father would ask Simon about it, so I left the cabin to tell Simon what I'd said and he agreed to back me up. This was a close call and I was very careful for the rest of the voyage since I knew my father would be watching. As we sailed further and further south toward the equator, the cabins got really hot, with only a slight breeze coming through the porthole. We shed more and more of our clothing and some of us began walking around without our shirts on. The dining room became stifling and we started taking our meals outside to eat sitting in a deck chair.

We got to meet almost all the other passengers, some of whom we knew from Lisbon, and it wasn't too long before Simon and my father organized a poker game. As I've mentioned, my father was a very good poker player and won most of the time. While the stakes weren't high, it was still considerable for people who had no income. The overall mood on the ship was one of relief that we had finally escaped death at the hands of the Nazis once and for all. While news of the war in those days was still not very encouraging, we convinced ourselves that the Allies would win the war and end Hitler's rule once and for all.

～

Two days before we arrived in Jamaica, Mr. Jacobson, the American representative of the Jewish Joint Distribution Committee, called a meeting in the dining room of the ship and told us that the Joint, as it was sometimes known, would look after us financially and attend to our cultural and spiritual needs. He also told us the British government was concerned about the possibility of spies among us and had requested that we be placed in a camp under close supervision until the Chief Aliens Officer of the Criminal Investigation Department (CID) could complete an investigation of everyone on board.

We were all upset about this news since we had been told that once we landed in Jamaica we would be free. Mr. Jacobson assured us this was indeed the case, but that there was still a war going on and Britain was concerned about enemy agents who would be in a position to inform the Germans about shipping traffic in the Atlantic. He emphasized that the facility wasn't an internment camp and we would be free to come and go and enjoy the same liberties as the women and children who had recently arrived there from Gibraltar.[1] Of course we were all worried about the use of the word "camp" but ultimately we understood the British concerns. Nobody asked if there were any Jews on the island, not expecting such a remote area to have a Jewish population. Mr. Jacobson handled the situation with great finesse and nobody believed that a Jew would ever sell another Jew down the river. Unfortunately, that was exactly what happened.

We arrived in Kingston, Jamaica on February 8, 1942, and disembarked the next day. The border control officers stamped our passport with the notation: "Permitted to land at Kingston, Jamaica but restricted to close supervision pending result of thorough investigation."

It turned out that there was a Jewish community of long standing on the island. The first Jews had apparently arrived in Jamaica with Columbus early in the sixteenth century and had evidently prospered. In 1831 an act that made it illegal for Jews to be elected members of the

---

1   Because of the proximity of the island of Gibraltar to both Franco's Spain and Mussolini's Italy, the island fortress of Gibraltar, a British possession, was considered to be in harm's way. For this reason its civilian residents – mainly women and children – were evacuated, first to England and then, in 1941, over concerns for their health, to Jamaica, with its more familiar tropical climate.

Corporation of Kingston was repealed, declaring that "Persons professing the Jewish Religion are entitled to exercise and enjoy the same rights, privileges, immunities and advantages to which His Majesty's other natural born subjects are entitled." Jews achieved prominence in Jamaica and enjoyed a secure existence.[2]

We boarded awaiting buses for the trip to the camp, which was about eleven kilometres from downtown. As we drove through the streets of Kingston it became immediately apparent how different our new surroundings were. We had hardly ever met a black person in Europe and the closest I had come was meeting the Abyssinian "prince" in Lisbon. The bus ride was uncomfortable as the buses were dirty and, with 25-degree Celsius temperature, we were hot in our heavy European clothing. Our luggage was to be brought by trucks later in the day. When we drove through the camp gates we noticed that the enclosure was ringed with barbed wire, prompting concerns about what we were in for. The buses stopped in front of a huge mess hall that turned out to be the dining room where we would eat all our meals.

Once all the buses had arrived and unloaded, there were about four hundred of us. We sat down on the benches and Mr. Jacobson greeted us. Next to him were two Jamaican gentlemen, whom he introduced as Mr. Rae, the camp commandant, and Mr. Brown, the deputy camp commandant. As Mr. Rae spoke, Dr. Biederman, who spoke some English, translated for the German-speakers and Mr. Jacobson for the Yiddish-speakers. We were assigned rooms in a barracks and told that families would be kept together. When we looked around we saw that there were many barracks connected to the mess hall by covered walkways. Shortly after the introduction, Mr. Rae

---

2 Moses Delgado (1789–1842) played a key role in the fight for Jewish civil liberties in Jamaica. Richard Stern and Ernest Altamont da Costa both served as mayors of Kingston in 1896–1897 and 1925–1927 respectively.

drove off in his chauffeur-driven car, leaving Mr. Brown to attend to the details.

Each barracks had twenty-four rooms separated by wooden partitions that were about two metres high and the beams supporting the angular roof were almost three metres above us. The open space of about half a metre between the exterior wooden wall and the slanted roof line allowed for ventilation. There were twelve rooms off each side of a central hallway and each barracks had four entrances, one from each side in the middle of the barracks and one entrance at each end. Each room had a window with a wooden shutter but no glass, a steel bed with a thin mattress and mosquito net, a chair and table and hooks on the wall to hang clothing. Between two barracks facing each other were two small buildings with showers, toilets, wash basins and laundry tubs, one for men and the other for women. The toilet stalls had swinging doors that just barely hid the person using the stall. We wondered if they were designed for midgets. My parents and I were assigned adjoining rooms and the Prisels were assigned a room across the hall from us. Our luggage arrived later in the afternoon – we would have to live out of our suitcases for now, but nobody complained because we were sure that this temporary arrangement would end once the investigation was completed.

The next day a nurse arrived to take blood to test for tuberculosis. The young nurse assigned to me had a problem finding a vein and after she pricked me a third time, I fainted. This was the first time in my life that I had this reaction and discovered that the sight of blood didn't agree with me.

That afternoon Simon Prisel and I ventured into the upper camp that was occupied by women and children from Gibraltar. During the rainy season the camp's two exit gates became a problem because the sand would wash over the roads leading to the camp, making them slippery. All the medical facilities and administrative offices, as well as the post office, school and canteen were up there too. Mr. Rae and his family and Mr. Brown and his family occupied two beautiful houses next to the main entrance to the camp. Across from the houses was the Catholic convent. The people in the upper camp had their own church and the Catholic diocese in Jamaica looked after their spiritual needs. There was a police station located at the other gate with a police force of about ten men. We were told that their main duty was to patrol the grounds and keep drifters out. I would soon discover that Mr. Rae, unknown to his bosses, had other ideas.

When the Catholic priest, Father Feeney, came to visit us on the third day we were at the camp and expressed his desire to assist us in whatever way he could, he hinted that his relationship with Mr. Rae was not very pleasant. He suggested that the married Mr. Rae was a womanizer and took advantage of his position at the upper camp. He was warning us to be on our guard.

The first shock of realization that our stay in the camp would not be a short one came on April 13, 1942, when the CID withdrew the landing restrictions they had placed on us but did not permit us to move out of the camp. I decided to distract myself by focusing on learning English as fast possible – I had no doubt that I could master it as quickly as I had learned French. I snapped up everything I could find in English and frequented the small library in the upper camp. But because Gibraltar is Spanish-speaking, most of the books were in Spanish. Even the lessons at the school for the Gibraltarian children were taught in Spanish, so other schools had to be found for the children in our camp. There weren't that many young children in our camp as most were either below school-age or teenagers. This time around my father couldn't do anything for me and I had to find my own way.

Henry and Maurice Feigenbaum, Maurice Tempelsman, Adolf Lipmanowitz, Trudy Gross, Lizzi Eckstein and I – all teenagers – were enrolled in local schools, including Jamaica College, Kingston College and Kingston Technical School. Every morning the camp station wagon picked us up and drove us into town, and then came back for us at the end of the school day. I went into the equivalent of second-year university and passed with 89 per cent in 1943. It was interesting that we had to write all our test papers in duplicate because they were sent by boat to either the University of London or Cambridge University for marking. Since there was a danger of the boat being torpedoed, the school had to keep a copy.

About a month after our arrival in Jamaica we had a visit from another priest who, to our amazement, spoke Hebrew. He wore a typical clerical collar that we identified with Catholic priests. He asked us how we were doing and whether we were happy in the camp. Needless to say he got an earful. He listened politely and left after about an hour later without any comment. Father Feeney happened to come by on a walk the following day and we asked him who the priest was who had visited us the day before. Father Feeney laughed out loud and informed us that he was Rabbi Henry P. Silverman, the spiritual leader of Kingston's United Congregation of Israelites. He told us that there were about three hundred Jewish families in Jamaica and they had a very active congregation with a synagogue in Kingston, and that rabbis in England frequently wore a clerical collar.

Rabbi Silverman never visited again; Father Feeney did more for us than the good rabbi. The Jewish community of Jamaica, with very few exceptions, did nothing to assist us and, at worst, ignored our existence. We never had a visit from any member of the Jamaican Jewish community during our whole stay in the camp. On the contrary, they almost seemed to resent our presence. Louis Alberga was the president of the United Congregation of Israelites when we arrived; he was followed by Leslie R. Mordecai and then Vernon Henriques. Frank Lyons was vice president during this time. None of these gentlemen ever visited the camp. Undoubtedly, the driving force for compassion would have been Rabbi Silverman, but this was not to be.

Soon after we arrived, my mother offered her services to manage the kitchen at the camp – she was well-qualified for the position given her experience in Lisbon. Mr. Rae turned down her offer without giving it any consideration. He only wanted his hand-selected people in charge of any activities involving purchasing so it would all go through him. He was the master of all purchases, be it trucks or paperclips. Not even Mr. Brown had any purchasing rights and he left in disgust not too long after we arrived. Mr. Lopez was in charge of the food supply, but he could only order from suppliers that Mr. Rae had approved. Mr. Lopez's family ran a large grocery store, wholesale and retail, at Half Way Tree, but he was not allowed to purchase any food items from them until he became commandant toward the end of the camp's existence.[3] The meat was second-rate and some of the vegetables were close to the throw-out stage. The cooks accomplished marvels with what they had and nobody dared to complain. There were three cells in the police station and people who complained too much frequently occupied them.

The lower camp where we were housed had been unoccupied prior to our arrival as it had originally been designated for the women and children of Malta. Both Gibraltar and Malta were subject to frequent air-attacks by the Germans and it was thought best to protect the women and children, by sending them to Jamaica. After the evacuation of the women and children from Gibraltar, the British government wanted to send the Maltese women and children, but their husbands insisted on sending a delegation to check out the facilities. After their visit, they told the British that they wouldn't allow the evacuation because they found the facilities inadequate and certainly didn't wish their relatives to be governed by a black man. By the standards of the day, it was indeed surprising that the British government had placed a black man in charge of white people. At that time, no person of colour could be a member of any of the leading clubs such as the Liguanea Club or be part of Jamaican high society. There was a strict division between blacks and whites. Black or coloured people weren't allowed to swim in the Myrtle Bank Hotel swimming

---

3 Half Way Tree is an area of Kingston, the capital of Jamaica.

pool. We didn't suffer from those prejudices and we were astounded to discover this phenomenon.

Within four months of our arrival in Jamaica I spoke enough English to visit Mr. Higgins, the chief administrative officer of the CID, to request a release from the camp. He told me that the only way any of us could leave the camp was to leave the island.

While I attended school, I frequented the Myrtle Bank Hotel to swim and eat lunch. My English was now good enough to allow me to converse with people and I met a number of the local people at the pool. One of them was John Pringle, a member of one of Jamaica's prominent, but not too affluent, families. He had graduated from Jamaica College and was at a loss what to do. He introduced me to a number of his friends and I found a way to escape the drudgery of the camp during the day and into the evening. One day John told me that he intended to join the Jamaican army officer-training school and suggested that I do the same. While this triggered feelings of revenge against the Germans in me, I couldn't see myself sitting in the fort at Newcastle in the Jamaican Blue Mountains waiting to fight the Germans. I did visit the local Royal Air Force (RAF) office but was told that they wouldn't accept me because I had been born in Germany. They also suggested the officer-training school of the Jamaican army, which sometimes sent a contingent to Britain to fight. John became a first lieutenant and was appointed aide-de-camp to the governor, Sir John Huggins, because of his family background.

I met Mrs. Wilson and her daughter, Barbara, at the swimming pool. Mrs. Wilson, an attractive woman in her mid-forties, although slightly overweight, was quite wealthy and always made advances to us youngsters. After John became a first lieutenant, he decided to marry Mrs. Wilson and live a comfortable life. Another person I met was Aaron Matalon and we became good friends. Aaron was Flo and Joe Matalon's third son and the eldest of the Matalon children in Jamaica. His two older brothers had joined the army and were fighting in Europe, while his two younger brothers were at school in

Kingston. Aaron's parents were extremely nice people and after I met them they wanted to meet my parents. There was a bit of a communication problem even though my parents were more fluent in English than they ever were in French.

The first meeting went extremely well and Mrs. Matalon liked my mother very much. After that, they got together frequently. Aaron wanted to improve his father's business and modernize it, but his uncle, Moses Matalon, was the wealthier of the brothers and it bothered Aaron very much. Moses Matalon had a big store on Harbour Street and Aaron's father had a little store on Princess Street. Both were in the textile business, but Aaron believed that his uncle was more outwardly successful because he was more aggressive than Aaron's father, who was quite happy "making a living" for his family. Aaron was engaged to Marjorie DeMercado and the DeMercados had a beautiful old house on South Camp Road. Marjorie's mother had remarried a ne'er-do-well who was living off the DeMercado money. Marjorie's sister Barbara was a beautiful little girl and if she had been a few years older I could have fallen in love with her. Aaron frequently took me along when he visited Marjorie and we all had a very good relationship. The Matalon family was a marvellous example of solid family bonding and the only time Aaron rebelled was when his father prevented him from changing the business. My feeling was that sooner or later Aaron would break away because he was bursting with anger at being restricted in his ambitions.

The Taylor family – Mervis and Hermann Taylor and their three boys and two girls – lived next to camp and were extremely kind to us. Hermann was an easy-going well-to-do Jamaican. His family owned a medium-sized department store managed by Hermann's brother and Hermann collected dividends from it. He owned a number of race horses and indulged in any form of gambling he could find. He was a compulsive gambler who bet large sums on the races, at times causing the family financial embarrassment. While his wife, Mervis, a compassionate lady, was a practicing Jew, Hermann was an agnostic.

The boys never went to synagogue, although the two girls frequently accompanied their mother to Saturday morning services.

Bobby Taylor and I became friends and he taught me how to ride horses. His father's race horses needed exercising so Bobby and I would ride the horses over to the Hope Botanical Garden, a fifteen-minute trek through the back roads. Once we got to Hope Garden, we would have a great time eating oranges, bananas, pineapples and mangos right off the trees. The flowers at the Garden were exquisite and the varieties endless. I went riding with Bobby at least once a week, but never had to clean the horses since their groom took care of it. The lane we rode through on the way to Hope Garden was fairly narrow and the fields on both sides were fenced off by barbed wire. One day, as we were galloping through the lane, Bobby called out from behind me not to shift my weight and to rein in my horse. I didn't know what was going on, but I tightened the reins and brought my horse to a stop. From somewhere behind me Bobby warned me not to get off the horse until he had caught up to me. When he came up alongside me, he pointed to the girth, which had broken – if I had shifted my weight, I would have been thrown into the barbed wire with a most bloody result.

Bobby frequently had his friends over for parties and always asked me to join them. The festivities always lasted way past the 10 PM curfew imposed by Mr. Rae and experience had shown that Rae, to prove his authority, wouldn't grant late permits. Little did he know that we had made an opening between the Taylor estate and the camp and I came back whenever I pleased. I just had to make sure to walk between the barracks when I returned. On one occasion, when I was stopped by a policeman, I said that I hadn't been able to sleep and had gone for a walk since we weren't restricted to quarters.

One night Mr. Taylor gave a birthday party for his wife and the festivities went on into the late hours. Just before 10 PM, I told Mr. Taylor that I had to leave and he insisted on telephoning Rae to ask him to extend my hours. Rae refused, which infuriated Mr. Taylor.

It was not customary for a black man to refuse a reasonable request from a white man. Mr. Taylor wouldn't hear of my leaving and said that he would show this Rae not to fool with a Taylor. It reminded me of a joke about a Jewish man who bought himself a big pleasure boat and invited his parents for a cruise. When they came aboard he greeted them wearing his captain's cap. His father looked at him and said, "By your mother you are a captain, by me you are a captain, but by a captain you are no captain." By the Gibraltarians and by us, Rae was a camp commandant, but by the Jamaican white folks he was no commandant. Bobby and I never disclosed to anybody the secret entrance we had created into the camp, so when Mr. Taylor insisted on driving me back to the camp around midnight, he took me to the gate. The guard let me in, but the next morning I was called to Mr. Rae's office. He informed me that since I had gone against his orders I was now confined to camp for four weeks with the exception of attending school. I told him that this wouldn't stand up for long and he got very angry and told me to get out of his office. I wasn't too worried about Rae's punishment – I knew I could always get out through the fence at the Taylor estate without anybody knowing.

That evening I visited Bobby and told Mr. Taylor what had happened. He told me not to worry about it and that he would take care of it the next day. After I got back from school I was again called to Rae's office and was ushered in to see Mr. Brown. He told me that Mr. Rae had decided to be more lenient and had lifted my restrictions. I later learned from Mr. Taylor that he had called the general manager of Barclays Bank, who was the chairman of the camp committee, and had asked him to instruct Rae to lift the restriction forthwith. That is what happened and from that time on Rae and I were on a collision course. He realized that I had outside connections and his power was limited to the occupants of Gibraltar Camp.

There was a comical Austrian couple in the camp named Mr. and Mrs. Neruda. Mr. Neruda was about 188 centimetres tall and weighed about 100 kilograms, and she was about 135 centimetres tall and weighed about 50 kilograms. Before the annexation of Austria, Mr. Neruda had been a member of the Austrian national bridge team. They had fled to Holland in 1938 and ended up in Portugal. Mr. Neruda became a bridge teacher in the camp and charged a nominal amount for lessons. He taught me bridge and was a very good teacher. We played at least twice a week and many of us became Neruda's pupils. When you were Neruda's partner and didn't know what to lead, he would boom across the table, "Lead what your heart desires" and laugh heartily. After two years the Nerudas left for Cuba and I hope he continued teaching people the king of card games.

My mother played cards with some of the ladies almost every afternoon while my father mainly played poker. One late afternoon when I came home my mother asked me to fetch her a glass of water. As I returned with the water I tripped and fell forward, turning the hand holding the glass inward and landing on it with all my weight, smattering the glass to pieces. The shards went into the ball of my hand and I had a very deep gash. It wouldn't stop bleeding, so I walked to the hospital. The matron thought there might be pieces of glass embedded in the wound and had me driven to Kingston General Hospital. There the doctor closely examined the wound, extracted two little pieces of glass and then instructed the nurse to stitch it up. The nurse was very young and inexperienced and she had trouble pushing the needle through my skin. She also forgot to give me a local anesthetic to dull the pain. After she tried a few times, I suggested that she call a more experienced nurse to stitch me up, which she graciously did.

I continued to have a fairly active love life during our stay in the camp. There were two lovely women, Lilly and Betty, living across the hall from my room. Betty had managed to escape from Paris with her six-year-old son, Claude, when the Germans arrived and she had made her way first to Lisbon and then to Jamaica. I found Betty extremely attractive, but knew she was having an affair with another man in the camp. One evening when I came home late from one of my trysts, Betty's door was open and I stopped to say hello. She invited me in and closed the door. I was puzzled but expectant. We both sat on her bed and she just had a dressing gown on. Her hand moved over mine and I took this as a sign of consent; this was the beginning of a long sexual relationship with no strings attached on either side. I would sneak into Betty's room late at night and we both enjoyed our torrid sex affair. We had to be careful not to make any noise, so we put her mattress on the floor.

It was different with Lilly. She wasn't satisfied with my lovemaking abilities and became my teacher. Somehow I doubt if there was anything to do with lovemaking that Lilly didn't know or hadn't experienced. She was the third woman in my life who contributed to my sexual training. While Betty was a dainty woman, Lilly was a seductress and she enjoyed having a young boy at her beck and call. She would let me know when she wanted me to come to her room; at any other time I wasn't welcome. When once I had an urge and knocked softly on her door, she turned me away and I was grateful for Betty's more accommodating nature.

~

When the first Pesach (Passover) arrived while we were living in the camp we heard nothing from the Jewish community in Kingston and addressed ourselves to the JDC in New York. Mr. Rae certainly didn't offer any assistance when he was approached nor did he accommodate a separate section in the kitchen for the kosher Jews. Fortunately for them, the individual families created their own cooking facilities outside their respective barracks and ate only foods such as fish, vegetables and fruit that were not subject to the *kashruth* laws. We were still restricted to the camp since the Pesach started on the evening of April 1, 1942, and the CID didn't clear us until April 13, 1942. Mr. Rae made no attempt to communicate with the Jewish community in Kingston, even though we had requested him to do so. Mr. Jacobson had made provision for us to receive a supply of matzah, kosher wine and Haggadot, books that tell the story of the Jewish exodus from Egypt. In answer to a telegram to the JDC in New York, we received news that the shipment would arrive in Kingston around March 20. On the evening of April 1, we had a communal seder dinner in the mess hall led by one of the Orthodox Jews. We asked him, in deference to the circumstances, to agree to an abbreviated version, which he reluctantly did. However, it was stipulated that the Orthodox Jews could remain to read additional sections of the Haggadah after most of us had left.

This disregard for us on the part of the Jamaican Jewish community continued as the Jewish New Year approached on September 12, 1942. Rabbi Silverman didn't come to the camp to ask us about our preparations for one of the holiest of days in the Jewish religion, nor did the president or vice president of the congregation in Kingston. Prayer books were sent from New York and even a small Torah was included in the shipment. It would not have been possible for us to hold our New Year's services without a Torah and even though the synagogue in Kingston had several Torah scrolls, they didn't offer to help.

It is unusual for Jews to ignore other Jews, particularly at New Year's, but the local Jewish community in Kingston set a record. It would have been customary to invite us to attend the services at the synagogue and the majority of us were not adverse to driving on Saturday or on the High Holy Days. They treated us as if we were lepers and only later a few of them, such as the Matalons, had any contact with us. We never did figure out why they acted that way but undoubtedly their spiritual leader, Rabbi Silverman, played a significant role in this indifference. I frequently saw Rabbi Silverman at the swimming pool of the Myrtle Bank Hotel, but never spoke to him. I couldn't bring myself to address him as "rabbi," which to me meant a teacher and the title of a Jewish religious leader. During the Middle Ages the rabbi, in addition to being a legal scholar, began to assume the role of teacher, preacher and communal leader. Silverman failed on all counts. He should have taken a page out of the book of Rabbi Leo Baeck, who stayed in Germany to minister to the poorer German Jews who couldn't flee from the Nazi tyranny and ended up in a concentration camp.[4] Father Feeney was more compassionate than the rabbi and visited us on a regular basis. The only thing Father Feeney did not condone was our fraternizing with the Gibraltarian girls. When Father Feeney caught us trying to date a girl from Gibraltar, he would instruct her mother to forbid her daughter to go out with us.

Our camp community created an internal committee to represent our interests. It was comprised of Dr. Platts, an English-speaker, Mr. Tempelsman, a diamond dealer from Antwerp, my father, and two other gentlemen. They were to regulate the affairs of the people and act as a buffer between Rae and the residents. It didn't take long to figure out that we needed to establish a united front to face Rae and prevent him from taking any unjust actions. The committee was also charged with looking after the financial interests of the people and communicating with American Jewish organizations such as the Hebrew Immigrant Aid Society. One incident that comes to mind about the interaction between the committee and Mr. Rae involved our Pesach celebrations in 1943. Dr. Platts told Rae that Passover was approaching and requested certain kitchen facilities to prepare the traditional dishes. Mr. Rae challenged Dr. Platts, accusing us of playing games with him because the year before we had celebrated Passover on a different date. Mr. Rae was evidently unaware that the Jewish calendar follows a partially lunar cycle different from the Gregorian.[5]

---

4 After he refused to leave his fellow Jews in Germany by accepting offers of refuge in North America, Leo Baeck was deported to the camp in Theresienstadt (Terezin), where he continued to be a source of inspiration and comfort to his fellow prisoners.

5 The Gregorian calendar, named for Pope Gregory XIII who proclaimed it in 1582, is the purely solar dating system that is now in general use for civil matters around the world; the Jewish calendar, based on principles outlined in the Torah

The camp had its own hospital administered by a matron and six nurses. Most of the nurses were professionals from Gibraltar, but the matron was Jamaican. She was a very nice middle-aged woman who tried everything possible to run an efficient hospital. The camp also had its own medical doctor and dentist tending to the more than 1,500 inmates, but patients needing surgery were sent to the Kingston General Hospital.

Dr. Gideon was a general practitioner and in his case "general" was the operative word. One illustration of this was his treatment of Mr. Fedderman. The Feddermans had come from Antwerp and, like many of us, had made their way through France and Spain to Portugal. While they were in transit through Spain their son, who was of military age, was detained and they were told that he couldn't continue on with them – he would be placed in an internment camp. They were given the choice of either travelling to Portugal without him or returning to France with him. After great soul-searching and with great regret, they decided to continue their flight to Portugal. Their daughter, Suzy, told me that Mr. Fedderman had had severe pains in his toes and had gone to see Dr. Gideon. After a preliminary examination, Dr. Gideon informed Mr. Fedderman that his teeth were the cause of the pain because an infection had spread a poison through his system that was creating the toe problem. He suggested that Mr. Fedderman have all his teeth pulled to relieve the pain. Mr. Fedderman asked the doctor if he was absolutely sure that without his teeth his aliment would be cured. Dr. Gideon assured him this to be the case, whereupon Mr. Fedderman removed both his dentures, placed them on Dr. Gideon's desk and said, "What now?" Apparently Dr. Gideon specialized in advising patients to lose their teeth. Even

---

and now used primarily for religious purposes, relies on a lunisolar system that takes into account both the position of the sun and the phases of the moon. This means that Jewish holidays fall on different days of the Gregorian calendar in different years.

my father was subjected to it. If it weren't for the fact that both the doctor and dentist were on the government payroll, one might have suspected some sort of collusion.

~

What we had feared at the beginning of 1942 became a reality later that year: the Nazis continued their systematic destruction of the Jews of Europe. In June they mandated the wearing of the yellow Star of David in Holland and France with the word "Jew" printed in the local language. We learned of the start of the mass gassings in Treblinka and Auschwitz.[6] We also learned the Lodz ghetto had been totally decimated – among the tens of thousands murdered must have been my mother's sister and her family. In August seven thousand stateless Jews had been arrested in unoccupied France and, soon after, Hitler publicly reiterated his intent to eliminate all Jews; Jews in German concentration camps were transported to camps in Poland. Later that year, the first deportation of Jews from Norway to Auschwitz began.[7] At the end of 1942 the Allies condemned the mass murder of Jews and promised to punish the perpetrators.[8] This was like closing a barn

---

6 The Treblinka death camp was one of facilities explicitly created for the implementation of Operation Reinhard, the Nazi plan for the mass murder by gassing (with carbon monoxide fumes) of Polish Jews living in German-occupied Poland. The first massive deportations to Treblinka II from Warsaw began on July 22, 1942. The testing of hydrogen cyanide had been going on at Auschwitz since 1941; the four main crematoria and gas chambers at Auschwitz II-Birkenau that used Zyklon B to release the cyanide fumes became operational in July 1943. For more information, see the entries for Auschwitz and Treblinka in the glossary.

7 All Jewish males in Norway over the age of fifteen were arrested and all Jewish property confiscated on October 26, 1942; deportations to Auschwitz by ship and by train began on November 19.

8 By the end of 1942 the Allies could no longer claim ignorance of the brutal treatment and mass murder of European Jews. In the face of incontrovertible evidence

door after the animals had fled. Why did the Allies not bomb the railroads and rail connections to the camps? Why did they not supply arms to the inmates of the ghettos?

In December 1942 we had an influx of about a hundred Dutch Jews who arrived from Spain on the SS *Marques di Comillas* and were assisted by the Dutch government-in-exile in London. At that time there were no ships sailing to Curaçao or St. Maarten from either Portugal or Spain, but there were vessels sailing to Jamaica. The Dutch government-in-exile had made the deal in London for the Dutch Jews to proceed to Jamaica. One Dutch family, the Katzes, consisted of twenty-five members, all of whom were saved. The senior Mr. Katz was one of the leading Dutch art dealers in Dieren. One day he was visited at his gallery by Reichsmarschall Hermann Goering, who looked at the paintings of the famous Dutch school.[9] He selected four paintings and asked Mr. Katz how much he wanted for them. Mr. Katz replied that he didn't wish to sell them, but would give them to the Reichsmarschall if he would to arrange for twenty-five members of his family to leave Holland for either Spain or Portugal. Goering agreed and after Mr. Katz delivered the paintings, a passenger railway car was readied and the twenty-five members of the Katz family boarded it. Two SS men accompanied the car to the French-Spanish

---

that was being widely reported in the press and growing public pressure, the governments of Great Britain, Belgium, Czechoslovakia, Greece, Luxembourg, the Netherlands, Norway, Poland, the Soviet Union, the United States, as well as the National Council of France, issued a joint statement condemning "in the strongest possible terms this bestial policy of cold-blooded 'extermination' and making a "solemn resolution to ensure that those responsible for these crimes shall not escape retribution." The statement did not offer any direct assistance to the beleaguered Jews of Europe, but it was the first international acknowledgment that they were being systematically slaughtered.

9 The Dutch School of painting, also known as Dutch Golden Age painting, generally spanned the seventeenth century and includes such Dutch masters as Rembrandt and Peter Paul Rubens.

border where they disembarked. The Dutch underground had made arrangements through the government-in-exile for the Katz family to continue on to Jamaica. Mr. Katz had taken a great risk when he delivered the paintings to Goering – before delivering them he had hired a forger to make copies of the paintings and gave the forgeries to Goering. Mr. Katz hid the originals in a safe place so that he could retrieve them after the war.

I witnessed first-hand the fact that Mr. Katz always went after what he wanted. I had bought a cigarette case in a Kingston store that had a sliding cover and a spring for each cigarette. When one moved the sliding cover, a cigarette would pop up. Mr. Katz saw it and asked me where I had bought it. He went to the store, but there weren't any left, so he offered to buy mine. I had paid five shillings for it and he offered me five pounds if I were to sell it to him. Fortunately, I didn't need the money and refused his offer.

In 1943 the camp fell prey to the infamous dengue fever epidemic. Dengue fever is characterized by the sudden onset of a high fever, rash, severe headaches, nausea and vomiting. The epidemic started in the upper camp and spread to us within days. Generally, the rise in temperature reaches its peak on about the fourth day and then falls back to normal. The greatest danger is within the three-to-five-day period when the disease can be fatal to someone with a weak constitution. The matron and her nurses did an exemplary job of trying to contain the spread of the fever and worked many overtime hours in the hospital and at the barracks. Some of us were hospitalized and I was one of them because I had developed a slight heart murmur by doing strenuous exercise during the hottest hours of the say. So, on day two of my attack, the matron decided to hospitalize me. One of the reasons may have been that the matron had become quite friendly with my parents who had, by then, acquired a substantial knowledge of English.

The days I spent in the hospital gave me a chance to get to know the Gibraltarians and their concerns better. One of the few men in the group told me why the Maltese had refused to come to Jamaica. He said that if their own men had known what this was like, they would have also elected to stay in Gibraltar. Since a number of them spoke little or no English, they felt uncomfortable in a country where English was the only official language.[10] To make matters worse, Rae refused to let any of their people cook, so they had to eat food that was foreign to them. Because of this, the majority of the inhabitants refused to eat in the mess hall and prepared their own food. The quantity of food they ordered was supposed to feed all the people, but it often fell short and they often wondered where some of the food had disappeared to, or whether it was ever delivered. It was eye-opening to hear how disappointed these people were by the treatment they had received at the hands of the British and how they would have preferred to have been under Spanish rule, even though they were not too fond of Generalissimo Franco.

On the fourth day of my illness, my temperature rose to over 40 degrees Celsius and I was hallucinating. The nurses worked hard to get my temperature down and the next morning I woke up almost fever-free. There was some talk that dengue fever could cause male impotence, but two nights later one of the nurses helped me prove that I wasn't so afflicted. I left the hospital confident.

Simon Prisel and I frequently went for walks after sundown and we usually went to Papine, a small village about three kilometres from the camp, to buy meat and vegetables. Both Simon's wife and my mother cooked dinner to supplement the food served in the mess hall. Breakfast and lunch were bearable, but when it came to dinner the cook had little imagination. My mother never made a second offer to assist them, even though many people in the camp who experienced her management in Lisbon urged her to do so. She had

----

10 While English was also the official language in Gibraltar, most of the local people spoke either Spanish or a form of Andalusian Spanish known as Llanito or Yanito.

assessed the situation quite rightly and knew that it was useless to try – because she was my mother, Mr. Rae wouldn't have even given her a job as a dishwasher. There was always a lot of haggling at the market, but vegetables and fruit were extremely cheap. Another item that was of first-class quality was the Blue Mountain coffee, undoubtedly one of the world's best. The coffee served in the mess hall wasn't very good, so we brewed our own.

Simon also had a number of affairs while we were in the camp – he could be quite a womanizer. I remember one incident in which we met two attractive young Jamaican women on our way back from Papine one evening. Simon was interested in having an encounter with one of them, but his English was very poor, so I had to act as middleman. As we walked into a field with them and sat down, the young women couldn't stop giggling. I assume that it was because they weren't used to sitting with white men, but they didn't reject our advances.

Jenny Weinreb had a crush on Simon. He knew it and frequently went for walks with her. Jenny's mother was horrified that her daughter would keep company with a married man and tried to stop it. Of course, it's always a mistake to try to prevent a child from doing something to which a parent objects. Jenny was quite tall, with a lovely figure, and very intelligent. Whenever Simon disappeared on one of his escapades, he would tell his wife, Ruth, that he was spending time with me. As a result I would have to make myself scarce while Simon pursued his love interests. He usually knew where I was and would come and fetch me afterward. Ruth was an avid card player and was quite content to spend her evenings playing cards and looking after their baby girl.

~

While my parents and I were in Jamaica, my brother, Heini, was in regular touch with us. He had left the internment camp in New

Brunswick and moved to Toronto, Ontario. Heini was planning to join the Canadian army and after the war study at the University of Toronto. The geographical distance between us was not as great as it had been when we were in Europe and we hoped to see him soon after the hostilities were over. He sent us a photograph from his high school graduation and pictures of himself horseback riding and working in the fields. He was now twenty years old and my parents were proud to see that he had overcome the hardship of the camp and was proceeding with his education.

~

There was a Mr. Fluegelmann in the camp who was a lawyer from Germany. I had met him at the Jewish Refugee Committee in Lisbon. Mr. Fluegelmann's only purpose in life seemed to be to annoy people to the point that they would start screaming at him. He always found something to make them angry and get them to lose control. He would berate them in any manner he could and when he had a person good and mad he would start laughing and then walk away. He picked on a different person every day and eventually it was my turn. I had observed him for quite some time and knew that the only way to defeat his manipulations was to stay calm. He began by telling me that I must be a slow learner since at my age I still needed to go to school and that he had already started university at my age. Then he told me that my father cheated at poker. He elaborated on all these points and when he saw that I wasn't getting mad, he began to scream, "What's the matter with you? Don't you understand what I'm saying? Are you that stupid?" When he still didn't get a rise out of me (and it took all my willpower not to scream back at him), he turned and walked away, and never started in on me again. That taught me a lesson – to always control my temper and to not let others get me mad.

Simon's playing around got him in trouble when Mr. Fluegelmann learned about it. One evening he started to malign Simon, accusing him of being a poor father and a bon vivant. He said things about Ruth that implied she hadn't been faithful to Simon in Lisbon and that their child might be somebody else's. Simon got so mad that he physically attacked Fluegelmann and I had to separate them.

At that very moment, a policeman walked by. All he saw was Simon attacking a man and not the reason behind it. He promptly placed Simon under arrest, even though I explained what happened. Simon asked me to go with him to the police station to interpret. Of course, I readily agreed. I explained what happened to the sergeant in charge, but the policeman said that I was involved in the struggle, so my explanation of trying to separate them fell on deaf ears. The sergeant ordered both Simon and me to be placed in a cell for the night and let Mr. Rae sort it out in the morning. We were surprised at that decision since we could have gone back to our barracks and appeared before Rae in the morning. In response to this ridiculous ruling, we decided to sing all night and keep the policemen awake. We ignored their pleas that we shut up and there was nothing they could do about it. When morning came, we were hauled before Mr. Rae and the sergeant explained what I had told him. Again I repeated that I had merely come with Simon as an interpreter and was detained by the sergeant. He let Simon off with a warning and told me that he could hold both of us, but decided not to do so. I looked him straight in the eye and said, "I believe that this is a very wise decision on your part." Rae understood very well what I meant.

One young lady who was in our camp with her parents and grandmother became very friendly with Rae. We wondered for a while how Rae knew about some of the complaints we were planning to register with the JDC in New York since most of the complaints were promptly attended to by the camp administration before we even had a chance to lodge them. While we welcomed this sort of remedy, we were interested in finding out who the informer was. We then learned that Rae had been seen in a compromising position with this young lady, confirming our suspicions. She maintained that he merely gave her lifts into town, but we discovered that she would deliberately walk down Mona Road, the route to the Mona Hotel, the one used by Rae when he went into town or to the hotel. To use that road one had to leave camp by the back gate, the one my parents and I used whenever we went to see the Taylors. As soon as we learned of the young woman's treachery, we were careful not to have any significant conversations within earshot of her or her parents.

The Mona Hotel was a brisk walk from the camp and my parents and I occasionally visited for 5 o'clock tea. They served an excellent English tea with all the trimmings such as scones with clotted cream and finger sandwiches. Whenever we went for tea I would go for a swim in their small pool and think of the one at the Myrtle Bank Hotel in Kingston, which was never crowded.

The Myrtle Bank Hotel was the leading hotel in Kingston and was owned by the United Fruit Company, which had offices in the annex building of the hotel. The buffet lunch frequented by Kingston's business community was served in the garden. Formality was the order of the day and ties and jackets were required – if necessary, men could borrow them in a small room off the lobby. Mr. Levy, the general manager of the hotel, insisted on keeping up this decorum. The hotel and grounds were a sea of white – not even light-skinned coloured people were allowed to buy tickets to the swimming pool. One time I invited Elly, a Dutch girl in camp with us, to join me for a swim. When she arrived, she told me that she couldn't buy a ticket because the cashier told her that the pool was full. At first I was puzzled since very few people were around the pool, but I suddenly understood what was happening. Elly was quite tanned and had crinkled hair. I went up front and talked to the cashier who knew me, explaining that Elly was in fact a white Dutch girl.

In 1944 the Issa family bought the hotel from the United Fruit Company. Abe Issa was looking after it while his brother Joe ran the family business, A. E. Issa & Sons Ltd. Mr Issa, Sr., the founder of the company, was semi-retired and had been appointed a justice of the peace – he enjoyed meting out justice from the bench. He fined me five shillings when I was charged with riding on the steps of the streetcar. He was aware that I was a friend of his son Abe but that didn't influence him. Later that same day he saw me at the Myrtle Bank Hotel, and said, "Come on, I'll buy you lunch to make up for the fine I imposed on you." He was a marvellous old man and told me some of the hardships that he had encountered when he first arrived in Jamaica from Lebanon.

He had started out by travelling the countryside selling textiles. He told me that he had carried the merchandise on his back and showed me the permanent marks made on his shoulders from the rope he used to carry his wares. When he had enough money, he bought a horse and carriage and then advanced to a wholesale store and later a department store. The two leading department stores in Kingston were owned by the Issas and the Hannahs, both from Lebanon. There was a story that Issa Sr. made a trip to New York and checked into the Plaza Hotel frequented by both his sons, Joe and Abe. One of the hotel's assistant managers was behind the desk when Mr. Issa checked in. When he saw the name and Kingston, Jamaica, the assistant manager asked if he was related to Joe and Abe Issa. He informed him that he was their father and the man said, "But Mr. Issa, you don't want a room, you want a suite, the same one that your sons always occupy." Whereupon Mr. Issa answered, "My sons can afford it, their father has money," and insisted on registering for the room.

Abe Issa was a very pleasant man and a bit of a playboy while his brother Joe had a more serious nature. When I was introduced to Abe at the Myrtle Bank Hotel by John Pringle, we took an immediate liking to each other. When he heard that I was living at the Gibraltar Camp, Abe's first reaction was to ask me whether I had transportation and when I said that I took the bus, he insisted on driving me back. On the way we stopped at his gorgeous mansion, almost a replica of the White House in Washington, and I had the pleasure of meeting his wife, Lorraine, a most gracious lady.

It was always hard for me to understand why he was having affairs when he had such a lovely wife. Wanda Gideon, the widow of Dr. Gideon of Montego Bay comes to mind. After her husband's death, Wanda visited Kingston a few times a month and always stayed at the hotel on Duke Street, not far from the synagogue. One evening when Wanda was in town, Abe had invited me to the Liguanea Club for dinner and brought Wanda along. We became very silly and Abe challenged me that he could drink me under the table. I accepted the dare and we started drinking. Abe didn't realize that over the time that I had been in Jamaica my system had developed a tolerance for more and more alcohol without any side effects. It wasn't too long before poor Abe slid under the table fairly drunk. I called in the chauffeur and between the two of us we got Abe into the car. I told the chauffeur to drive Wanda back to the hotel and then we would take Mr. Issa home. When we got to the hotel, I escorted Wanda to her room and she asked me if I would like to come in. How could I be rude to the lady and refuse? I went down and told the chauffeur to take Mr. Issa home and that I would take a taxi. When I met Abe at the Myrtle Bank a couple of days later, he wanted to know what happened and I told him that I had taken care of Wanda. I didn't tell him that I had had to sneak into camp through the Taylor estate secret entrance that night.

Abe's sister Bertha was a lady of leisure who also enjoyed an active sex life. Her husband was South American and worked as a manager in one of the family's department stores. Unfortunately, he couldn't keep his hands off the salesgirls and Bertha caught him at it. As a result, he was booted back to where he had come from and Bertha's favours were freely dispensed. A number of us had brief sexual encounters with her and only Robert Broekman lasted for any length of time.

⁓

One of the newspapers we received from New York was the *Aufbau* published there in German. My father read it every week and it kept us posted on the sufferings of the Jews who were still in Europe. That year – 1943 – was sort of mixed. January saw the first armed resistance against deportation in the Warsaw ghetto, but in March the first crematorium in Auschwitz began operations.[11] In April discussions between US and British delegates at the Bermuda conference on how to help the victims of Nazi terror proved fruitless.[12] But the main tragedy was the uprising and destruction of the Warsaw ghetto between April and May. It showed that Jews would strike out against the Nazis if they had the means to do so, which the free world continued to deny them. In June Heinrich Himmler ordered the liquidation of all the ghettos in the occupied eastern territories including Lvov, Częstochowa, Bialystock, Minsk, Lida, Vilna, Belorussia, Riga and Kraków.

On the war front, Field Marshal Paulus surrendered to the Soviets at the end of January; the organized Axis resistance in Africa ended; Japanese troops retreated across the Yangtze River; the Allies invaded Sicily and, in September, landed on the Italian mainland and the Italians sued for peace; the Allied leaders conferred in Cairo at a meeting attended by General Chiang Kai-shek of China, Franklin Roosevelt, and Winston Churchill.[13] Finally, the war had begun to

---

11 The first instance of armed resistance in the Warsaw ghetto occurred on January 18, 1943, in response to the Germans' attempt to deport the remaining Jews. The main Warsaw Ghetto Uprising began in mid-April. For more information, see the glossary.

12 The Bermuda conference was convened by the US and Great Britain in Bermuda on April 19, 1943. The stated purpose of the conference was to deal with the issue of wartime refugees, but given the fact that the JDC and World Jewish Congress were not permitted to attend, the Americans refused to consider allowing more Jewish refugees into the US and the British refused to consider Palestine as a safe haven for Jewish refugees, no viable solutions emerged from the discussions.

13 German Field Marshall Friedrich Paulus surrendered to the Soviet army on January 31, 1943; the organized Axis resistance in Africa ended on May 12, 1943; the

turn in the Allies' favour – for the Jews, however, the slaughter continued unabated.

We had news from Uncle Arno in London that Aunt Herta had died of a heart attack. She had left the factory to go home to prepare dinner and the bus in front of her was hit by a German bomb and most passengers killed. When she got home, she telephoned my uncle to tell him how upset she was by this experience. My uncle arrived home to find her sitting on the sofa, dead.

Toward the end of summer 1943, I met Henry Fowler, principal of the Priory School, the most exclusive private school on the island. When he learned that I was fluent in French, Henry asked if I would consider becoming the school's French teacher as the last one had returned to England for military duty. We agreed on a generous salary and I was set to start in September. I had to obtain a work permit from Mr. Higgins at the CID, but Henry didn't think that this would be a problem. He gave me a letter stating there were no French teachers available for his school. Mr. Higgins authorized the request – and then I had to go and see Rae. He took two days to give me an appointment and when I told him I was taking a position as French teacher at Priory School, he told me that I should make a written request and he would consider it. I replied that my visit was merely a courtesy and that Mr. Higgins had already granted me a work permit. I said that

---

Japanese completed their retreat across the Yangtze River on February 13, 1943; the Allies invaded Sicily on July 9–10, 1943, and landed on the Italian mainland on September 3, 1943, prompting the Italians to seek an armistice with the Allies. Italy declared war on Germany on October 13, 1943, following the capture of Mussolini by Italian partisans and the collapse of his Fascist government. Churchill and Roosevelt met in Cairo on November 22–26, 1943, to discuss plans for the Normandy invasion. They also issued a declaration, with Chinese leader Chiang Kai-shek, announcing their intention to strip Japan of all territories seized since 1914 and restore Korean independence. When the Cairo meeting was concluded, Churchill and Roosevelt flew to Tehran, Iran to meet with Soviet leader Joseph Stalin.

I wanted him to instruct the people at the gate that there were to be no restrictions on my comings and goings. I also mentioned that the governor's two daughters were pupils at the school. He said he would consider my request; I found out that later that day he issued those instructions.

I had about six weeks to prepare to become a French teacher. Henry paid me an advance on my salary and I went to Sangster's bookstore to purchase everything I could find relating to French instruction. I returned to camp loaded down with books and closeted myself for the next few days, coming out only for meals. My parents were extremely proud that I had a job and was the first person in the camp to obtain a work permit. One advantage that I had was that I could remember the way my private French teacher in Brussels had taught me and I even found a copy of the textbook he used. This became my preferred text book and I convinced Henry Fowler to buy copies of them for the school. After about three weeks, I had written out a complete syllabus for the first semester and submitted it to Henry.

Henry Fowler had been a Rhodes scholar in 1935 and had established the Priory School in 1943. His girlfriend, a very domineering person, had great influence over Henry and the staff had to cater to her. Getting on her bad side made life at Priory not only miserable but short-lived. There were six teachers altogether, including Henry Fowler, Jon Laidlaw and his wife, and two others whose names I don't recall. Jon was the mathematics teacher and an amateur painter.

One day when Jon and I were between classes, he casually mentioned that he would like to write a new mathematics textbook for Grades 1 to 3. It was his contention that if one made the subject interesting for children at that age, they would continue to find it interesting for the rest of their study years. He showed me an outline of his proposed book and because of my own interest mathematics, I asked him if I could collaborate with him on it. From then on, between classes and after the end of the school day, Jon and I worked together on a new mathematics book for pre-teens.

When we had almost completed the first draft, we decided to work on the final revisions on a vacation in the Blue Mountains during the Easter break. We drove to Gordon Town and from there we rode on donkeys up to the hotel. It was a small, elegant guest house set in an old-fashioned garden situated on a ridge with a 360-degree view of the Blue Mountains, Kingston, the Hellshire Hills and the plains of St. Catherine and Clarendon. It was very cool up there and in the evening a sweater and jacket were not only a requirement for dining but a necessity for warmth. I had not felt so pleasantly invigorated since our arrival in Jamaica and if it were not for the donkey ride, I would have liked to introduce my parents to what seemed to be the coolest spot in Jamaica. While we were there Jon told me an amazing story about his father who had a twin who lived in Africa. One evening while Jon was in his bedroom in Scotland reading, his father came in and told him that his twin brother had just died. It was later established that his father's twin did indeed die at the very time his father told him it happened.

The mathematics exercise book was about forty pages and consisted of a number of well-conceived games that taught four basic functions. The child had to complete each exercise and therefore the book could only be used once. We had done some testing of the book with children at our school but this was far from a scientific test since they were older than the children the book was designed for. We approached the publisher of the *Daily Gleaner*, Jamaica's leading newspaper, with the draft.

The *Daily Gleaner* had been founded in 1834 by brothers Jacob and Joshua de Cordova, Jewish merchants in Kingston. The current publishers gave us one printing estimate and we got another one from the government printing office. Both quotations were higher than we could afford and Henry could not be persuaded to participate financially. It was my idea to sell advertising for the exercise book and I undertook to do so. My first contract came from Abe Issa and the second from Sangster's bookstore. I sold enough advertising for us to be able to afford a first print run. While Henry was not willing to contribute any funds, he insisted on being the book's distributor and having the school's name printed on the cover. We printed one thousand copies and sold about five hundred within four weeks. A second printing was arranged about three months later. By then Jon and I had divided up the profits and it was agreed that I would be paid half a penny for each book sold. Before I left Jamaica I collected about four payments; while they weren't substantial, they did help.

The school consisted of a main building with various classrooms and two outdoor, open satellite buildings. The French classes took place in one of the satellite buildings. The average class consisted of about eight to ten pupils and altogether there were about sixty children in the school ranging in age from seven to sixteen. Fortunately, I looked much older than my eighteen years, and Henry must have thought so too and never asked me how old I was. During the first semester I always stayed two lessons ahead of my class, but by the second semester I had built up my confidence and considered myself a pro. My teaching was acceptable to Henry and he offered to keep me on for another year. He knew that I would leave Jamaica as soon as possible, but he wouldn't likely have any problem hiring a French teacher from Europe once the war was over.

It was always pleasant to escape the constant heat, so Bobby and I frequently drove with the girls of the moment up to Newcastle, where the British troops were quartered. Newcastle is about 1,200 metres up and only about twenty kilometres from Kingston up a steep, narrow and tortuously winding road. One of the many fine houses along this road was Bamboo Lodge, which was settled in 1730 as a Cottage Farm and may have been the first coffee plantation on the island. The great house subsequently became a naval recuperation station.

Many of my evenings and nights were spent at the Glass Bucket Club, near Cross Roads, and the Silver Slipper Club, down by the sea. The Glass Bucket was owned by Joe Abner and his wife, an overpainted blond. There was a variety show every night with local talent selected by Abner. Kingston had very little to offer by way of cultural events so the night clubs were the only distraction. There were some movie theatres, the largest being the Carib at Half Way Tree that showed fairly current movies, but most of the theatres had very poor air circulation and at times the stench was overwhelming. On the other hand, the private clubs, such as Liguanea, were mostly dinner places with monthly dances and offered no entertainment. Scotch and soda was cheap and it was difficult to spend one pound sterling during the course of the evening. Abner always had a good jazz band playing. Songs like "You Must Remember This" were making the rounds and were frequently requested by the patrons.

The Silver Slipper Club was more of a "mixed club" where the better-off native Jamaicans would make an appearance. It was not unusual to see the prominent politician Alexander Bustamante with his girlfriend, Gladys Longbridge, enjoying the dancing. It was also the hang-out for young white men and their girlfriends. The club was ringed by a number of little bungalows that were available by the hour or night. We all knew not to greet people we knew when they had female company unless the other party gave a sign of recognition. This was the accepted way of life and if you didn't play by the rules, the owner of the club would soon send you into permanent exile. From the open upstairs one had a magnificent view of the sea and the twinkling lights of the homes across the bay. Some of my friends preferred this club to the Glass Bucket, particularly the ones who were either engaged or had serious intentions but were looking for fun. It was astonishing sometimes to encounter these pillars of Jamaican business at the club with their "secretaries."

Henry Fowler, headmaster of the Priory School, was one of the founders of the Little Theatre Movement in Kingston and I asked if I could be of help. The company was preparing to produce the musical *The Vagabond King* by Rudolf Friml. This operetta made its debut in New York in 1925 and Noel Vaz was ambitious in bringing it to Kingston's Ward Theatre. The plot is a very simple one: Paris is under siege by the Burgundians, and its people are frozen and starving. The filthy beggar-poet François Villon infuriates Louis XI with his criticism of the king's inaction. As a delightfully conceived punishment, Louis offers Villon the job of grand marshall for twenty-four hours. If he accepts, he can try to free Paris and he'll also be able to pursue the beautiful Lady Katherine, whom he has worshipped since he glimpsed her in church. However, he will also hang at the end of the twenty-four hours. Should Villon remain in the tavern with his faithful mistress, Huguette? Or should he risk all?

Nothing of this dimension had ever been produced at the local level and the critics condemned it to utter failure. Fortunately for Noel, he had access to one English actress, Margaret Whiting, who was living in Kingston with her boyfriend, Henry Lopez, a Jamaican dentist. They were not welcome in the "in" society since Henry was black. Margaret was given the part of Catherine de Vaucelles and Henry played King Louis XI. As Francois Villon and Huguette, the other two leads, we cast two Jamaican singers. The total cast, aside from the musicians, was about thirty-five actors and actresses. Rehearsals were mostly in the evening and after three months of intense rehearsals, the opening night finally arrived. During all this time I had filled a number of tasks assigned to me by Noel, including being a stand-in and a stage-manager and director when Noel was detained. It was great fun and I enjoyed the experience of theatre. The musical set a record with its twelve performances, which was the first time any play had had more than three shows in Kingston. Some of the songs such as "Only a Rose," "Some Day" and "Vagabond King Waltz" became very popular on the island and one could hear to them in the nightclubs. Soon after putting on *The Vagabond King*, Noel produced *Arsenic and Old Lace* and I worked with Noel on that one, too. Alas, it did not receive as warm a reception.

The Ward Theatre was primarily used for visiting American artists who were brought to the island by the local impresario, Stephen Hill. However, it was also the arena for the formation of the Jamaican

Labour Party founded by Alexander Bustamante in 1943.[14] The artists usually appeared for no more than two performances, which were a 75 per cent sellout. Stephen smartly tied their trips in with their appearances at the American armed forces base at Fort Simmonds, so his costs were greatly reduced. I talked him into giving some free tickets to the camp so that some of our people who could not otherwise afford it would be able to attend. When I advised Rae of this opportunity for some of the camp residents, he agreed to give them passes and also provided a station-wagon for transportation. I assume that he wanted to change his image, as this was shortly before he left the job.

After our theatre rehearsals, we often stopped at the Glass Bucket for a nightcap. By then I was considered a regular. I would meet Bobby Taylor there and he was always obliging in picking up whoever was my present girlfriend at the time. Other regulars were Ferdie Martin, the Haitian consul general, and Milton Walstrom, a vice consul at the American consulate. Ferdie got himself into trouble by augmenting his income with some illegal foreign exchange transactions under cover of diplomatic immunity. He beat a hasty retreat back to Haiti for a few months, but then returned and the matter was conveniently quashed.

One evening Milton brought along George Edwards, a fellow countryman who held a senior position in the US Department of Labour and was stationed in Jamaica to recruit temporary farm workers to meet US war needs. The venture was so successful in Jamaica that it was repeated year after year, and the plan extended to other West Indian Islands. George was living at the Myrtle Bank Hotel and

---

14 Bustamante's party won 22 of 32 seats in the first House of Representatives elected by universal suffrage, making Bustamante the unofficial government leader, serving as minister for communications until the position of chief minister was created in 1953. Jamaica was granted independence from Britain in 1962 and Bustamante served as the independent country's first prime minister until 1967.

made trips into Jamaica's interior to hire as many people as he could. One evening when we were leaving The Bucket, he offered to drive me back to camp and I gladly accepted. We had barely pulled out from the parking lot when I felt George's hand on my thigh and moving toward more intimate parts. I took his hand and put it on the car seat and told him I liked him as a person, but was a confirmed heterosexual. George respected my attitude and never made a pass again. We became very good acquaintances and I was interested to learn about the life of homosexuals. George was actually bisexual – he had been married twice and had two children. I introduced George to the lead dancer of the Jamaican Ballet whom I had met during my theatre days and they were both happy with that introduction.

Another American on the island was a scrap dealer from New York. Apparently, there were thousands of tons of scrap on the island that were not being gathered by anybody and Mr. Jakob had come to recognize that fact. His trucks would go into the countryside and pick up anything they could find, including old automobiles and machinery. Since Jamaica had no scrap dealers, the scrap would be left by the road or in backyards and Jakob picked it up for next to nothing. He chartered small freighters to transport the scrap to the States where he received a substantial price because of the shortage during the war.

~

On August 20, 1944, a disastrous hurricane swept through Jamaica almost completely destroying the coconut industry. Many homes, as well as schools and other public buildings were badly damaged and some were completely demolished. It was a Sunday and I was in bed reading while the winds howled outside my closed shutters. We hadn't been warned about the hurricane and suddenly the barracks roof disappeared and I was staring up at the dark sky. The roof landed with a loud crash about three metres away between two barracks. I jumped out of bed and rushed to the next room to check on my parents. The only concrete building in the camp was the mess hall and we decided, along with many other people, to wait it out there. Most of the electricity in and around Kingston was disrupted as the electric wire poles and cables were uprooted and scattered across the roads. The storm lasted about two hours in our area and just as quickly everything became still. We returned to our rooms and tried to make the most of sleeping under the stars.

The next day Mrs. Kipper went into labour and required more help than the camp hospital could provide. There were no drivers available because of the hurricane, so I offered to drive Mrs. Kipper and her husband to the Kingston General Hospital. Little did I know what I was offering to do. When we left the camp we discovered that the roads were covered with fallen trees, some overturned automobiles and live electric cables. It took quite a bit of fancy driving to avoid all this while trying to keep the car from jerking too much. A normal drive of about twenty minutes took over an hour to complete. When we arrived at the hospital there were a lot of emergency cases. If I hadn't known Dr. Ferreira, the chief medical officer, poor Mrs. Kipper might have had to give birth in the waiting room. Dr. Ferreira immediately attended to her and when I left with her husband a few hours later, they were the proud parents of a baby boy. The trip back to camp took a long time too. The damage to property was enormous and many residences were without roofs or windows. The police and army had personnel out to prevent looting, particularly in the downtown area where many shop windows had been smashed. As I drove through the area I was reminded of what I saw in Germany in the days after Kristallnacht on November 9, 1938.

~

I met Count Alfred de Marigny in 1944, when he came to Kingston right after he was found not guilty of murdering his father-in-law in Nassau, Bahamas. Alfred was an impoverished French nobleman married to Nancy, one of Sir Harry Oakes's daughters. The story circulating at the time was that he had murdered Sir Harry in the heat of a passionate argument about Alfred's spending habits. I met Alfred de Marigny at the swimming pool of the Myrtle Bank Hotel, where he was stretched out on a deck chair next to mine. When I addressed him in French his face lit up and he was delighted to speak to somebody in his native tongue.

He told me that Sir Harry was a person who never forgot a grudge and his killer could have been any number of people whom he had intentionally ruined. As an example he recounted the story of when Sir Harry had first arrived in Nassau. He'd gone for afternoon tea to the British Colonial Hotel wearing shorts and a short-sleeved shirt. The maitre d' informed him he couldn't be served unless he wore a tie and jacket. This wasn't unusual in British enclaves and, as I've mentioned before, was the practice at the Myrtle Bank Hotel dining room. Sir Harry demanded to speak to the manager after being told that they didn't care who he was and that rules were rules. After an unproductive meeting with the manager he stormed out of the hotel. He proceeded to visit his friend and lawyer, Harold Christie, and instructed him to find a way for Sir Harry to acquire the British Colonial Hotel. In due course, he gained control of the hotel and the day after went back for tea in shorts and a short-sleeved shirt. When the maitre d' again told him that he couldn't be served, he again asked to see the manager. When the manager arrived, he looked at the two of them and told the maitre d' that Sir Harry now controlled the hotel and that they were both fired.

Alfred mentioned that Axel Wenner-Grenn, a wealthy Swedish industrialist who owned Paradise Island, a small island almost connected to Nassau, and the Duke of Windsor were German sympathizers and that Paradise Island accommodated German submarines undergoing repairs. He believed there was some connection between Sir Harry's murder and this political affiliation. De Marigny mentioned it was easy to blame him because he was the obvious outsider in an otherwise closed British society. As a Jew, I could identify with those feelings. Sir Harry Oakes had made many enemies in his business career and private life and de Marigny thought he was a likely candidate for a frame-up. It appears that Sir Harry's political beliefs didn't agree with the influential citizens of the island.

De Marigny was saddened by his marital break-up and felt that his wife Nancy's family's efforts to rupture their relationship had been successful. He never expressed any opinion as to his wife's position on his own trial and subsequent verdict. I found de Marigny a delightful, cultured fellow and never gave thought as to whether he was guilty or if the truth was more convoluted. The material question was still why the Duke of Windsor, who at that time was the governor of the Bahamas, tried to keep the news of the murder from being publicized off the island.

$\sim$

We continued to follow news about the war very closely and celebrate every Axis loss and every Allied victory. Most of our information came via the BBC in London and some from the *Daily Gleaner*. We began to feel a sense of relief, but our joy was tempered by the news that Jews in Poland were being slaughtered. By the middle of May 1943, the Warsaw ghetto was no more – although we were all proud of the Jewish uprising against the Nazi tyranny. We heard about the valiant Danes whose underground operation had saved about seven thousand Jews through evacuations to Sweden.[15] But we also learned that Italian Jews were being transported to the death camp in

---

15 When Hitler ordered the arrest and deportation of Danish Jews on October 1–2, 1943, many Danes took part in a clandestine collective effort to evacuate about eight thousand Danish Jews by sea to nearby Sweden. Virtually the entire Danish Jewish community was saved in this single operation.

Auschwitz. Italy's declaration of war against the Germans in October 1943 may have hastened that process.[16]

When 1944 began we were feeling more optimistic about the war, but our mood changed to full elation once we learned of the invasion of the Allied troops in Normandy, France on June 6, 1944.[17] By September US troops were at the German border. We would later find out that even though the Germans were aware that the war was lost, they proceeded with their plan to rid Europe of Jews. In November, while the Soviet troops were approaching Budapest, Hungary, Adolf Eichmann deported 38,000 Jews from Hungary to various camps.[18] At the end of that month Heinrich Himmler ordered the destruction of the crematoria at Auschwitz-Birkenau as the Nazis tried to hide evidence of the death camps.[19]

~

I've mentioned before that my father was an avid reader of the *Aufbau*, the weekly Jewish newspaper written in German and published in

---

16 When the Allies landed in southern Italy in September 1943, the Nazis occupied northern and central Italy and began deporting Italian Jews who mainly lived in the north. In all, the Germans deported about eight thousand Jews from Italy to Auschwitz. But because Italian authorities had very often obstructed the deportations, many Italian Jews succeeded in hiding or escaping to Allied-occupied areas of Italy in the south. More than 40,000 Jews survived the Holocaust in Italy.

17 The invasion of Normandy in France by a massive combined force of British, Canadian and American troops known as D-Day.

18 Adolf Eichmann was a high-ranking SS officer who oversaw the deportation of Jews to slave-labour and death camps all over Europe and the implementation of the Nazis' "Final Solution."

19 As Soviet and Allied forces pressed into German-occupied territory, Heinrich Himmler ordered the destruction of the Auschwitz-Birkenau gas chambers and crematoria. The same was done at other death camps such as Treblinka, Sobibór and Bełzec, where the SS tried to destroy and conceal the evidence of their mass murders.

New York. Even though the copies we received were at least three weeks old, he read the news voraciously. He noticed in the paper that a few outfits in New York were offering the sale of food parcels for shipment from the United States to families in Europe and that there were still certain shortages in the US of items that were plentiful in Jamaica. Coffee, sugar, jams and marmalades, dried fruits, etc. were items my father thought could be shipped from Jamaica. We wrote letters to a number of the advertisers and made a deal with Knopf and Company, New York, one of the largest shippers. Knopf advertised it in their offerings and it was not long before we received the first order and cheque.

There was a Chinese food wholesaler close to Aaron Matalon's father's store and over the time I visited Aaron I got to know one of the sons of the Chinese food wholesaler. We had to be careful that they didn't find out exactly what we were doing since they could easily undercut us. We told them that we were sending parcels to the US and although they had a hard time understanding why the Americans needed food from Jamaica, they packed all the goods into individual cartons. We had rented a small room near the main post office where we did all the labelling and addressing and then carted the parcels to the post office. We eventually sent as many as 250 parcels a week since their was great demand for sugar and coffee.

All through the rest of 1944 and into 1945 we were actively engaged in this business. I would get to the office every day after finishing my teaching and soon my father decided that we could do our own packing and buy the food items from different wholesalers. As soon as an order came in we tallied the items required, ordered them and had them delivered to the office. My mother took an active part and we hired two additional workers who closed and tied the cartons. My father even added a few import lines such as textiles, which he sold to the stores. The business continued until we left Jamaica in 1948.

As the war moved in favour of the Allies, the men from Gibraltar prevailed upon the British government to repatriate their wives and children and no longer expose them to the dreary life in the camp. The Atlantic Ocean was no longer a German submarine hunting ground and the sea voyage from Jamaica to Gibraltar was considered safe. So, at the beginning of 1945, the upper Gibraltar camp was closed and all the women and children returned to home.

The Dutch refugees were moved from Jamaica to Curaçao in 1944, following complaints by the Dutch inmates to their government-in-exile in London. My friend Nico Katz was one of them, as were my girlfriends Vrouwtje and Sinny. At various times I had had entanglements with each of them, but the affair with Sinny had taken on more serious overtones than I intended. Sinny was very much in love with me and did everything she could to get me away from Vrouwtje. However, I was in love with another girl named Lizzi who, at the time, was not as responsive. All the parents, including Lizzi's, were not exactly enamoured at the thought of me near their daughters – I had acquired quite a reputation for promiscuity. A beautiful girl named Trudy was responsive to my advances, but her father, one of the camp's cooks, told my parents to tell me to stay away from their daughter. My parents said that they had no intention of controlling who I saw and suggested that the cook exercise influence over his daughter. The more he tried to control Trudy, the more she wanted to please me in every way. My main standbys, however, were still Lilli and Betty, and they were a handful.

That same year, 1944, Cuba once again offered to issue visas to us in Jamaica. After more than two years of camp living, the possibility of change was appealing. A number of people, including the Prisels, took the opportunity and left for Cuba toward the end of the year. Even my bridge teacher, Mr. Neruda, left, much to my regret. The group remaining in the camp was reduced to about eighty people. All these empty barracks and reduced services played on the emotions of those remaining and more fights broke out between them.

My parents and I considered going to Cuba but decided against it. Aside from my teaching, we had a thriving business that increased in volume every week and fortunately nobody knew about it. We had registered a company, E. Mann & Sons, and opened a bank account at the Canadian Bank of Commerce. So we elected to stay and watched, with regret, some of our friends leave. People realized that my parents and I had distanced ourselves from almost all the others and they ascribed it to my position as a teacher. My parents spent very little time in the camp since they left in the morning and worked in the office. Most of our meals were eaten outside the camp and it was really only on Saturdays and Sundays that any of us stayed in the camp.

My father was a very calm person and I hardly ever heard him raise his voice, so when I encountered his wrath I knew it was something serious. This happened on the first Passover seder night in 1944. That year it was early in April – April 7 – and, as he had in previous years, my father held the services on the veranda of our barracks. He usually invited a few people and my mother did all the cooking. On the day of the first seder I met one of the nuns from the convent for our usual walk in the woods. She was a young nun, in her early twenties, whom I had come to know when we both walked to Papine one afternoon. The first time I had met her was while she was in hospital with dengue fever. She always went out on her day off.

She was a beautiful woman whose mother was a black Jamaican and father a British soldier who had been stationed at Newcastle in the 1920s. Her father refused to acknowledge his daughter and once he returned to England they never heard from him again and her mother had trouble making ends meet. Once her daughter reached school age, she enrolled her in a Catholic school and after she graduated she became a nun. She was quite intelligent and had come to realize there were three ways for her to live her life: as a prostitute, as some white man's mistress, or as a nun. She chose the latter.

That particular day she had telephoned me at Priory School to tell me that it was her day off. After our second encounter we agreed that it would be wiser if we were not seen leaving camp together. Our meeting place was just before reaching Papine, on a lane that led into the hills. She didn't attract any attention because she wore regular street clothes except when she was on duty. On the rare occasion we met in the camp, we barely acknowledged each other. As it happened, Henry Fowler called a staff meeting that day and I didn't get out of school until around 5 PM, which was the time we were supposed to meet. Fortunately, she was still waiting when I arrived at around 5.30 PM, but everything seemed to go wrong that day. We went to our usual hiding place, which was a cut-out we found in the hill area that was totally private; nobody could see us from the outside. For the first time, we both fell asleep and when we woke up it was already dark outside and it was clear that I had missed the seder.

I immediately realized the predicament I was in because I knew there was no way I could be back in camp before 10 PM. We almost ran all the way back and I just beat the clock. When I got to the camp and saw my father's face, I saw how hurt he was. This was the time he lost his usual composure. He didn't scream at me; rather his voice was ice-cold as he told me that he had never been so ashamed and that he had called off the seder because I wasn't there to ask the traditional Four Questions.[20] Ironically, the very first question is, "Why is this night different from all other nights?" I knew the traditional reply, but in my heart there was another answer – I had hurt my father with my philandering and I swore to myself that it would never happen again. On the second night of Passover my parents invited the same people and my father never said a word about the previous night or why I hadn't been there.

∼

By April 1944 we were all pretty certain that the Allies would win the war and discussions ensued about the possibility of returning to

---

20 At the Passover seder, the youngest child traditionally asks four questions designed to elicit information about the nature of the celebration.

Europe. The majority of the Dutch contingent said that they would return to Holland and the Katz family certainly intended to do so. Those of us who had come out of Germany almost unanimously agreed that we would not return. I was filled with disgust for a nation that had so quickly and resolutely turned against its citizens and perpetrated such murders. At that time we weren't aware of the enormity of the Nazi horrors but what we did know caused us to regard the German people as barbarians, willing to cooperate in this incredible devastation of life.

We often reflected on our good fortune at being so far removed from the scene of the atrocities perpetrated not only against Jews but others. We should have understood how far the Nazis would push, particularly when they realized that they had lost their battle for the so-called Thousand-Year Reich and that the destruction they had wreaked on so many other nations would soon be repaid.[21] Sadly, this fed their drive to speed up the deportations and mass killings. Josef Goebbels, the minister of propaganda, accused the Allies of cruelty over their destruction of Dresden, ignoring what the Nazis had done in England. He deplored the indiscriminate bombing of civilians, turning a blind eye to what the Nazis had done to the Warsaw population.[22]

---

21 Hitler had made clear in various speeches that he anticipated that his empire (Reich) would "last a thousand years." The phrase "Thousand Year Reich" was also calculated to create a pseudo-religious aura of a millennial state.

22 On February 13–15, 1945, twelve weeks before the surrender of Nazi Germany, the British Royal Air Force and US Army Air Force carried out massive attacks on the German city of Dresden, using both high explosive and incendiary bombs. The attacks destroyed most of the city centre and caused 24,000–40,000 civilian casualties. During the November 1944 civilian Warsaw uprising against the occupying German forces, 150,000–200,000 Polish civilians were killed. The Germans then levelled about 35 per cent of Warsaw, dynamiting it block by block. The German air force bombed Warsaw in 1939 and 1944.

The impending end generated a feeling of euphoria that the Germans were not only losing, but that the destruction of Germany was in progress. We no longer differentiated between Germans and Nazis, and the July 1944 attempt on Hitler's life did not alter our opinions.[23] After all, this was not a war fought about principles but for the enslavement of conquered countries. "Deutschland, Deutschland Über Alles" (Germany Above All Else), the national anthem, was to be the only anthem of a European continent governed from Berlin.

Were eighty million Germans responsible for the killings, atrocities and brutalities committed in their name or do we shift the guilt to Hitler and his cohorts? History is filled with examples of people rising against their governments, but the German people cooperated with Hitler's gang. They came out in droves to greet and pay homage to Hitler and squealed in delight at his pronouncements. They went along with his genetic breeding schemes to produce an "Aryan" race. They cheered him on when he reneged on all international agreements. They delighted when he conquered countries through the blitzkrieg. They felt proud when his soldiers invaded and occupied France and the Netherlands and would have praised him had he brought England to its knees. They celebrated when the German army was at the walls of Moscow. They condoned the killing of Jews and promoted laws for the protection of animals. They stole from Jewish households and businesses while professing to be law-abiding citizens. German soldiers shot women and children, claiming to do so on orders from their superiors. They devised some of the worst cruelties known to man while faithfully attending church services. There is nothing to support the idea that even a significant minority of Germans were prepared to leave the country – as Thomas Mann had – because they couldn't condone Hitler's machinations.

---

23 On July 20, 1944, a group of German officers attempted to kill Adolf Hitler by detonating a bomb during a meeting he was attending. The plot failed and most of the conspirators were executed or forced to commit suicide.

~

My days were filled with teaching and my nights with cavorting. My salary and the additional income from the food parcels provided a lifestyle that afforded me the luxuries that were available. I wasn't concerned about my future and was waiting for the war to end to decide what to do next. I liked Jamaica since it had offered me not only a home during these turbulent days but peace of mind, an education, friends and a safe haven. The camp was an experience that contributed to the formation of my character and taught me to be tolerant toward all people. My disagreements with Rae educated me in the wisdom of having powerful connections. I also realized that I would probably never have a real friendship because true friendships are formed during one's early school days and Hitler's ascent to power had prevented that. Another lesson I learned was never to run with a crowd, but to always follow my own intuition.

The end of the war was near. On May 2, 1945, we heard an announcement from the BBC that Hitler was dead and that Admiral Karl Doenitz had been appointed as his successor. We had previously heard that Heinrich Himmler had made approaches to the British and Americans with a peace offer.[24] This was resolutely refused because it didn't include the Soviet Union.

On Tuesday, May 8, 1945, we woke up to the announcement from the BBC that peace now reigned across Europe. The official announcement by Churchill, Truman and Stalin was made later in the day. Germany had surrendered unconditionally and the document was signed at General Dwight D. Eisenhower's headquarters by Colonel General Alfred Jodl, chief of staff for the Wehrmacht. Jodl was accompanied by General Admiral Hans Georg von Friedeburg,

---

24 Himmler had indeed quietly sounded out the British regarding the possibility of a separate German surrender, hoping to avoid a Soviet invasion of Germany.

commander-in-chief of the German navy. Hitler was reported to have committed suicide in his bunker in Berlin.

It had been five years, eight months, and six days since Hitler invaded Poland and struck the spark that set the world afire. Our ordeal was over. We were alive and needed to pick up the pieces of our shattered lives. Japanese capitulation followed on August 15 after President Harry Truman authorized the dropping of the atomic bomb on Hiroshima.[25] On May 23 Himmler was captured but committed suicide before he could be brought to trial. The Nuremberg Trials were announced in November to bring all the German war criminals, including Goering, Schacht, Hess, and more to justice.[26]

I wondered, would we also investigate why the Allies permitted the slaughter of so many Jews in the camps? Why nothing was done to assist the Jewish resistance fighters? Why the railroad tracks leading to the camps weren't bombed? Why the Americans wouldn't permit the *St. Louis* passengers to enter? Why the Canadians had refused to grant immigration permits to Jews? Why the Jews of the United States did so little to save the German Jews? Why some two-thousand-odd Jews were deported from Britain to Canada and Australia?

This was a bittersweet time for us. Celebrations were mixed with mourning for relatives lost in the concentration camps and elsewhere. It was over, though, and fortunately my immediate family came through it without loss of life. I still had two uncles from my extended family and I lost two uncles and two aunts. How blessed we

25 The bombing of Hiroshima on August 6, 1945, together with the subsequent bombing of Nagasaki on August 9, prompted the Japanese government to sue for peace.

26 Following Germany's surrender on May 7, 1945, the occupying Allied forces established a war crimes tribunal in the German city of Nuremberg where, from November 21, 1945 to October 1, 1946, twenty-two of the major Nazi leaders and their collaborators stood trial for war crimes.

were considering how whole families were wiped out in the camps and the war.

At the end of May we were moved up to the convent building as the nuns had left once the Gibraltarians were no longer there. These were much better living accommodations – the convent contained not only many rooms but also excellent kitchen facilities and a dining room. The new camp commandant was Mr. Lopez, who had formerly been in charge of the food supply. Messrs. Rae and Brown were gone and Mr. Lopez was free to purchase wherever he wanted. The improvement in the culinary department was immediate and Mr. Lopez removed all restrictions including the guards at the gatehouse. He kept a couple of the policemen on duty, primarily for our protection. He and his family moved into the house that had previously been occupied by Rae and Lopez's daughter, Celia, for whom I developed a strong attachment.

My parents and I discussed our next steps. We were anxious to reunite with my brother and considered emigrating to Canada. We had decided some time ago that we would not return to Europe since there was nothing left for us there. During one of our nightly outings I asked the US vice consul if he would issue me a visitor's visa to the United States and he agreed. On December 21, 1945, I was issued the visa and three days later I received a return visa to Jamaica from the colonial secretary's office.

I was looking forward to the journey because it meant that I would see my brother again. After having served in the Canadian army, he had followed through with his plans and enrolled at the University of Toronto. It had been more than six years since I had last seen him. We had missed growing up together and my brother Heini was now my brother Howard. I wondered if we would be able to recoup the time lost and build a meaningful familial relationship.

Our lives were full of these little ironies, of lost opportunities, void of childhood friendships, growing up too fast, and facing life-threatening situations. I wondered how much of these experiences would be reflected in our future. On a more practical level, I had also decided to visit the purchaser of our food parcels to see if we could increase the volume or add to our clientele. My father had suggested that I look around for other items we could import to Jamaica.

The Fifth Exodus

"What makes this Exodus different from all the previous ones?" On all the previous journeys I had always been thinking about how to stay alive and hoping to have a future. On December 26, 1945, I embarked on a banana boat destined for Tampa, Florida. We made an overnight stop in Port Antonio to load some additional freight and then proceeded to our destination. There were six nuns on board returning to the States and ten British soldiers returning home. I met an acquaintance, the son of the Jamaican Railway president. Together we took advantage of a delay in departure and rushed out to buy a case of rum and two cases of scotch. The trip was uneventful but even if something had happened I doubt we would have been aware of it. The nuns were horrified as we imbibed and toasted anything and everything that happened on the ship and at sea. The soldiers were only too happy to assist us and even the captain joined us. The nuns thought the ship would never reach its destination with such a degenerate crowd aboard. One of the nuns had known Albert Rich when he was married to his first wife and was not aware that he had divorced and remarried – the woman who was travelling with us was his second wife. The nuns were convinced that Albert was living in sin and that the Good Lord would punish us all; Rich for his moral transgression and me and my acquaintance for our self-indulgent behaviour. We landed in Tampa on December 31, 1945, and Albert and his wife invited me to spend New Year's Eve with them. I do remember that the morning after an all-night binge, on January 1, 1946, we walked down one of the main streets of Tampa singing "June Is Busting Out All Over."

~

In my life there have been three important events that have determined my destiny: January 30, 1933, when Hitler came to power; May 10, 1940, when Hitler invaded Belgium; and May 8, 1945, when Hitler was defeated. These three dates mark the events that affected our survival. The war stopped me from having a normal childhood.

In Germany I was the "Jew boy"; in Brussels I was the "dirty German"; in France I was "undesirable"; in Portugal I was the refugee; in Jamaica I was simply a non-entity. So for those twelve years I was a pariah in an exploding world. How would the balance of my existence be shaped? Would these experiences guide my fate and lead me into a future of normalcy to experience an ordinary life? Only time would tell.

A Jew has never had the benefit of the glory of the past but must live for the present and the future. Since the war, I have probably lived with deeply engrained "Jewish suitcase syndrome" – with a virtual suitcase always packed, ready to move on a moment's notice. I wonder if the Jews will ever enjoy a peaceful existence without racial persecution?

I am a survivor.

Glossary

AJB (French) L'Association des juifs en Belgique (Association of Jews in Belgium), known in Flemish as the Jodenvereeniging in Belgie (JVB). It was established by the Nazis in November 1941 to consolidate all the Jews in Belgium under one administrative umbrella. Ostensibly created to organize Jewish schools, oversee the welfare of the Jewish population in Belgium and facilitate Jewish "emigration," the AJB's main tasks were in fact to implement the Germans' anti-Jewish measures and facilitate the transport of Jews in Belgium to compulsory labour and death camps. Like the Judenräte in occupied Eastern Europe, officials of the AJB were in a difficult position. Some members of the AJB were affiliated with the Belgian Resistance and worked to rescue Jewish children through their orphanages and underground networks. *See also* Judenrat.

aliyah (Hebrew; literally: ascent) The term used by Jews and modern Israelis to refer to Jewish immigration to Israel. It is also the term used for "going up" to the Torah in a synagogue to recite special blessings.

American Jewish Joint Distribution Committee (JDC) Also known colloquially as the "Joint." The JDC provided material support for targeted Jews in Germany and other Nazi-occupied territories and facilitated their emigration to neutral countries such as Portugal and Turkey. As Nazi persecution accelerated in Germany between 1933 and 1939, the organization accelerated its aid to German Jews and helped 250,000 of them escape the country. When the German armies swept toward Paris in May 1940, the JDC moved its offices to Lisbon, Portugal, where it continued to help thousands of European Jews find permanent refuge in the United States, Palestine, and Latin America. Between 1939 and 1944, JDC officials helped about 81,000 European Jews to find asylum in various parts of the world.

Aryan Originally a nineteenth-century anthropological term used to describe an Indo-European ethnic and linguistic grouping, the word "Aryan" was used in Nazi racial ideology to denote a Germanic "master race."

Auschwitz (German name for the Polish town Oświęcim) A town in southern Poland about thirty-seven kilometres from Krakow and the name of the largest complex of concentration camps built nearby. The Auschwitz complex contained three main camps: Auschwitz I, established in May 1940 mainly to hold Polish prisoners; Auschwitz II-Birkenau, a mass-murder facility built in 1942; and Auschwitz III-Monowitz, a slave-labour camp built in October 1942. In 1941 Auschwitz I was the testing site for the use of the lethal gas Zyklon B as a method of mass killing. The Auschwitz complex was liberated by the Soviet army in January 1945.

bar mitzvah, bat mitzvah (Hebrew; literally: one to whom commandments apply) The age of thirteen when, according to Jewish tradition, boys become religiously and morally responsible for their actions and are considered adults for the purpose of synagogue ritual. A bar mitzvah is also the synagogue ceremony and family celebration that mark the attainment of this status, during which the boy is called upon to read the Torah publicly. In the latter half of the twentieth century, liberal Jews instituted an equivalent ceremony and celebration for girls – called a bat mitzvah – which takes place at the age of twelve.

Battle of Britain After the fall of France, Germany turned its attention to achieving air superiority over Great Britain in preparation for invading Britain. The effort to incapacitate the Royal Air Force by both bombing airfields and waging air battles – and the successful British defence – is known as the Battle of Britain. It lasted from July through September 1940.

blitzkrieg (German; literally: lightning war) The term used to describe the attack of an all-mechanized force (infantry, armour and air) that concentrates on a small section of the enemy front and then moves forward without ensuring the security of its flank. The term can also refer to the period of Germany's "lightning attack" on Western Europe in the early part of World War II.

Bund Deutscher Mädel (BDM). The "League of German Girls" was the female wing of the Hitlerjugend (Hitler Youth), of which it was formally a part. The task of the BDM was to prepare women for motherhood so they would raise children educated in the ways of National Socialism and indoctrinated with "racial pride." *See also* Hitlerjugend.

chametz (also chometz; Hebrew). Those foodstuffs that, because they are produced by, or associated with, leavening and fermentation, must be removed from Jewish households during the festival of Passover. *See also* matzah; Passover.

conversos Jews who were forcibly converted to Catholicism to avoid death and expulsion in fourteenth and fifteenth-century Spain and Portugal. *See also* "crypto-Jews" and "marranos."

crypto-Jews. Conversos who secretly maintained their adherence to Judaism.

Dachau Established in March 1933 primarily to house political prisoners, the Dachau camp, located about sixteen kilometres north-

west of Munich in southern Germany, was the Nazis' first concentration camp. A crematorium was constructed next to the main
camp in 1942 and the camp remained in operation for the entire
period of the Third Reich.

Danzig (German, Gdańsk in Polish). City state and seaport situated at the mouth of the Vistula River on the Baltic Sea, located
about 340 kilometres from Lodz and 500 kilometres from Berlin.
Danzig belonged to Germany prior to World War I but was made
an autonomous "Free City" by the peace settlement following it.
Under the authority of the League of Nations throughout the in-
terwar period, Danzig/Gdańsk was a major point of contention
between Germany and Poland, with the latter maintaining special
economic rights in the area and acting as the representative of
city state abroad. In September 1939 the Germans occupied and
immediately re-annexed the city. During the war the city endured
heavy Allied and Soviet bombardment by air and during the Soviet capture of the city in March 1945 the city was largely destroyed.
In the post-war settlement agreed by the Allies the city became
part of Poland.

fifth column A term first used by the Nationalists in the Spanish
Civil War of 1936–1939 to refer to their supporters within the territories controlled by the Republican side. Because these people
were helping the four columns of the Nationalists' army, they were
deemed to be their "fifth column." Since that time the expression
has been used to designate a group of people who are clandestinely collaborating with an invading enemy.

Gestapo The German secret police; the name is actually an acro-
nym for Geheime Staatspolizei (Secret State Police). The Gestapo
were a brutal force that operated with very few legal constraints
in dealing with the perceived enemies of the Nazi regime within
Germany. *See also* SS.

ghetto A confined residential area for Jews. The term originated in
Venice, Italy in 1516, with a law requiring all Jews to live on a seg-

regated, gated island known as Ghetto Nuovo. Throughout the Middle Ages in Europe, Jews were often forcibly confined to gated Jewish precincts. During the Holocaust, the Nazis forced Jews to live in crowded and unsanitary conditions in a dilapidated district of a city. Most ghettos in Poland were enclosed by brick walls or wooden fences with barbed wire. The Warsaw ghetto was the largest in Poland with over 400,000 Jews crowded into an area of 1.3 square miles.

Haggadah (Hebrew, pl. Haggadot; literally: telling) The book of the Passover seder service. *See also* seder; Passover.

Hermann Goering (also spelled Göring) Hitler's designated successor and commander-in-chief of the Luftwaffe (German air force). After World War II, Goering was convicted of war crimes and crimes against humanity and sentenced to death. He committed suicide before the sentence could be carried out.

Hitlerjugend (HJ) Known in English as the Hitler Youth, Hitlerjugend (HJ) was founded in 1926. By 1935, 60 per cent of the German youth – boys and girls – were members of the HJ and in December 1, 1936, all other youth groups were banned. In 1939 HJ membership was made compulsory for youths over seventeen, after which membership comprised 90 per cent of German youth. Boys over the age of ten were eligible for membership, but in 1941 membership became compulsory for them as well. The focus of the paramilitary organization was to create soldiers for the Third Reich who were properly indoctrinated in Nazi ideology. The girls' branch of the HJ was the Bund Deutscher Mädel (see the glossary entry).

Hitler Youth. *See* Hitlerjugend.

Jeunesse de Pétain Upon assuming the leadership of the collaborationist Vichy regime, Maréchal Pétain set out to create a reactionary "Révolution Nationale" that would instill deeply conservative values throughout France and replacing the French trinity of

"Liberty, Equality, Fraternity" (*Liberté, Égalité, Fraternité*) with "Labour, Family, Fatherland." (*Travail, Famille, Patrie*). Part of his campaign to capture the hearts and minds of French youth was the establishment of the paramilitary youth organization Jeunesse de Pétain – formally called Chantiers de la Jeunesse Françaises – an organization that closely paralleled the Hitlerjugend in Germany and was committed to creating a profoundly conservative France.

Judenrat (German, plural Judenräte) Jewish Council. A group of Jewish leaders appointed by the Germans to administer and provide services to the local Jewish population under occupation and carry out German orders. The Judenräte appeared to be self-governing entities, but were under complete German control. The Judenräte faced difficult and complex moral decisions under brutal conditions and remain a contentious subject. The chairmen had to decide whether to comply or refuse to comply with German demands. Some were killed by the Nazis for refusing, while others committed suicide. Jewish officials who advocated compliance thought that cooperation might save at least some Jews. Some who denounced resistance efforts did so because they believed that armed resistance would bring death to the entire community.

judenrein (German) Free or cleansed of Jews. Used by the Nazis to describe an area from which all the Jews had been removed, this word deliberately carries connotations of cleanliness and purity; at the same time it suggests that the presence of Jews defiles a location.

Kashruth (Hebrew; also Kashrut) A system of rules that regulates what can be eaten, how food is prepared and served, and how meat and poultry are slaughtered. Foods that are prepared according to these rules are considered to be kosher. See also kosher.

Kindertransport The best-known initiative to get German Jewish children out of Nazi Germany and bring them to the UK between December 1938 and September 3, 1939, the government-sanctioned but privately funded Kindertransport rescued nearly 10,000 children under the age of seventeen. The 1,400 children under the age of fourteen who went to the US between 1934 and 1945 did so through a program known as "One Thousand Children" that was initiated and run by private and communal organizations. Individual Jewish religious schools in both the UK and the US also offered rabbinical training to German Jewish youths so that they would qualify for exit visas before 1939. A February 1939 US government initiative to admit 20,000 Jewish child refugees from Nazi Germany to the United States failed to get Congressional support.

kosher (Hebrew) Fit to eat according to Jewish dietary laws known as Kashruth. *See also* Kashruth.

Kristallnacht (German, equivalent of the English "Night of Broken Glass") The pogrom that took place in Germany on November 9–10, 1938. Over the course of 24 hours, 91 Jews were murdered, 25,000–30,000 were arrested and deported to concentration camps, 200 synagogues were destroyed and thousands of Jewish businesses and homes were ransacked. Planned by the Nazis as a coordinated attack on the Jews of Germany, Kristallnacht is often seen as an important turning point in Hitler's policies of systematic persecution of Jews.

Maginot Line A line of massive border fortifications built by the French after World War I to prevent another German invasion.

marranos. *See* crypto-Jews.

matzah (Hebrew, also matza, matzoh, matsah; in Yiddish, matze) Crisp flatbread made of white plain flour and water which is not allowed to rise before or during baking. *Matzah* is the substitute for bread during the Jewish holiday of Passover, when eating bread and leavened products is forbidden. *See also chametz*; Passover.

Mein Kampf (My Struggle), Adolf Hitler's manifesto for his National Socialist movement appeared in two volumes in 1925 and 1926 (though the second volume was dated 1927). The book combines autobiography with an delineation of Hitler's racist, antisemitic, ultra-nationalist, anti-democratic and anti-Marxist ideology.

minyan (Hebrew) The quorum of ten adult male Jews required for certain religious rites. The term can also designate a congregation.

Nuremberg Laws. Announced at the annual party rally held in Nuremberg in September 1935, the Nuremberg laws institutionalized and codified the racial theories inherent in Nazi ideology. The edicts stripped Jews of their civil rights as German citizens and separated them from Germans legally, socially, and politically. Under "The Law for the Protection of German Blood and Honour," Jews were defined as a separate race rather than a religious group. Whether a person was "racially Jewish" was determined primarily by ancestry (how many Jewish grandparents a person had). Among other things, the law forbade marriages or sexual relations between Jews and Germans.

Passover (in Hebrew, Pesach) One of the major festivals of the Jewish calendar, Passover commemorates the liberation and exodus of the Israelite slaves from Egypt during the reign of the Pharaoh Ramses II. Occurring in the spring, the festival lasts for eight days and begins with a lavish ritual meal called a seder during which the story of the exodus is retold through the reading of the Haggadah. With its special foods, songs and customs, the seder is the focal point of the Passover celebration and is traditionally a time of family gathering. During Passover Jews refrain from eating *chametz* – that is, anything that contains leavened barley, wheat, rye, oats, and spelt. The name of the festival refers to the fact that God "passed over" the houses of the Jews when He set about slaying the firstborn sons of Egypt as the last of the ten plagues aimed at convincing Pharaoh to free the Jews.

Reform Judaism Also known as Progressive Judaism, Reform Judaism emerged in nineteenth-century Germany in response to the previous century's rise in secularism in Europe, the Haskalah (Jewish Enlightenment) and Jewish emancipation, which allowed Jews more social and economic freedom. The Reform movement introduced a variety of changes in Jewish observance including incorporating German into religious services in place of, or in addition to, Hebrew.

Reichstag Fire Decree The more commonly used name for the Order of the Reich President for the Protection of People and State that was passed by German President Paul von Hindenburg on February 28, 1933, the day after the burning of the German parliament building in Berlin. It suspended the right to assembly, freedom of speech, freedom of the press and other constitutional protections, including all restraints on police investigations. The passage of the decree was an essential step in establishing the Third Reich as a one-party totalitarian state.

Rosh Hashanah (Hebrew) New Year. Autumn holiday that marks the beginning of the Jewish year and ushers in the High Holy Days. *See also* Yom Kippur.

SA The abbreviation for Sturmabteilung (German) for "assault division," usually translated as "storm troopers") The SA served as the paramilitary wing of the Nazi party and played a key role in Hitler's rise to power in the 1930s. Members of the SA were often called "Brown Shirts" for the colour of their uniforms, which distinguished them from Heinrich Himmler's all-black SS (Schutzstaffel) uniforms. After the 1934 purge within the Nazi party known as the "Night of the Long Knives," the SA was effectively superseded by the SS.

seder (Hebrew; literally: order) A ritual family meal celebrated at the beginning of the festival of Passover. *See also* matzah; Passover.

Shabbat (Hebrew; in Yiddish, *Shabbes, Shabbos*) Sabbath. The weekly day of rest beginning Friday at sundown and ending Saturday at sundown ushered in by the lighting of candles on Friday night and the recitation of blessings over wine and bread; a day of celebration as well as prayer, on which it is customary to eat three festive meals, attend synagogue services and refrain from doing any work or travelling.

shiva (Hebrew; literally: seven) In Judaism, shiva is the seven-day mourning period that is observed after the funeral of a close relative.

Simchat Torah (Hebrew; literally: rejoicing in the Torah) The Jewish holiday that marks the conclusion of the annual cycle of readings from the Torah and the beginning of a new cycle. The holiday is a particularly joyous one, marked by singing and dancing with the Torah scrolls in synagogue and involvement of children in the synagogue service.

SS The abbreviation for Schutzstaffel (Defence Corps), the SS began as Adolf Hitler's elite corps of personal bodyguards. Its leader, Heinrich Himmler, expanded his domain to include all of Germany's police forces. The SS was comprised of the Allgemeine-SS (General SS) and the Waffen-SS (Armed, or Combat SS). The General SS dealt with policing and the enforcement of Nazi racial policies in Germany and the Nazi-occupied countries. An important unit within the SS was the Reichssicherheitshauptamt (RSHA, the Central Office of Reich Security) whose responsibility included the Gestapo (Geheime Staatspolizei). The SS ran the concentration and death camps, with all their associated economic enterprises, and also fielded its own Waffen-SS military divisions, including some recruited from the occupied countries.

Sturmabteilung. *See* SA.

tallis (Yiddish, in Hebrew, *tallit*) A prayer shawl worn by an adult Jewish male when praying at prescribed times.

tefillin (Hebrew) Phylacteries. A pair of black leather boxes containing scrolls of parchment inscribed with bible verses and worn by traditionally observant Jewish men on the arm and forehead at prescribed times of prayer as a symbol of the covenantal relationship with God.

Treblinka One of the camps created as part of Operation Reinhard, the Nazi plan for murdering Jews in German-occupied Poland using poison gas. A slave-labour camp (Treblinka I) was built in November 1941 in the Generalgouvernement, near the villages of Treblinka and Małkinia Górna, about 80 kilometres northeast of Warsaw. Treblinka II, the killing centre, was constructed in a sparsely populated and heavily wooded area about 1.5 kilometres from the labour camp. The first massive deportations to Treblinka II from Warsaw began on July 22, 1942. The people who arrived packed into railway freight cars were separated by sex, stripped of their clothing and other possessions, marched into buildings that they were told contained bathhouses and gassed with carbon monoxide. From July 1942 to October 1943 more than 750,000 Jews were killed at Treblinka, making it second only to Auschwitz in the numbers of Jews killed. Treblinka I and II were both liberated by the Soviet army in July 1944.

Vichy France The Franco-German armistice of June 22, 1940, divided France into two zones: the northern three-fifths to be under German military occupation and the remaining "free" southern region – known as Vichy France after the town in south-central France where its administrative centre was located – to be under nominal French sovereignty. The Vichy government was led by Maréchal Philippe Pétain.

Warsaw Ghetto Uprising The Jewish insurgency that arose within the Warsaw Ghetto in German-occupied Poland in opposition to the Nazis' efforts to liquidate the ghetto and transport the remaining population to the Treblinka death camp. Launched against the Germans on January 18, 1943, the most significant portion of the rebellion took place from April 19 to May 16, 1943, and ended when the poorly armed and supplied resistance was crushed by German troops.

Winterhilfswerk (Winter Aid Program) The annual drive by the Nazi People's Welfare Organization (Nationalsozialistische Volkswohlfahrt) that ran between 1933 and 1945 and was designed to provide food and fuel to the German people. Its slogan was "None shall starve nor freeze."

Yom Kippur (Hebrew) The Day of Atonement, a solemn day of fasting that culminates the ten days of repentance that begin with Rosh Hashanah. *See also* Rosh Hashanah.

Maps & Photographs

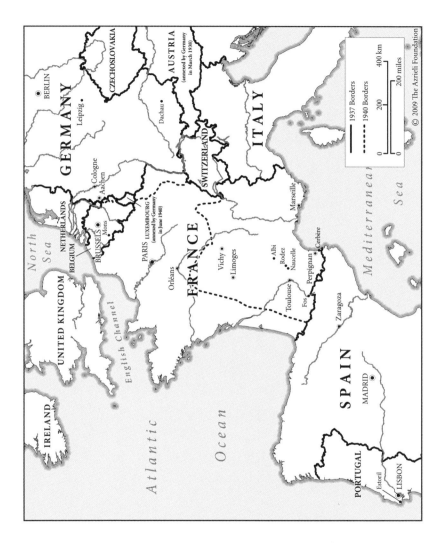

North Sea

IRELAND

UNITED KINGDOM

English Channel

Atlantic

Ocean

GERMANY

BERLIN

Leipzig

Cologne
Aachen

NETHERLANDS

BRUSSELS
BELGIUM

Mons

PARIS

LUXEMBOURG
(annexed by Germany
in June 1940)

FRANCE

Orléans

Vichy
Limoges

Albi
Rodez
Naucelle

Toulouse

Fos

Perpignan
Cerbère

CZECHOSLOVAKIA

AUSTRIA
(annexed by Germany
in March 1938)

Dachau

SWITZERLAND

ITALY

Marseille

Mediterranean
Sea

SPAIN

MADRID

Zaragoza

PORTUGAL

Estoril

LISBON

1937 Borders
1940 Borders

0   200   400 km
0   200 miles

© 2009 The Azrieli Foundation

Fred Mann (left) with his brother, Heini. Leipzig, May 11, 1932.

1 Left to right: Fred Mann's father, Emanuel Mann; his mother, Zelda Mann; his paternal grandmother, Fannie (Feige) Mann; and his paternal grandfather, Ferdinand (Feiwel) Mann. Leipzig, date unknown.

2 Uncle Josziu (far right), Aunt Karolin (second from right) and others at Café Garai. Berlin, 1930s.

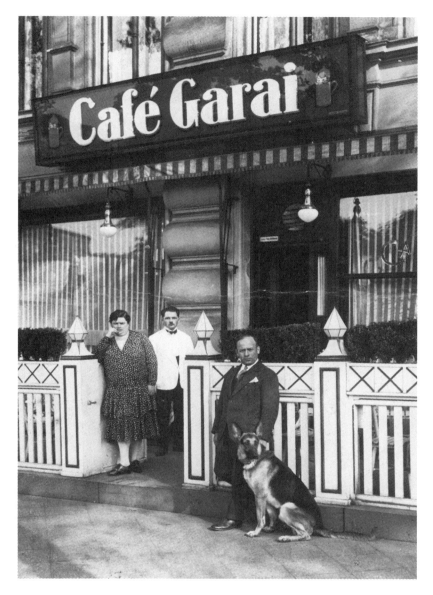

Aunt Karolin (left) and Uncle Josziu (right) in front of Café Garai with one of the waiters and their German shepherd.

Fred Mann's German identity card issued in Leipzig, July 11, 1939.

German birth certificate issued two years later, on February 27, 1941, with "Israel" added to his name.

Fred Mann in his Boy Scout uniform.

Fred Mann's Aunt Rena (seated on the right) with her husband, Kurt Berliner (seated on the left), in Camp des Milles, France, 1941.

Fred Mann's French ration card issued just three days after France signed an armistice with Germany.

A page from Emanuel Mann's passport showing visa stamps from Siam (Thailand), Portugal and Jamaica.

Another page from Emanuel Mann's passport showing transit visa stamps from the Spanish consulate in Marseilles and exit visa stamps from Vichy France.

1 New Year's Eve, Lisbon, 1941. Left to right: Tibor Braun, Trudy Braun, the count, Antonine Mueller (Trudy's mother), Zelda Mann, Fred Mann, and Emanuel Mann.

2 The Jewish Refugee Committee canteen run by Fred Mann's mother. Lisbon, 1941–1942.

3 Fred Mann's identity card from the Jewish Refugee Committee in Lisbon showing that he was working for them.

The Mann family travel papers showing consular notations and stamps that mark their journey from France to Jamaica, 1940–1942.

1 Zelda Mann on her arrival in Jamaica, February 1942.

2 Playing cards at Gibraltar Camp in Jamaica. Fred Mann is seated second from the right.

3 The Mann family at Gibraltar Camp, Jamaica. Left to right Emanuel Mann, Fred Mann, Zelda Mann

E. MANN & SONS
EXPORT & IMPORT
GENERAL MERCHANDISE

MR. M. L. MANN

JAMAICA, B. W. I.

Fred Mann (centre) with friends in Jamaica.

Business card for the export business that Emanuel and Fred Mann operated in Jamaica from 1944 to 1945.

1 Fred Mann with his brother, Howard (Heini) in Toronto, 1950s.

2 Veronica Mann, Fred's wife, in Saltzburg, Austria (date unknown).

3 Uncle Josziu in Canada (date unknown).

Index

The Azrieli Foundation

The Azrieli Foundation was established in 1989 to realize and extend the philanthropic vision of David J. Azrieli, C.M., C.Q., MArch. The Foundation's mission is to support a wide spectrum of initiatives in education and research. The Azrieli Foundation is an active supporter of programs in the fields of Jewish education, the education of architects, scientific and medical research, and education in the arts. The Azrieli Foundation's many well-known initiatives include: the Holocaust Survivor Memoirs Program, which collects, preserves, publishes and distributes the written memoirs of survivors in Canada; the Azrieli Institute for Educational Empowerment, an innovative program successfully working to keep at-risk youth in school; and the Azrieli Fellows Program, which promotes academic excellence and leadership on the graduate level at Israeli universities. Programs sponsored and supported are located in Canada, Israel and the United States.

Israel and Golda Koschitzky Centre for Jewish Studies

In 1989, York University established Canada's first interdisciplinary research centre in Jewish studies. Over the years, the Israel and Golda Koschitzky Centre for Jewish Studies has earned national and international acclaim for its dynamic approach to teaching and research. While embracing Jewish culture and classical study in all its richness, the Centre also has a distinctly modern core, and a strong interest in the study of the Canadian Jewish experience. York was the Canadian pioneer in the study of the Holocaust. The Centre maintains its strong commitment to the study of the Holocaust through the research, teaching, and community involvement of its faculty, its graduate diploma program in Advanced Hebrew and Jewish Studies, and its unique program of Holocaust and anti-racist education – developed in cooperation with the Centre for German and European Studies – for Canadian, German and Polish education students.